RECREATION PROGRAMMING FOR DEVELOPMENTALLY DISABLED PERSONS

RECREATION PROGRAMMING FOR DEVELOPMENTALLY DISABLED PERSONS

Edited by
Paul Wehman, Ph.D.

Assistant Professor of Special Education
Department of Special Education
Virginia Commonwealth University

University Park Press
Baltimore

DED

UNIVERSITY PARK PRESS
International Publishers in Science and Medicine
233 East Redwood Street
Baltimore, Maryland 21202

Copyright © 1979 by University Park Press

Typeset by American Graphic Arts Corporation.
Manufactured in the United States of America by Collins Lithographing and Printing Co., Inc.

Library of Congress Cataloging in Publication Data

Main entry under title:

Recreation programming for developmentally disabled persons.

  Bibliography: p.
  Includes index.
    1. Handicapped—Recreation—Curricula.
2. Recreational leadership. I. Wehman, Paul.
GV183.5.R4   790.19′6   78-14554
ISBN 0-8391-1295-5

CONTENTS

CONTRIBUTORS

Paul Bates, Ph.D., Department of Special Education, Southern Illinois University, Carbondale, Illinois 61802

Paul Bates is an Assistant Professor of Special Education at Southern Illinois University, who specializes in interpersonal skill training of mild to moderately retarded adults. In addition to holding an M.S.W. degree, he has earned his Ph.D. from the University of Wisconsin-Madison, Department of Studies in Behavioral Disabilities. Previously he was a coordinator of a community transition project at Lincoln Developmental Center in Lincoln, Illinois. This project was directed toward transitioning institutionalized severely and profoundly retarded adolescents back to their communities. Paul Bates has also written several articles on vocational programming of the severely developmentally disabled.

Nancy Briggs, M.Ed., Exceptional Play, Inc., P.O. Box 1015, Lawrence, Kansas 66044

Nancy Briggs is employed by Exceptional Play, Inc., where she is involved in product design, educational and consumer research, and supervision of production of fabric products. Her educational background includes post-master's work in Special Education at The University of Kansas and graduate and undergraduate degrees in Family and Child Development and Home Economics from Kansas State University. She was project coordinator for the Personnel Training in Early Childhood Special Education program at The University of Kansas. Formerly a graduate assistant for the Kansas State University Infant and Child Care Center, she created and implemented "Playground Special"—a summer recreation program for the developmentally disabled.

George Giacobbe, Ph.D., Department of Special Education, Virginia Commonwealth University, Richmond, Virginia 23284

George ("Doc") Giacobbe is an Assistant Professor of Special Education at Virginia Commonwealth University. At one time "Doc" was a professional violinist and played with various orchestras, string quartets, and even a country and western band. He was a Music Therapist Aide at an institution for retarded children. In the army Dr. Giacobbe was involved in psychological evaluations of children at Walter Reed Hospital, and he has participated in a teacher-training program affiliated with Hillcrest Children's Center in Washington, D.C. He earned his Ph.D. at the University of Georgia. For several years "Doc" was a special education teacher at a Boys' Home. He continues to enjoy playing and listening to music.

Richard M. Graham, Ph.D., Department of Music Therapy, University of Georgia, Athens, Georgia 30602

Richard M. Graham is Professor of Music and Director of Music Therapy Programs at the University of Georgia. He has worked with developmentally disabled individuals, ranging from very young children to the lderly. Dr. Graham has directed workshops in music for the young, atypical child for the Council for Exceptional Children. He has been lecturer and visiting professor at numerous universities and colleges throughout the United States, Canada, and South America. He is a former President of the National Association for Music Therapy, Inc.

Carol Granger, M.S., O.T.R., Hickory Hill School, 3000 Belt Boulevard, Richmond, Virginia 23220

Carol Granger, is currently employed as the Occupational Therapist at Hickory Hill School in Richmond. She coordinates therapy services for the severely, profoundly, and multihandicapped children in this program. Before working with the Richmond Public Schools, Ms. Granger was the Director of Activity Therapy services at Southside Virginia Training Center in Petersburg, Virginia. She earned her Master's degree in Occupational Therapy in 1973 from the Medical College at Virginia Commonwealth University.

Ada D. Hill, Ed.D., Department of Special Education, Virginia Commonwealth University, Richmond, Virginia 23284.

Ada D. Hill, is a special educator and Assistant Professor of Special Education at Virginia Commonwealth University in Richmond. She earned her Bachelor of Arts degree from St. Augustines College, her Master of Science degree from Virginia State College, and her Doctor of Education degree at The American University. Her professional experience includes regular and special education, classroom teaching, and program development. She has lectured and has served as a consultant for several agencies and school systems. Dr. Hill has authored several articles in the area of special education.

Jo Ann Marchant, M.Ed., 5046 West Belmont, Richmond, Virginia 23225

Jo Ann Marchant is a teacher of severely and profoundly retarded children in the Richmond Public Schools. Ms. Marchant has a Bachelor's degree in Psychology and a Master's degree in Special Education and has taught retarded children for nine years. In recent years she has become extremely active in developing data-based programs for severely handicapped children, especially in behavior management and play skill development. Considered an outstanding teacher by her colleagues and students' parents alike, she has been an excellent model for student teachers, practicum students, and graduate interns in teacher-training programs in Virginia.

Adelle Renzaglia, Ph.D., Department of Special Education, University of Virginia, Charlottesville, Virginia 22092

Adelle Renzaglia is an Assistant Professor of Special Education at the University of Virginia. She received her Ph.D. from the University of Wisconsin, Department of Studies in Behavioral Disabilities. Dr. Renzaglia has been deeply involved in habilitative programming for severely and profoundly retarded adolescents for several years and co-authored *Habilitation Practices with the Severely Developmentally Disabled, Vol. I,* a widely disseminated research monograph from the Rehabilitation Research and Training Center at Madison, Wisconsin. Her previous work was at Anna State School, Anna, Illinois, where she was involved in behavioral programming of profoundly retarded persons. Dr. Renzaglia's current interests include teacher training and applications of discrimination learning to instruction of the severely handicapped.

Phillip S. Strain, Ph.D., Middle Tennessee Mental Health Institute, 3411 Belmont Boulevard, Nashville, Tennessee 37215

Phillip S. Strain is Supervisor of Research, Children, and Youth, at Middle Tennessee Mental Health Institute, Nashville, Tennessee. Dr. Strain earned his doctorate at George Peabody College for Teachers and has taught at The American University in Washington, D.C. He has been a prolific writer, and his research on the social behavior of behavior-disordered children has stimulated new thoughts and program policy by special educators. Dr. Strain's current research interests have centered on the effects peers have on handicapped children in social situations.

Paul Wehman, Ph.D., Department of Special Education, Virginia Commonwealth University, Richmond, Virginia 23284

Paul Wehman is an Assistant Professor in the Department of Special Education at Virginia Commonwealth University in Richmond. For several years he has been extremely involved in the development and dissemination of play and leisure skill programs for severely handicapped persons. Previously at the University of Wisconsin, where he earned a Ph.D. from the Department of Studies in Behavioral Disabilities, he also has conducted applied research in vocational training of the severely and profoundly handicapped. He was a clinical psychologist at Lincoln Developmental Center from 1972 to 1974. Dr. Wehman's current research interests lie in recreation curriculum development and vocational placement of severely retarded adults.

Becky Williams, B.A., Exceptional Play, Inc., P.O. Box 1015, Lawrence, Kansas 60044

Becky Williams is Vice President and co-founder of Exceptional Play, Inc. Her specialty is the design and evaluation of play materials and equipment for the disabled. In addition to her work with Exceptional Play, she is currently pursuing a master's degree at The University of Kansas, where she received a B.A. degree in Child Development and Sociology. Previous work experiences include teaching at the preschool level and serving as Mental Health/Psychological Services Coordinator for an area Head Start Project. She is a member of the National Association for Retarded Citizens, The American Association for the Education of the Severely/Profoundly Handicapped, and the Council for Exceptional Children (including CEC-MR, DEC, and DOPHHH).

Ron Williams, M.S., Exceptional Play, Inc., P.O. Box 1015, Lawrence, Kansas 60044

Ron Williams is President and co-founder of Exceptional Play, Inc. In addition to his management responsibilities with Exceptional Play, he is actively involved in the development of new products, including play materials for the disabled and playground structures for both normal and disabled populations. Formerly on the faculty of the School of Business at The University of Kansas, he taught courses in Organizational Behavior, Management of Small Business, and Business Policy.

PREFACE

Services for developmentally disabled individuals have been expanding dramatically in recent years. With mandatory legislation, landmark right-to-treatment and right-to-education court decisions, and continued parental support, developmentally disabled persons of all ages are receiving more attention. As this movement continues, increasing emphasis is being placed on the nature and quality of education and habilitative services that are provided. Among these services are recreation and leisure skills. Leisure skill programming addresses the question: *What do developmentally disabled individuals do after school or after work, on the weekends, and during free time at home*?

This is an important question, because without constructive use of leisure time many severely developmentally disabled children and adults may have to be institutionalized. Families will be able to cope more effectively and will be more accepting of their situation if the handicapped child uses free time appropriately and does not require constant supervision. Furthermore, as many educators and recreation specialists are well aware, handicapped individuals learn other skills more quickly through the use of play and leisure activities.

The chapters in this text grew out of a need to provide specialized information on programming recreation and leisure skills for developmentally disabled persons. An effort has been made to address the topical areas that have been discussed and inquired about most frequently by teachers. These include: What curricula are available? Where can I get materials? What methods do I use with the severely and profoundly handicapped? What is the outlook for community recreation programs? Can severely developmentally disabled individuals learn social interaction and cooperative game skills? The chapters in *Recreation Programming for Developmentally Disabled Persons* address these questions directly and begin to offer answers.

The initial chapter, which I developed, is a recreation curriculum for developmentally disabled individuals of all ages and functioning levels. Leisure skills are categorized into several areas and specific skills generated within each category. Although this curriculum is still in the process of field testing, it provides an important starting point for systematic selection of leisure skills.

In Chapter 2, Becky and Ron Williams and Nancy Briggs have pulled together important information relating to selection and design of recreation materials. As the owners of *Exceptional Play, Inc.,* they are in an excellent position to identify the scope of problems in this area and to present some viable alternatives. This chapter is *must* reading for all teachers, therapists, and administrators involved in the play material selection process.

The third chapter involves developing free-play skills with toys in developmentally disabled children. This chapter was written by myself, and there is a strong emphasis on teaching severely and profoundly handicapped children how to interact with toys. This is a practical chapter, directed to teachers and other practitioners who are faced with starting a toy play program.

Phil Strain and Ada Hill contributed the fourth chapter. Their work reviews and synthesizes literature on developing social interaction skills and cooperative behavior in severely developmentally disabled children and preschoolers. The theme of this excellent chapter is the efficacy of peers as change agents in social interaction situations. This chapter will be especially helpful to preschool teachers working with developmentally delayed children.

In Chapter 5 Jo Ann Marchant has described the importance of games and hobbies with developmentally disabled individuals. As a teacher of a class of severely retarded children, she has been in the enviable position of field testing many instructional skill sequences developed for selected games. These sequences and data are shared in her chapter.

The increasing need for community-based recreation programs is discussed in Chapter 6 by Adelle Renzaglia and Paul Bates. This important chapter describes a logical model of recreation program development for working with developmentally disabled persons in the community. The strong emphasis on normalization sets the tone for the suggestions that Renzaglia and Bates offer.

The seventh chapter, developed by Carol

Granger and myself, focuses on sensory stimulation, an area not usually associated with recreation programming. However, because of the critical nature of sensory stimulation with many low functioning, severely developmentally disabled individuals, this chapter has been included. Relevant literature is reviewed, and many program guidelines and activities in auditory, tactile, visual, and gustatory stimulation are provided. The development of sensory awareness is an important prerequisite to exploratory play skills.

The final chapter was written by Richard Graham and George Giacobbe and is devoted to music programming for developmentally disabled persons. This chapter will be helpful to all teachers who wish to use music in recreation and leisure skill programs. It will be especially helpful, however, to the music teacher looking for specialized information relating to the developmentally disabled child. Numerous musical selections are provided.

An Appendix of references and resources, including an annotated bibliography, is also provided. This detailed appendix should be a valuable tool for teachers, practitioners, and researchers in locating relevant information about recreation programs. It is hoped that this material will bring the field up to date with what is presently available in the recreation and leisure skill area for developmentally disabled individuals.

This book represents the efforts of a group of professionals interested and competent in leisure skill program development. It is our attempt to share information with others concerning how to help developmentally disabled persons acquire and maintain a repertoire of leisure skills.

I would like to thank several people, in addition to the contributors, for their support and assistance in completing the manuscript. Special thanks go to Charlotte Parks and Pat Pleasant for their, as usual, highly efficient typing of the manuscript. I also want to acknowledge and thank the many undergraduate and graduate students who allowed me to "bounce" ideas off them. This also applies to the staff and students at Hickory Hill School in Richmond.

Paul Wehman

To Kent, Therese, and Claiborne

RECREATION PROGRAMMING FOR DEVELOPMENTALLY DISABLED PERSONS

1 TOWARD A RECREATION CURRICULUM FOR DEVELOPMENTALLY DISABLED PERSONS

Paul Wehman

Recreation and leisure time activity have assumed a rapidly expanding role in the lives of people in American society. Most individuals welcome time away from school or work and carefully plan ways to use free time. For young children this may involve free play with toys and with other children. Adolescents and adults may become involved in sports activities, in an assortment of hobbies, social events, and clubs, or in simply watching television, going to the movies, or reading a book.

Developmentally disabled persons are no different in their need for recreation and leisure. In fact, involvement in leisure activities may help develop social skills, language, and motor skills, depending on the type of activities selected. Handicapped children and adults may become better accepted by peers when actively involved in community-based recreation activities. Perhaps the fundamental reason for helping developmentally disabled individuals acquire a range of leisure skills, however, is that they usually have an abundance of free time. This is reflected in evenings, weekends, holidays, and summer time for children, in a lack of adult services in many communities, and in high unemployment rates which interfere with the disabled person's job prospects, as well as in the excessive time that those individuals placed in state institutions have. Clearly a large burden falls on the family or foster parents to find constructive leisure activities for handicapped individuals (Berryman, 1968; Stanfield, 1973).

In considering the delivery of recreation services to developmentally disabled persons it must be recognized that:

1. An important goal in leisure education is to teach individuals to select from a range of leisure skills. Leisure skills should be diversified and should reflect the different types of recreation, i.e., sports, table games, hobbies, that are engaged in by nonhandicapped peers.

2. Most developmentally disabled persons will require, to a varying extent, some form of instruction, supervision, and follow-up to ensure that the skill(s) is acquired (Day and Day, 1977). Furthermore, even when skills are developed, generalization and retention will not occur unless specific instruction is provided.

The purpose of this chapter is to delineate a recreation curriculm for developmentally disabled persons. This curriculum outlines and describes a logical scope and sequence of leisure skills that may be taught to developmentally disabled individuals of all ages and functioning levels.

CHARACTERISTICS OF DEVELOPMENTALLY DISABLED PERSONS

Before delineating the curriculum, a definition of the term *developmentally disabled* is provided. Specific behavioral characteristics of developmentally disabled persons are also provided. Because this book is relevant for all ages and functioning levels of developmentally disabled individuals, an effort is made to discuss characteristics of preschool children, adolescents, and adults that may influence the type of recreation program they will receive.

Developmentally disabled refers to any "disability attributable to mental retardation, cerebral palsy, epilepsy, or autism and is attributable to any other condition of a person found to be closely

1

related to mental retardation because such condition results in similar impairment of general intellectual functioning or adaptive behavior to that of mentally retarded persons" (Public Law 94-103, 1975). Therefore, this text is directed to staff that work with children and adults who are labeled mentally retarded, cerebral palsied, severely epileptic, and autistic.

Preschool
Developmentally Disabled Children

Developmentally delayed infants and toddlers differ from normal children on many behavioral dimensions. They do not show the same rate of motor development, language is grossly impaired, self-care skills are usually deficient, and little affect or positive emotion is displayed. While nonhandicapped preschoolers display social and cognitive growth through expanded exploration of their environment and surroundings, developmentally disabled preschoolers, particularly those who are more severely involved, rarely explore spontaneously.

There is a limited amount of social interaction observed in delayed toddlers. Attending skills are not well developed, and only loud sounds or gross changes in visual stimuli will result in orienting responses.

This general lack of sensory awareness, and the limitations in exploratory behavior, are most notable in severely delayed preschoolers, and drastically reduce the emergence of normal play activity. Through exploring the environment the nonhandicapped child acquires knowledge, both through imitation and sensory feedback.

Attending to relevant cues in the environment is the initial step in sensory awareness and responsiveness. It is also crucial in the development of visual tracking and searching skills, and imitative behavior. An analysis of the play deficits of developmentally disabled young children reveals the following dilemma. If a child does not attend, or is unaware of his surroundings, the opportunity to gather new information about the environment cannot occur, thereby inhibiting the development of more advanced and complex play activity.

For example, a child who attends to a peer playing with a new toy that makes pleasant sounds may be able to imitate the play behavior when given the same toy at a later time. Moreover, attending to a wide assortment of sounds, visual

stimuli, and tactile stimuli that are present enables a child to cope physically with the environment.

Through exploratory behavior a child is provided with the sensory imput and feedback that many theorists feel is the basis for intelligence (e.g., Piaget, 1951). Furthermore, it has been theorized by Ellis (1973) and empirically supported (e.g., Berkson and Davenport, 1962) that sensory deprivation, or lack of sensory input, may lead to stereotypic, self-stimulatory behavior in institutionalized mentally retarded populations. This may be nonfunctional head weaving, body rocking, or finger flicking, and is commonly observed in the severely and profoundly retarded. There can be little doubt that the sterile and stimulus-deprived ward environments of most institutions for the retarded exacerbate the tendency for stereotypic behavior.

Thus far, it has been emphasized that many developmentally disabled preschoolers do not attend well or imitate, and thus do not display the social awareness usually typical of normal young children. However, another behavioral characteristic of this population, which is also important, is the limited number of events that are reinforcing to these children. Developmentally disabled persons typically require greater amounts of reinforcement, more frequently, and with reinforcement contingencies that are labeled clearly. Social reinforcement, or approval, often is not a sufficient motivator to encourage exploration on the part of delayed preschoolers, and tangible reinforcers may have to be used initially.

This presents an inherent difficulty in programming play skills for the child with substantial handicaps. Noted writers in the area of play (Ellis, 1973) and leisure (Neulinger, 1974) have observed that play should be pursued for the joy of engaging in an activity, without external consequence. Play behavior ought to occur as a result of the intrinsic reinforcement derived from the activity. However, without external reinforcement presented contingent on play activity or exploratory behavior, severely involved preschoolers may display little sustained activity.

School-Age
Developmentally Disabled Children

Once a child has begun to explore the environment and to act on a variety of different objects, at least two broad categories of play should be encouraged: 1) more complex and sustained toy play, and 2) greater frequency of social interaction patterns. Ideally these play behaviors may be developed concurrently through the careful selection of play materials and efficacious teaching procedures.

While the nonhandicapped child displays these behaviors with little instruction, the developmentally disabled youngster is deficient in behaviors that are critical to the acquisition of these skills. As with the younger child, deficits in visual tracking and searching skills, and a general failure to learn in other than intentional learning situations, e.g., incidental learning (Hardman and Drew, 1975), creates serious problems in the development of play skills. Equally problematical is the characteristic lack of spontaneity with play materials, which is observed frequently.

A major reason for inappropriate play behavior is that the handicapped child has not been taught appropriate behavioral alternatives for using play materials and has not learned the reinforcing value of certain toys. This is not to imply that no attempt has been made at instructions; rather, the issue is one of which combination of teaching procedures, materials, and curricula has been utilized, and how carefully do the elements meet the specific learning characteristics of the child.

Limited cooperative play and lack of social interaction between peers are also typical characteristics. Independent or isolated play has been noted frequently (e.g., Paloutzian et al., 1971). The child may play well alone and be able to amuse himself appropriately for a short period of time; however, the duration of play activity is usually brief if there is no supervision or assistance.

When there is little peer interaction during play sessions, children fail to develop higher level social behaviors, such as cooperative and competitive play. In short, independent play is a lower stage of social development, which may only provide sensory input from inanimate objects. Affective feedback cannot be gained until children begin to interact.

Lack of social interaction is a dominant characteristic of many handicapped children, and is one with which the present text is concerned. This limitation grossly impedes the development of language and communication skills, and unfortunately minimizes the effects of play as a potent medium of social development. Moreover it is generally accepted that, if social interaction is not encouraged at a young age, the long range outlook for competent social behavior is not bright.

In designing an effective leisure skill program for developmentally disabled children, behavioral strengths and weaknesses of the individual child must be analyzed. This should include assessment of attending skills, incidental learning abilities, language behavior, gross and fine motor skills, social responsiveness, and reinforcement preferences. Once behavior is analyzed, instructional procedures, materials, and curricula then may be prescribed for the optimal development of leisure behaviors.

Developmentally Disabled Adults

The leisure problem of developmentally disabled adults has been documented previously (Benoit, 1955; Stanfield, 1973). It involves primarily the difficulties in providing leisure time experiences that are commensurate with the mental age of the adult and that are not dehumanizing, e.g., pushing a baby cart around the room. Also involved is the selection of durable materials that will hold up under intensive use.

Developmentally disabled adolescents and adults learn slowly and display a limited behavior repertoire. Their level of cognitive development is often similar to nonhandicapped children. Furthermore, they frequently exhibit poor gross motor behavior and lack coordination. Perceptual-motor skills may not be well developed, and this influences the performance of actions that require fine motor skills.

What compounds these deficits with severely developmentally disabled individuals is that their physical stature is usually normal and fully developed. Full physical development, accompanied by such grossly limited intellectual functioning, poses a problem as to the optimal types of instructional procedures and materials that should be employed.

Generalization of skills to other environments and in different situations is also more difficult in older developmentally disabled persons, particularly the mentally retarded (Wehman, Abramson, and Norman, 1977). Transfer of training is an area in which most retarded people require some programming; younger retarded children, however, may make generalizations more readily.

A further characteristic of the more severely handicapped that should also be noted are the excessive inappropriate social behaviors. Stereotypic rocking behavior, self-abuse, verbal and physical aggression, and strange sounds are indicative of the more severe types of behavior excesses exhibited by the severely and profoundly mentally retarded. These behaviors stand in the path of habilitation of many severely retarded people and often develop in an attempt to gain attention. Unfortunately such characteristics give rise to labeling the severely or profoundly retarded adult as "dangerous" or "crazy," with the net result being that many recreation specialists are reluctant to work with this population.

This brief overview of the learning and behavior characteristics of developmentally disabled persons is intended as a preface to a discussion of recreation curriculum development. It is emphasized that the learning potential of this population should not be confused with the traditional level of development that has been observed frequently. Unquestionably, developmentally disabled individuals are capable of considerably more complex skills than they typically have performed, but only provided that individualized instructional procedures and materials are employed, and only if the instruction is continuous throughout the full life span of the individual (i.e., from birth through adulthood).

RATIONALE FOR RECREATION CURRICULUM DEVELOPMENT

A logically planned leisure skill curriculum can provide the basis for three critically important instructional areas in programming: 1) skill assessment, which will facilitate the initiation of a program, 2) sequencing and order of presentation of materials, and 3) evaluation of student progress made in the curriculum. The implications of each of these points should be evident. For example, assessment instruments and data collection strategies should be determined by the format, preciseness, and sequencing of the curriculum being used.

Second, careful sequencing of structured recreation programs would lead to skills being acquired more rapidly and would give inexperienced teachers direction in training. Free play may be enhanced through different curriculum guidelines, which provide the optimal antecedent events for different play situations.

The curriculum provides the "what" of an instructional program. It tells the teacher which skills can be taught to the student and in what order. In recreation this is particularly important because of the necessity for presenting a range of leisure skill choices to the student.

Evaluation may be conducted with one individual in the number of skills or games acquired, or with several individuals, or across the curriculum, which is designed to tap different dimensions of cognitive or behavioral development. The curriculum should be organized in a hierarchy that provides a logical behavioral sequence which becomes progressively more advanced. Evaluation of the individual's success through the curriculum sequence is facilitated by observation and recording procedures.

In short, a leisure skills curriculum should be the basis of a comprehensive recreation program that is aimed at accelerating development in developmentally disabled persons. It should emphasize normalization and provide opportunities for self-initiated leisure time skills.

There are few curriculum efforts in this area. The I CAN project is one curriculum that has been produced by a group from Michigan State University (Knowles, Vogel, and Wessel, 1975). In this physical education–based curriculum, which was designed for trainable level retarded children and youth, aquatics, body management, fundamental skills, and health fitness are the four program content areas. Within each content area are performance modules. Materials have been specially designed for content areas, and an accountability system has been developed to evaluate whether or not performance objectives have been met.

It would appear that curriculum development efforts should be interdisciplinary in nature. Physical education specialists, recreation therapists, educators, and occupational therapists must all have input into content areas. The sequencing and task analysis of content areas are critical, particularly as the more severely involved receive regular physical education recreational services. Also, it may be beneficial to receive increased input from rehabilitation counselors who can provide support for leisure time problems of developmentally disabled adults. This is a neglected area in the recreation literature.

DEVELOPING A
RECREATION CURRICULUM

Because greater efforts are required to formulate recreation curricula, the question then becomes one of determining which methods can be used to generate fresh ideas and correct sequencing. One strategy that is often fruitful is the use of task-force groups comprised of professionals or students with different service orientations. Each task-force group is charged with establishing program content and sequencing for a given recreational area, e.g., socialization, over a specified period of time.

Group members might generate ideas initially from close scrutiny of what nonretarded peers engage in for activity in the designated program content areas. Sequencing and task analysis of activities should be based on normal child developmental sequences of learning. Specificity of task analysis and instructional methodology included in curricula packages are determined by the target functioning level of students or clients.

After first drafts of curricula are generated, a field-testing phase is implemented in which portions of curricula are evaluated empirically for economy of use, correctness of sequencing, tapping of appropriate content areas, etc., with the target population in different settings. With subsequent criticisms and modifications, a revised curricula package can be prepared.

The development of a recreation curriculum is an exciting area, and one which has great potential utility for those involved with developmentally disabled persons. It is mandatory that more attention be paid to this area. With the growing commitment to behavioral training methods and precision teaching, well-planned and sequenced curricula must be the logical program content base of learning material.

In an effort to expand earlier leisure skill curriculum work (Wehman, 1976) into a more comprehensive scope and sequence, a recreation curriculum for developmentally disabled persons is delineated below. Table 1.1 provides a proposed recreation curriculum for developmentally disabled persons. It has not as yet been thoroughly field tested, but it has come through the task-force brainstorming and analysis stage. It represents an attempt at a comprehensive identification of leisure skills and is based largely on an analysis of what nonhandicapped children and adults do

with their free time. It should be remembered, however, that the skills depicted are representative of the different categories and levels. There is little doubt that many more skills can be generated.

The six levels in Table 1.1. are to be viewed as separate subdomains or categories of recreation. There is no presumption that one category must precede the next, e.g., passive leisure before sports. Rather, the emphasis is on developing a skill repertoire.

The balance of this chapter is devoted to describing each tier in the recreation curriculum outlined in Table 1.1. There is also a brief discussion involving how to use the curriculum for assessment and instruction.

Toy Play

The top level of the recreation curriculum involves toy play. This is an area that reflects cognitive, motor, and social development in children (Piaget, 1951) and may provide an effective medium for assessing the general functioning level of developmentally disabled children. The way in which children interact with toys and with other peers in a free-play situation may provide a gross profile of the child's skill level. In clinical situations, especially, a number of behavioral indices may be evaluated, thereby providing observational data on the child's exploratory behavior, relationship to parents and peers, language, cognitive development, and persistence. Preferred toys can be evaluated as potential reinforcers as well.

The toy play level has been organized into a familiar progression (Parten, 1932; Barnes, 1971; Wehman, 1977) of increasingly more advanced toy play. This begins with the early developmental stages of exploratory play. In this stage the child is becoming aware of objects and people in the environment and may play with objects in a repetitive and nonfunctional way. Most profoundly retarded children and adults play in this way without systematic leisure skill instruction because they have not developed to a more advanced stage.

Independent play, parallel play, and associative play are the following stages through which children typically can be expected to develop. Independent play reflects appropriate toy play by the child alone; in parallel and associative play the child continues to move closer to social interaction with peers.

Table 1.1.   A recreation curriculum for developmentally disabled persons

Level I: Toy play

Exploratory play	Independent play	Parallel play	Associative play	Cooperative play	Symbolic play
1. Acts on toy or play objects.	1. Plays appropriately alone with wide range of materials.	1. Plays independently with wide range of materials in close proximity to others.	1. Initiates interaction with peers in play situations for short periods of time.	1. Exhibits mutual participation and peer interaction during play.	1. Engages in dramatization and imaginative/pretend play.
2. *Representative activities:* Reaches for objects; bats at objects; grasps and squeezes toys; makes regular oral contact with toys; shakes objects; throws toys; engages in high rate self-stimulatory actions with toys.	2. *Representative activities:* Uses playground equipment; uses following toys: blocks, puzzles, dolls, stacking rings, top, snap beads, play phone, pull toys, ball, musical instruments, tricycle, Lincoln Logs, books, water colors, hula hoop.	2. *Representative activities:* Swings on swing next to peer; builds block tower near peer; bounces ball near peers; colors at table with peers.	2. *Representative activities:* Approaches peer with a toy; makes brief physical contact with peer during play; makes regular eye contact with peer during play.	2. *Representative activities:* Rolls a ball; builds with blocks; pulls a peer in a wagon; uses a toy phone; pushes a peer on a swing or down a slide; takes turns hitting Bop Bag.	2. *Representative activities:* Plays domestic make-believe with dolls, cars, trucks, blocks, house, and dishes; engages in dress-up activities; uses puppets, paper dolls; plays cowboys/Indians, doctor/nurse, cops/robbers.

Level II: Passive leisure

Simple attending	Spectator activities	Complex attending	Educational activities
1. Pays attention to visual or auditory presentations.	1. Travels to places and events in community for leisure.	1. Engages in passive activities that require greater cognitive/intellectual ability.	1. Becomes involved in fulfilling requirements of specific instructional courses.
2. *Representative activities:* Looks at pictures in books; listens to musical instruments; listens to radio; listens to record player; listens attentively to stories; watches television.	2. *Representative activities:* Attends movies; attends music concerts; attends carnivals and fairs; attends dance shows; attends circus; attends animal shows; attends church; goes to library.	2. *Representative activities:* Works crossword puzzles; engages in cooking outside; engages in observing nature; uses CB radio; writes letters; follows news/sports events.	2. *Representative activities:* Takes non-credit adult education classes; takes art and music lessons; takes GED test; takes vocational/technical courses at local junior college.

Level III: Game activities

Simple imitative group games	Complex group activities	Simple table games	Card games (matching and recognition games)	Complex table games	Table game sports
Peek-a-Boo; This Little Piggy; Where Is Thumbkin; Ring-Around-the-Rosie; Duck-Duck-Goose; I Spy; Simon Says; Follow the Leader; London Bridge; A Tisket a Tasket.	Relays; Tag; Hide and Seek; Hopscotch; Snake in the Gutter; Rhythm games; Twenty Questions; Memory games; Charades; Counting games; Car traveling games.	Candyland; Funny Face; Hi-Ho Cherry-O; Pig-in-a-Garden; Goldilocks and the Three Bears; Lotto; Gnip-Gnop; Tic-Tac-Toe.	Old Maid; Snoopy; Snap; Go Fish; Authors; Hearts; Rummy; Set Back; Concentration; War; Crazy Eights; Poker; Solitaire; Preacademic learning games.	Checkers; Clue, Man From Uncle; Monopoly; TV game show games; Easy Money; Dominoes; Scrabble; Chinese Checkers; Go to the Head of the Class.	Foosball; Table hockey; Electric bowling; Air hockey; Pinball machines; Bumper pool; Electric screen games

Level IV: Hobby activities

Simple hobbies
1. Requires limited fine motor skill.
2. *Representative activities:* Finger paints; cuts with scissor; colors with crayons; pastes; makes simple potholders; cares for plants and flowers; makes simple candle and vase arrangements.

Scrapbook and collections
1. Requires sustained interest in given collection of materials.
2. *Representative activities:* Coin collection; beer can collection; photograph album; models and dolls; stamps; care for a pet; picture diary; sports scrapbook.

Arts and crafts activities
1. Requires more advanced fine motor skills and instruction-following skills.
2. *Representative activities:* Baking; decorating; needlepoint; knitting; making dolls and model airplanes; mosaics; furniture building and refinishing; woodcarving; clay work; sculpture; leather crafts.

Life science activities
1. Requires understanding of basic concepts in science.
2. *Representative activities:* Becomes involved in horticulture activities; raises and breeds pets; follows stars, planets and other phenomena in universe; visits community facilities such as planetarium and aquarium.

Level V: Sports

Individual motor activities
1. Requires limited gross motor skill; ambulatory *or* nonambulatory.
2. *Representative activities:* Rolling on mat; sitting on swing; scooting; crawling; walking; jumping on trampoline; climbing; running; hopping; throwing.

Group motor activities
1. Requires limited gross motor skill; must have ability to cooperate in group of two or more.
2. *Representative activities:* Simple ball play; group barrel rolling; wheelchair relays; Follow the Leader; use of Teeter-Totter equipment; beanbag throw.

Noncompetitive sports
1. *Representative activities:* Boating; sailing; canoeing; dancing; camping; hunting; motorcycling; biking; tree climbing; skiing; sledding.

Individual competitive sports
1. Requires basic understanding of the concept of win/lose.
2. *Representative activities:* Croquet; jogging; weight-lifting; swimming; horseshoes; pool; ping-pong; wrestling; skating; tennis; badminton; handball; gymnastics.

Team competitive sports
1. Requires basic understanding of win/lose concept and ability to work with a team.
2. *Representative activities:* Football; basketball; baseball; soccer; softball; field hockey; volleyball.

Level VI: Socialization

Restricted socialization
1. Requires ability to interact appropriately.
2. *Representative activities:* Ability to initiate friendships; having a "close" friend; visiting relatives; ability to attend social functions under supervision.

Community socialization
1. Requires ability to interact appropriately; also, must be able to travel with minimal supervision.
2. *Representative activities:* Joins clubs such as Boy Scouts and sports clubs; becomes involved in community groups and activities such as United Way and works with nonhandicapped peers; takes short courses, music lessons, etc.

Sexual expression
1. Requires understanding of basic concepts in sex education.
2. *Representative activities:* Attends dances and parties with member of opposite sex; initiates and/or receives invitations to date; engages in physical contact with member of opposite sex.

Community contributions
1. Requires ability to interact appropriately, travel independently, and accept responsibility.
2. *Representative activities:* Engages in the following types of volunteer/service work: babysitting; companion service; work for the Red Cross and local hospitals; soliciting; political campaigns; church work.

Cooperative play is characterized by children playing together with toys. This involves taking turns, sharing toys, and helping peers during free play. Cooperative play should include the following response sequence:

1. Initiating interaction without teacher prompts
2. Sustaining the interaction for a reasonable period of time
3. Receiving the interaction in a socially appropriate way
4. Terminating the interaction in a socially appropriate way

Symbolic play may be considered the most sophisticated type of toy play. In this stage children can amuse themselves with few or no play materials. Make-believe play usually only occurs when children have gone· through the previous stages of toy play.

Because several of the chapters that follow are directed toward designing toys, toy preferences, and social interaction, an in-depth discussion of this level of the curriculum is not provided here. It should be recognized, however, that in this level, as well as in the other levels, an effort has been made to arrange material from simple to more complex activities.

Passive Leisure

The passive leisure level of the recreation curriculum encompasses those skills that require little physical movement and that are sedentary in nature. They include the leisure skills that are characterized by listening, watching, reading, talking, or writing and that necessitate minimal motor activity. Unfortunately, for many developmentally disabled individuals, recreation only involves passive leisure skills like watching television or listening to the radio.

Across the passive leisure level in Table 1.1, an effort has been made to identify skills that are progressively more complex in requirements. For example, simple attending skills involve only listening or attending to stories, television, the radio, or music. In spectator activities, however, the individual would be expected to attend recreation and sporting events or any community-based spectator activity.

Complex-attending passive leisure activities, on the other hand, would require more cognitive skills. These would include working crossword puzzles, birdwatching, and outside cooking. The final phase of passive leisure involves educational activities, such as going to night college, attending adult education classes, taking music lessons, or becoming involved in other types of structured courses.

Game Activities

Games represent a major aspect of any leisure skill program. In the recreation curriculum game activities have been subdivided into six levels, from simple imitative group games through more complex table games and table game sports. This subdivision represents one effort at sequencing clusters of skills.

Group games have been divided into the very simplistic type of games that young children play (e.g., Peek-a-Boo) to the more advanced games involving Hide and Seek and Charades. Group games are an excellent medium for children to learn preacademic skills and to take turns cooperatively.

Card games and simple table games also are identified as clusters of skills that children and adults play for fun. Simple table games follow a general start-to-finish sequence. Once an individual has acquired this sequence in several games, other table games will be acquired more rapidly (Wehman et al., 1978). Complex table games are those that do not follow the simple start-to-finish sequence and may involve backward moves (e.g., Checkers), or moves characterized by atypical direction (i.e., Chinese Checkers). Table game sports are a cluster of skills that represent a miniature-sized illustration of the real sport. Air hockey, pinball, and foosball are examples of table game sports that individuals can be exposed to and taught how to play.

Hobby Activities

Within the hobby activity level of the curriculum are scrapbook and collection activities, arts and crafts, and life science activities. Hobbies are defined as those activities with which an individual spends an extended period of time and which allow for personal development and growth. Typically hobbies require some degree of fine motor coordination and are rather passive in nature.

Hobbies can be a valuable outlet for developmentally disabled persons who live alone or who have limited social contact. Unlike many leisure activities, a hobby frequently results in a finished product in which an individual can take pride.

The subdivision of hobbies in the curriculum is arbitrary at best and represents an effort at depicting skills that require increasingly more advanced skills. Admittedly there is a fine distinction between certain arts and crafts skills and life science activities like horticulture. In either cluster of skills an individual easily could become deeply involved. The most important aspect of this division, as with several levels within the curriculum, is that related skills are clustered together. This should facilitate selection of leisure skills for instruction by teachers and recreation specialists.

Sports

Sports activity is an extensive area, which has been previously analyzed and sequenced in the I CAN curriculum (Knowles, Vogel, and Wessel, 1975). Clearly, as one level in this curriculum it is far too limited; more in-depth discussions of this area can be found in adaptive physical education texts. However, because of the substantial overlap between physical education and recreation, and the importance of adaptive physical education in individualized education programs, sports activities are critical to any recreation curriculum.

Sports have been arranged initially according to simple gross motor activities. Individual activities precede group activities. Noncompetitive sports, such as biking, tree climbing, dancing, and sledding, are identified as the next cluster of sports skills. It should be apparent, however, that the creative teacher can adapt any of the motor activities or noncompetitive sports to a point at which they can become competitive among peers.

Because competition is a facet of life to which all individuals must become accustomed and adjust, individual and team competitive sports are an important aspect of leisure skill training. The concept of win and lose characterizes many relationships and life situations, and the developmentally disabled person must learn how to win graciously and also how to accept defeat. Sports are an excellent medium for this development. Furthermore, there is probably no other level in the curriculum that provides the opportunity to work cooperatively with a team. The give and take required in a team relationship also may facilitate acceptance of developmentally disabled persons by nonhandicapped peers.

Socialization

The area of socialization as a level of leisure skill development is particularly difficult to sequence inasmuch as it is pervasive throughout several other levels of the curriculum. As the individual becomes more proficient and adept at spending leisure time with others, socialization with other persons usually will evolve.

There are, however, a number of socialization skills that represent a primary level of leisure time activities. Friendships, participation in community and social clubs, and relationships with members of the opposite sex are socialization skill areas that constitute a most fulfilling type of recreation.

Four areas have been sequenced horizontally within the socialization level. Restricted socialization involves the ability to interact appropriately with peers, although with little contact with the community. It is characterized by the gradual development of sustained friendships with peers. Community socialization is the next stage and moves the individual into social clubs and other community-based programs, which provide public visibility.

Once this level of social awareness has been attained, sexual expression and experiences with members of the opposite sex should take place. Expression of sexuality may be transmitted differently across all functioning levels of developmentally disabled individuals.

It is the expression of sexuality that those involved in leisure skill training for the developmentally disabled should be most concerned with. To move closer toward a standard of normalization, there is a need to encourage sexual integration during leisure activities and to help individuals acquire appropriate socialization skills when interacting with members of the opposite sex. Recreation is an ideal vehicle for such interaction to take place. Teachers must exercise care that they do not arrange social experiences that may be anxiety producing or aversive. It may be wise initially to role play how to act in certain situations, such as how to act at a dance, and provide supportive counseling with individuals.

Skills that are required for getting a date should be explained and practiced. How to use a telephone, asking a girl out, and learning how to accept rejection are social skills with which developmentally disabled adolescent and adult males should become familiar. Recreation programs should be planned with the explicit objectives of encouraging appropriate social and sexual behavior (Hamre-Nietupski and Williams, 1977).

The issue of sex experiences for developmentally disabled persons must be faced directly by those involved in leisure time programming. Sexual expression is a popular means of recreation for many nonhandicapped individuals. Certainly this should be no different for the developmentally disabled. Recreation therapists and educators must not shy away from this commonly avoided area of programming. Instead, different programming methods and strategies should be planned to facilitate such growth in retarded persons.

Perhaps what is required in encouraging sexuality in the more severely involved is an understanding that sexual expression need not be physical sexual actions and that, in fact, a large part of sexuality is the positive feelings and self-esteem often shared between men and women. If teachers are sensitive to this distinction, sexual expression can become a real part of recreation for developmentally disabled persons.

A final stage of the socialization level is reflected by the individual making tangible contributions to the community. This involves activities such as volunteer work, working in political campaigns, or church work. At this stage the individual is no longer only taking from society but is beginning to make a substantial impact on the community in the form of service.

HOW TO USE
THE RECREATION CURRICULUM

Assessment

This curriculum may be employed as a tool for assessing leisure skill competencies of developmentally disabled persons. Although still in an underdeveloped state, it provides a representative sample of skills across the recreational spectrum. The innovative teacher can arrange these skills into a behavior checklist format in which one of two types of responses can be made:

1. A simple yes/no indication of the individual's proficiency in the skill. This would allow an assessment of which skills can be selected for instruction.
2. A more detailed indication of the individual's level of proficiency with different skills. This could reflect a format such as:
   a. Does skill independently
   b. Does skill but needs verbal cue
   c. Does skill but needs model or demonstration
   d. Needs physical assistance to perform skill

It may be that only certain levels of curriculum are of direct interest to the teacher. In this case it will be appropriate to do a careful assessment of only the relevant level in the curriculum.

Instruction

There is an instructional sequence of activities that the teacher should follow in implementing skills within the curriculum. This sequence is presented below:

Step 1. Review the curriculum carefully. Study each category and the skills within each category.
Step 2. Select skills that appear to be commensurate with the student's ability level and interests. If the student is capable, have him become involved in selection of the skill(s) for instruction. Skills may be selected across tiers (horizontally).
Step 3. Write instructional objective for skill(s) and establish prerequisite skills.
Step 4. Task analyze the skill into smaller components depending on the functioning level of the individual.
Step 5. Identify instructional procedures and materials necessary to teach skill.
Step 6. Plan for transfer of training so the student will generalize skill across materials, persons, and environments.
Step 7. Review progress of student regularly. Select the next skill(s) and repeat sequence.

To illustrate how the curriculum can be employed, two skills have been selected. In one case, assume that a developmentally disabled child named Ricky is taught a skill at the sports level; in the second case, Norman, a developmentally disabled adult, is being trained in a skill at the socialization level.

By informal observation and review of the curriculum, it was decided that Ricky should be taught an individual sports skill. Jumping rope was the skill selected, and subsequently an instructional objective and a task analysis were written. These are described in Table 1.2.

Teaching procedures included specific verbal instructions and demonstration of how to do the skill. Jump roping was taught in a forward chaining sequence, that is, Step 1 was taught first and then Step 2 was taught. Each step was cumulatively added as Ricky became more proficient.

Table 1.2. Task analysis for jumping rope

Behavioral objective: Given a rope, the student will be able to jump (skip) 18 out of 20 times.

Steps:

1. Child approaches rope.
2. Child bends over.
3. Child grasps one end of rope with right hand.
4. Child grasps one end of rope with left hand.
5. Child has rope in both hands.
6. Child places rope behind heels of feet.
7. Child spreads legs slightly apart.
8. Child brings rope forward.
9. Child lifts up feet with jumping motion.
10. Child passes rope under feet.
11. Child completes jumping motion, his feet returning to the ground.
12. Child swings rope forward again.
13. Child lifts feet with same jumping motion.
14. Child repeats process.
15. With skipping motion, child lifts one foot.
16. Child alternates other foot.
17. Rope passes underneath foot.

Once Ricky had reached criterion on the skill, he was given instruction in a different training setting with other teachers. This was done in order to promote generalization.

In the second case, Norman was judged to be approximately at the stage at which he needed guidance and counseling in sex education and sexual expression. Asking a woman to go to a social club was the target behavior identified. The skill sequence, which is delineated below and is by Nietupski and Williams (1974), provides an excellent example of how this skill should be taught.

The following are task analyses of the skills required in Phases I, II, III, and IV:

Phase I: Teaching students to use the telephone to invite classmates and teachers to engage in selected recreational activities at the home of the caller at specified times when the target person[1] answers the telephone and either accepts or declines the invitation.

More specifically, when given a cue by a teacher to arrange for a recreational interaction, the student should perform the following series of skills:

1. Given a personal directory, the student should locate the name and telephone number of a target person.

2. The student should lift the receiver.
3. The student should dial the appropriate telephone number.
4. The student should greet the person who answers with "Hello" or "Hi."
5. The student should request to speak to the target person by saying, "May I speak to (*name of target person*)?"
6. The student should identify him/herself with, "This is (*own name*)."
7. The student should make a request for the target person to engage in the recreational activity at the student's home and at a specified time by saying, "Can you (*watch TV*) at my house at (*6:30*)?"[2]
8. The student should respond appropriately to the target person's answer by giving a proper closing routine, i.e.,

    If the target person accepts the invitation, the student must say something indicating that the invitation has been accepted (e.g., "See you then. Goodbye," or "Good, see you there. Goodbye.").

    If the target person declines the invitation, the student must say something indicating that an invitation had been declined (e.g., "Sorry, maybe next time. Goodbye," or "Too bad. Goodbye.").

9. The student should hang up the receiver.
10. The student should respond correctly when the teacher asks, "Can (*target person*) come over?"

Phase II: Teaching students to use the telephone to invite classmates and teachers to engage in selected recreational activities at the home of the caller at specified times when a nontarget person[3] answers the telephone but the target person is available and accepts or declines the invitation.

More specifically, when given the cue by a teacher to arrange for a recreational interaction, the student should perform the following series of skills.

---

[1] The *target person* is the person the student wishes to ask to engage in an activity.

[2] *Times:* Times were on the hour and the half hour and chosen to reflect typical times the activities take place (e.g., dinner, 6:30; sleep over, 8:00).

[3] A nontarget person is any person other than the target person who answers the telephone.

1. Given a personal directory, the student should locate the name and telephone number of the target person.
2. The student should lift the receiver.
3. The student should dial the telephone number of the target person.
4. The student should greet the person who answers with "Hello" or "Hi."
5. The student should request to speak to the target person by saying, "May I speak to (*name of target person*)?"
6. The student should identify him/herself with, "This is (*own name*)."
7. The student should wait until the target person says "Hello."
8. The student should identify him/herself to the target person with, "This is (*own name*)."
9. The student should make a request for the target person to engage in an activity at the student's home at a specified time (e.g., "Can you (*activity*) at my house at (*specified time*)?").
10. The student should respond appropriately to the target person's answer by giving a proper closing routine, i.e.,

    If the target person accepts the invitation, the student must say something indicating the target person accepted the invitation (e.g., "See you then. Goodbye," or "Good, see you there. Goodbye.").

    If the target person declines the invitation, the student must say something indicating that an invitation has been declined (e.g., "Sorry, maybe next time," or "Too bad. Goodbye.").
11. The student should hang up the receiver.
12. The student should respond correctly when the teacher asks, "Can (*target person*) come over?"

Phase III: Teaching students to use the telephone to invite classmates and teachers to engage in six recreational activities at the home of the caller at specified times when the conditions of Phases I (target person answers) and II (nontarget person answers) with the target person accepting or declining the invitations are presented randomly.

The response chains the students were required to perform were identical to the response chains de-

lineated in Phases I and II. Certain activities[4] were always paired with the target person answering, while other activities were always paired with a nontarget person answering.

Phase IV: Teaching students to properly receive, accept, or decline invitations via the telephone to engage in selected recreational activities.

More specifically, given the situation in which the telephone rings in a student's presence:

1. The student should pick up the receiver.
2. The student should give a proper greeting by saying "Hello" or "Hi."
3. After the caller says, "Hello, may I speak to (*student*)? This is (*caller*)," the student should identify him/herself to the caller by saying, "This is (*own name*)."
4. After the caller asks the student to engage in a selected recreational activity at his/her house at a selected time, the student should request the caller to wait while he/she asks permission by saying, "Please wait," or "I will ask."
5. The student should report to the control figure[5] (teacher), in another part of the room, at least the activity or place requested and correctly answer the control figure's questions regarding conditions of the request the student did not report (i.e., either time/place or time/activity). If the student could not relate one or more conditions of the request to the control figure, it was permissible for the student to request the information from the caller.
6. The student should report to the caller whether or not he/she can accept the invitation by saying "Yes," "Yes, I can come," or "No," "No, I cannot come."
7. The student should give the proper closing routine (e.g., "Goodbye").
8. The student should hang up the receiver.

Each of these cases are extremely abbreviated descriptions of how to use the curriculum for instructional purposes. The following chapters illustrate how to develop, implement, and gen-

---

[4] *Activity* refers to the skills necessary to successfully request someone to engage in an activity. See "Activities" section for the activities taught in the program.

[5] *Control figure* refers to the person who has control over whether or not the student can engage in an activity outside the home (usually a parent). The teacher played the part of this person and would direct the student to either accept or decline an invitation.

eralize recreation skills in developmentally disabled individuals within many areas of this curriculum.

PURPOSE OF TEXT

This book has been developed primarily for teachers and recreation specialists working with developmentally disabled individuals. The purpose of the text is to provide information on curriculum, instruction, and materials for recreation programs. This text will help teachers and other practitioners develop a repertoire of leisure skills in developmentally disabled persons.

Subsequent chapters examine in depth several levels of recreation curriculum. Current research in recreation is described and evaluated in the context of leisure skill program development. In several areas, such as community-based recreation, limited research is available, and an effort is made to provide new information and programs.

A final word is in order. Although the recreation curriculum delineated in Table 1.1 provides an important beginning toward a systematic approach to programming leisure skills, it is obviously only a beginning. It will be important in the future to:

1. Expand the range of skills to include much lower functioning individuals
2. Expand the total number of skills within each cluster
3. Field test and revise the sequence in order to establish the validity of the curriculum arrangement
4. Write behavioral objectives for each skill that will ensure accountability in recreation programs
5. Write a task analysis for each skill that accurately reflects an appropriate sequence
6. Write teaching procedures and activities for each skill that have empirical verification

Furthermore, there is no reason why this curriculum sequence cannot also be used as a recreation skill inventory for assessment and evaluation purposes. It is hoped that the curriculum will continue to stimulate more sophisticated program developments in leisure instruction.

REFERENCES

Barnes, K. 1971. Preschool play norms: A replication. Dev. Psychol. 5:99–103.

Benoit, E. P. 1955. The play problem of retarded children: A frank discussion with parents. Am. J. Ment. Defic. 60:41–55.

Berkson, G., and Davenport, R. K. 1962. Stereotyped movements of mental defectives. I Intitial survey. Am. J. Ment. Defic

Berryman, D. 1968. Leisure time and mental retardation. Train. School Bull. 58:136–146.

Day, R., and Day, H. M. 1977. Leisure skills instruction for the moderately and severely retarded: A demonstration program. Educ. Train. Ment. Retard. 12(2):128–131.

Ellis, M. J. 1973. Why People Play. Prentice-Hall, Englewood Cliffs, N.J.

Hamre-Nietupski, S., and Williams, W. 1977. Implementation of selected sex education and social skills programs with severely handicappped students. Educ. Train. Ment. Retard. 12(4):364–372.

Hardman, M., and Drew, C. 1975. Incidental learning in the mentally retarded: A review. Educ. Train. Ment. Retard. 10:3–9.

Knowles, C., Vogel, P., and Wessel, J. 1975. Project I CAN: Individualized curriculum designed for mentally retarded children and youth. Educ. Train. Ment. Retard. 10(3):155–180.

Neulinger, J. 1974. The Psychology of Leisure. Charles C Thomas, Springfield, Ill.

Nietupski, J., and Williams, W. 1974. Teaching severely handicapped students to use the telephone to initiate selected recreational activities and to respond appropriately to telephone requests to engage in selected recreational activities. In L. Brown, W. Williams, and T. Crowner (eds.), A Collection of Papers and Programs Related to Public School Services for Severely Handicapped Students. Madison Public Schools, Madison, Wis.

Paloutzian, R., Hasazi, J., Streifel, J., and Edgar, C. 1971. Promotion of positive social interaction in severely retarded young children. Am. J. Ment. Defic. 75(4):519–524.

Parten, M. B. 1932. Social play among school children. J. Abnorm. Psychol. 28:136–147.

Piaget, J. 1951. Play, Dreams and Imitation in Childhood. W. W. Norton, New York.

Stanfield, J. 1973. Graduation: What happens to the retarded child when he grows up? Except. Child. 6:1–11.

Wehman, P. 1976. A leisure skills curriculum for the developmentally disabled. Educ. Train. Ment. Retard. 11(4):309–313.

Wehman, P. 1977. Helping the Mentally Retarded Acquire Play Skills: A Behavioral Approach. Charles C Thomas, Springfield, Ill.

Wehman, P., Abramson, M., and Norman, C. 1977. Transfer of training in behavior modification programs: An evaluative review. J. Spec. Educ. 11(2):217–231.

Wehman, P., Renzaglia, A., Berry, G., Schutz, R., and Karan, O. C. 1978. Developing a leisure skill repertoire in severely and profoundly handicapped persons. AAESPH Rev. 3(3).

2 SELECTING, ADAPTING, AND UNDERSTANDING TOYS AND RECREATION MATERIALS

Becky Williams, Nancy Briggs, and Ron Williams

The purpose of this chapter is to describe a systematic approach to selection and design of recreation materials for developmentally disabled individuals. No list of "right" materials is presented. Instead, the emphasis is on explaining why there are not enough appropriate recreation materials for the disabled, and why selection and adaptation are such difficult processes.

Although no absolute rules or infallible answers are set forth here, important issues that must be considered in recreation material selection are discussed. We anticipate that the information presented will stimulate intelligent questions by those faced with identifying appropriate materials.

We make few promises for instant success in evaluating materials, influencing manufacturers, or finding creative solutions to materials problems. Practical approaches to these topics are offered, along with detailed suggestions. Finally an overall framework for organizing and understanding materials-related information and processes is provided. This model should be utilized in developing and implementing recreation skills for developmentally disabled individuals.

NEED FOR SYSTEMATIC SELECTION OF RECREATION MATERIALS

The Availability Problem

A frequent dilemma faced by those involved in recreation programming is "What materials are available?" The availability problem is what we call the entire spectrum of mismatches, dissatisfactions, ignorance, nonavailability, and general frustration with educational, therapeutic, and recreation materials and equipment. The origins of this problem are widespread; they stem from an entire system of teachers, therapists, manufacturers, parents, administrators, professional organizations, suppliers, and government. No single element in the system can correct the situation without a concerted effort by the others. Regardless of the causes, it is a simple task to identify the symptoms:

> "I've found some materials that might be appropriate, but I don't know how to choose the best one."

> "Everything I've found is either too difficult for my clients to use . . . or it's not durable enough . . . or it's entirely too expensive. I'm beginning to think that appropriate materials just don't exist.

> "I can find materials that are *almost* right for my clients, but I'm not sure if I can adapt them or if I should try to make them myself. When could I find the time to do it?"

These "symptoms" are a matter of concern in community recreation programs, in facilities for the elderly, in educational programs for young handicapped children, in rehabilitation programs for disabled adolescents and adults, and in many other facilities as well. Unfortunately these problems often lead to more questions than answers: Just what is the problem? Why should I care?

How did it get this way? How *should* it be? What can I do about it? Where can I get help?

Good Materials versus Bad Materials

The dilemma presented by these questions is particularly frustrating when the importance and the benefits of good recreation materials are considered. Numerous research studies suggest the positive effects that appropriate materials may have upon a variety of populations (Wehman, 1976). An overall increase in engagement, or in active use of available materials, has been demonstrated in geriatric populations (McClannahan and Risley, 1975), and among mentally retarded adults. Materials also can have an effect on specific types of behavior. Some materials may encourage social play (Quilitch and Risley, 1972), while others seem to reduce the frequency of disruptive behaviors (Hamad, Herbert-Jackson, and Risley, 1975). Specially designed play materials may result in longer periods of engagement and may even contribute to acquisition of preacademic skills (Bartholomew, 1976).

While these data suggest a number of benefits to be derived from appropriate materials, it is unfair to assume that good materials alone are responsible for a successful program. They still have to be used appropriately and in conjunction with adequately trained staff. On the other hand, poor materials will make it difficult to meet objectives, whether they are therapeutic, educational, or recreational in nature. Poor materials will make it difficult for disabled individuals to succeed, enjoy, or benefit from your program. And poor materials often represent a considerable waste of time and money for everyone involved.

Our Perspective on Populations

In addressing these issues and offering alternatives, we have chosen to focus on that segment of the population that can be considered "developmentally young." We look at the materials problem primarily as it relates to the severely/profoundly retarded, to the multihandicapped, and to crippled and other health-impaired persons of all ages, as well as to infants (normal or exceptional) and lower functioning geriatric clients. There are several reasons for taking this stance. First, materials can make a more significant difference here. Recreation materials have a much greater chance of being wrong for these groups than they do for the mildly or moderately impaired, or for normal children and adults. Thus, the selection, adaptation, and design processes are much more critical with the developmentally young.

In addition, toy play and gross motor activity are generally most suited to the capabilities and interests of these individuals. Persons who are less disabled are more likely to be interested in organized, more sophisticated activities, such as hobbies, crafts, structured sports, etc. This fact also supports the argument that the greatest need for appropriate recreation materials is likely to be among the severely developmentally disabled. Ordinary toys, games, and recreation equipment are much more usable by higher functioning disabled persons than by the developmentally young.

Finally, there is considerable value in focusing on the severely developmentally disabled when we look at any criteria for evaluating materials. We force ourselves to consider the maximum number of variables; we must be aware of the extremes of behavior and development, as well as the combinations; we must try to "exhaust the possibilities" of what might cause a material to be inappropriate. Once sensitized to all the important factors, it is easier to generalize to higher functioning populations, in which the criteria might be less stringent.

Our Perspective on Materials

In general we think of recreation materials in terms of toys, games, sports equipment, and playground apparatus. Of course, recreation materials also may include musical instruments, books and magazines, craft and hobby supplies, therapeutic materials, etc. Because of the significant problems involved in trying to classify materials into "either/or" categories, when many of the best materials can be used for many populations and for addressing many different goals, we have chosen to think of recreation materials as a spectrum, rather than as discrete types or categories. Our basic interest lies in play materials that are appropriate for activities including stimulation and exploration, manipulation, gross motor development, creative and constructive play, socialization, and other activities at the lower levels of development.

This outlook has two basic effects on the information presented in this chapter. First, those topics such as games, music activities, hobbies, and sports, which are covered in other chapters of this book, are not discussed specifically. Second, the information relating to selection, the acquisition process, and adaptations is presented in terms of the spectrum of materials rather than particular categories. This broad perspective encourages a more comprehensive, flexible approach to materials and their uses.

Critical Skills and Information

One purpose of this chapter is to explore the variety of competing factors that have contributed to the availability problem today. It is important that all of us understand how "the system" works and what we can do about it. But identifying and explaining the problem is not enough. That is why we have included specific characteristics and considerations for evaluating play and recreation materials, information on adaptation and creation of materials, and a wealth of references. We hope to give you a framework for understanding the problem, as well as the necessary tools for creating some solutions.

Recently publishers and educators have suggested criteria for evaluating instructional materials along several different dimensions (Bleil, 1975; Boland, 1976). While their approaches to educational curriculum materials are sound, the same criteria do not lend themselves adequately to recreation materials. These authors do, however, consider the importance of evaluating materials in relation to the overall program, environment, objectives, and client or student needs. This approach is similar to what we call "evaluating the match." We must shift our thinking from evaluating materials to evaluating the match (or fit) of materials with our own client populations and within our environments. This concept of the match appears repeatedly throughout this chapter and is described in detail in a later section.

In this chapter we assume some basic knowledge of six categories of information. Part of this information is specific to a teacher's participation in an ongoing recreation program, and the rest of it relates to general understanding and awareness of materials and their uses. Together, these six categories describe both the information and the skills required for evaluation of materials, prescription of materials and activities, selection of materials for purchase, and adaptation.

1. *Clients:* Know the population you are serving and get to know your clients as individuals; whether through formal assessment or observation. If you are a student, learn about the range of developmental disabilities and the importance of client abilities and limitations, needs and goals.
2. *Objectives:* Know your program goals, as well as individual objectives for your clients; know the basic methods and strategies for attaining objectives.
3. *Administrative issues:* Familiarize yourself with your program's overall priorities, requirements, budget limits, spending deadlines, space utilization, etc.
4. *Readily available materials:* Familiarize yourself with the materials currently being used in your program and in related ones. Find out what classroom teachers, therapists, and recreation personnel are using in your community . . . and if materials can be borrowed from various agencies on a trial basis.
5. *Commercially available materials:* Know what products are available from a variety of manufacturers and distributors in recreation, education, and related fields. Keep this information in a usable form rather than just as a pile of catalogs.
6. *Creative options:* Be aware of possible assistive devices, alternate teaching strategies, environmental modifications, methods for adapting materials and creating new ones. Assess time, money, skills, equipment, and plans necessary for pursuing these creative options.

To the extent that a teacher can increase the amount of information in each of these categories, the easier it will be to determine success in meeting the availability problem and obtaining "the match."

UNDERSTANDING THE AVAILABILITY PROBLEM

The *availability problem* is a term we use to describe the current lack of appropriate play materials, the increasing barrage of information and misinformation about such products, the lack of training and research in the field, the need for adequate selection and adaptation procedures, the corresponding frustrations, and the conflicting priorities that abound. This problem is not limited to the purchasers of materials (teachers, therapists, and parents) or to the ultimate consumers (disabled children and adults). Rather, it is a failure of the entire system of materials production, distribution, and use.

A Variety of Perspectives

The characteristics of materials and "the match" described below provide a clue to the multiple priorities of teachers and therapists, as well as an indication of the complexity of the materials themselves. By examining the values and perspectives of those who have an interest in solving this problem (and who have contributed to it as well), perhaps we can better understand why the system has not been working.

First, let us consider a hypothetical play material and its importance to the actual consumer, *the disabled child or adult.* Here the most basic issues include: Is this something I can play with, something to enjoy, and help me pass the time? Does this toy or game really work, or is it broken, lost, or used up? Can I even use this play material, or is it too difficult for me? And most of all, is it really fun?

For the *purchaser,* the questions are quite different: What is the educational or developmental value of this material? Will it help me attain the objectives I've established for my child or client? Is it really safe? And durable? Can I afford it? Will it require more supervision than I can give?

In some cases, there is an additional set of questions asked by a *supervisor or administrator:* Is this a cost-effective purchase? Is the material useful for many clients, for many activities, or will it just lie on a shelf? Does this fit in my current budget cycle? Will it comply with all the regulations under which we operate? How will I justify the expenditure to my superiors? Will the addition of this material lend credibility to our program?

The *manufacturer/supplier* of this hypothetical product also has his share of questions: How will this play material sell? How big is the market? Will it be profitable for me to manufacture or distribute it? Does it fit our current production capability or sales force? How much development or marketing cost will there be before sales begin? How serious are product liability problems? What are the payoffs associated with alternative products?

Obviously each of the "special interest groups" described above has its own perspective on materials. Each would also place different emphasis on the various characteristics and dimensions of the match of materials with the client. To the degree that these perspectives are not compatible, the system will not be successful in providing materials.

Looking at Manufacturers

Earlier we described the above perspectives as belonging to "those who have an interest in solving this problem (and who have contributed to it as well)." It is important that none of us falls into the easy trap of blaming others. Manufacturers, for example, are often accused of failing to provide materials that are needed. But part of the "blame" rests on consumers who have purchased unwisely or who have not demanded responsiveness from producers. While it is true that some teachers and therapists have approached manufacturers with pleas for "appropriate" materials, they usually have been unable to translate their feelings of frustration at the lack of materials into specific product descriptions, or even constructive guidelines, that the manufacturers could use. In addition these pleas often have been directed at the company's sales representatives. Many of them are unfamiliar with the needs of the developmentally disabled and are not knowledgeable of their company's product development and production processes.

While part of the availability problem can be traced to inadequate communication of needs, many manufacturers have avoided the special education market. They have clung to the belief that the market was too small to be profitable. The "special populations" components of larger companies have tended to be stepchildren at best. Preschool or early childhood product lines already handled by the company have been modified slightly, if at all, and marketed to special educators using different terminology (such as the jargon of P.L. 94-142). This has been especially true in the school supply industry, which includes books, furnishings, play equipment, audio-visuals, etc. Materials once referred to as "educational toys" sometimes appear in this category but are rarely designed specifically for the disabled.

The toy industry would seem to be the logical place to look for play materials for the disabled, but their manufacturing and marketing styles are geared toward short product-life cycles, high powered advertising, and sales in the multimillion dollar range. While some ordinary toys may be used satisfactorily in programs for the disabled, their occurrence is, unfortunately, accidental. It is unlikely that toy manufacturers as a whole will welcome the attention of special educators any more than they have appreciated the efforts of the Consumer Product Safety Commission or the Public Action Coalition on Toys. As mentioned by the editor of a major trade publication for the toy industry, "The manufacturers have long since decided that no matter how broad their efforts to please, nothing short of going out of business altogether will meet with the full approval of the self-styled vigilantes of manufactured goods" (Murn, 1977). He was, of course, commenting on consumerists who were demanding toys that were safe, durable, nonviolent, nonracist, and nonsexist.

It is unfortunate that toy manufacturers have been so resistant to public appeals for change. Nearly 30 years ago, the American Toy Institute studied the need for toys for hospitalized children (Langdon, 1948; Gips, 1950), but it is difficult to determine any resulting impact on the industry in general.

Some manufacturers in the sports and recreation industry acknowledge the existence of disabled persons. Adaptations of equipment for bowling, wheelchair basketball, and other games are becoming more available. In addition, New Games Foundation suggests many activities that require no equipment and that stress group participation and cooperation instead of individual and team competition.

Unfortunately few of the products and activities supported by this industry are relevant to the severely physically disabled. The same is generally true of playground equipment—in spite of the label "therapeutic" now used by several manufacturers to describe their products. They fail to recognize that materials, by themselves, are rarely therapeutic. Their value depends primarily on the ways in which the materials are used.

On the other hand, manufacturers and distributors of truly therapeutic, adaptive, and rehabilitative materials and equipment have provided few products for recreational activities. Their emphasis has been on health care and self-help skills, which can hardly be criticized. However, the conclusion to all of this is the frustration of knowing that

1. Few of the manufacturers in recreation-related industries are currently interested in serving the disabled
2. Few of the suppliers of therapeutic products are able to provide recreation materials

3. Few of the smaller, specialized manufacturers are able to distribute enough products on a wide enough basis to meet the need

Nevertheless, new federal legislation may prompt more manufacturers from "adjacent" industries to "get in on the act" by producing materials for the disabled. Before we rejoice too much at that prospect, we need to recognize one fact. While this trend may result in the availability of additional products, they may not be *appropriate* products. In other words, teachers may have more from which to choose, but they also will have more of an obligation to purchase carefully. Failing to buy a good product will tend to cause the manufacturers to stop making it. Conversely, buying a bad product will tend to cause the manufacturers to continue making it.

Prices are likely to be higher than expected for new play materials. This may result from the manufacturers' greater costs for development, production, and marketing of specialized materials. Or manufacturers may see increased services for the disabled as a new rainbow for themselves—with the accompanying pot of gold at the end. This perspective has even been suggested to manufacturers and suppliers as an enticement. Information directed to suppliers by the Council for Exceptional Children (CEC) has mentioned a $3.2 billion market for special education products and services by 1982 (an amount 30 times greater than that in 1977). Subsequent information has lowered that estimate to $2.5 billion. However, a recent attempt to identify the percentage of funds now being used (or projected for the future) for acquisition of materials resulted in no information. Apparently CEC is now unable to estimate the market so clearly identified in the recent past. Misleading manufacturers in order to get them into the market is a disservice to everyone. They will become disillusioned quickly if their attempts do not result in appreciable sales. They then will have "learned their lesson" and will avoid *any* products for the special education market in the future.

Looking Within Our Professions

It may be difficult to understand or empathize with the problems faced by manufacturers and suppliers. Nevertheless, it should be realized that recreation and developmental disabilities are very difficult markets with which to deal, both individually and in combination. They are constantly moving targets and are very confusing for many materials producers. However, part of that confusion is a reflection of the upheaval in fields related to both recreation and developmental disabilities.

Looking specifically at professionals who serve the developmentally disabled, it is unsettling to see the inconsistencies in terminology, the variations in populations served, and the differences in priorities. There is little agreement on whether special recreation materials are even desired, let alone necessary. Some believe that special materials are "anti-mainstreaming." Others say that such materials are required in order to meet program objectives. Many professionals seem to have had tunnel vision in that they focused on only one aspect of development, to the exclusion of all others. New emphasis is being placed on the need to serve the "total person," and more and more agencies are providing balanced programs of education, therapy, job training, recreation, etc.

Focusing on recreation for a moment, it is interesting to note the increased "status" of recreation and leisure activity in this country. Formerly in low positions on many priority and funding lists, recreation eventually may receive the attention it deserves. Currently professionals in public recreation are feeling the impact of federal legislation regarding accessibility of their facilities and programs to the developmentally disabled. They may be among the most vocal in expressing their need for special materials and equipment. At the same time, professionals in therapeutic recreation are trying to assimilate a coherent philosophy and strategy for providing their services to a greater number of disabled individuals.

Additional and improved recreation programs are becoming more common as we learn about the importance of play in early development and the relevance of leisure activity to both mental and physical health. In addition to the differences in opinion and emphasis within the service delivery system, there are also the pressure and uncertainty caused by Public Law 94-142. Educators are unsure of their funding channels and confused about their potential liability for lack of student progress. Recreation personnel are trying to determine the best ways of providing mandated activities in physical education, therapeutic recreation, and leisure. No one is sure of the potential advantages of the Individualized Education Programs (IEPs) and their role in materials selection and evaluation.

For the time being, when special educators and recreation personnel begin to evaluate materials to use with their newly written IEPs, they are faced with a barrage of advertising claims, product information, and technical specifications. This is potentially valuable for the trained materials specialists but tends to unnerve the average teacher or therapist. The problem becomes one of comparing apples and oranges, when peaches are what is really desired.

A balanced approach to advertising standards and product evaluation is suggested in a magazine article originally directed to parents.

> By suggesting that special materials are critical for the disabled child, ordinary toys of proven value may be set aside. [On the other hand,] there are certainly situations where new materials are necessary and should be obtained. But if a frisbee will suffice, call it a frisbee, not a motor control device (Audette, 1973).

Further advice and support for the confused professional may be available from some of the newer information systems such as NIMIS, IRUC, and TRIC. Newsletters of various organizations sometimes offer information regarding new products or those that have been evaluated in their facilities. Many universities have an Instructional Materials Center, or someone on the faculty in special education, recreation, or occupational therapy, who can offer assistance. A few communities have organized "toy libraries" of play materials that are available on a loan basis to families with disabled children.

Unfortunately many information systems and service agencies seem to duplicate the efforts of similar groups. They seem to emphasize the dissemination of information and products, without attending to the feedback function that is necessary for increased and improved play materials. They fail to provide specific enough information to help the professional choose from among multiple entries within each "search" category. The net result is that the individual is provided with all sorts of apparent alternatives, but with virtually no help in evaluating them. And no systematic information is provided to manufacturers with respect to needed changes and desired new products.

Although currently a "weak link" in the system, with increased efforts by producers and consumers alike, the information systems and service organizations may have the potential to alleviate part of the availability problem.

Summarizing the Availability Problem

In attempting to help provide a broader understanding of the availability problem, we have described various perspectives at work within the system. The conflicting values and priorities of the ultimate consumer, the purchaser, the administrator, and the manufacturers are all too obvious. We also have explored some of the inconsistencies and some of the pressures acting upon both producers and consumers. Each group is so concerned with its own operations and problems that it is surprising that appropriate recreation materials can be found at all. What remains is the necessity for: 1) developing an overall view of the system in functional terms, 2) facilitating communication among groups within the system, and 3) improving the acquisition process as a whole.

CHARACTERISTICS OF PLAY MATERIALS AND "THE MATCH"

When we begin to examine play and recreation materials, we soon learn that the phrase "a simple toy" is terribly misleading. Many of us have tended to underestimate the complexity of play materials, just as play itself has been underestimated. We have selected and purchased materials on the basis of superficial characteristics, and have failed to consider the more subtle variables related to our environments and the individual users. We have failed to look "beyond the obvious" in terms of creative utilization and adaptation of materials. In short, we have not really known what to look for, and we have not understood what we have seen.

Let us assume that our major goal is to identify "appropriate" play and recreation materials. When we look at a material (or a photograph or a plan for one), we want to be able to say, "Yes, that's what I need," or "Well, that's worth trying," or "No, just forget that one." And we want to be reasonably sure that our judgment is accurate. Unfortunately this ability may take more skill and effort than we realize. How can we possibly hope to succeed at such a complex task?

Because we are trying to assess or predict appropriateness, let us consider the most effective procedure available. Obviously, the best way to evaluate a material is to *use it.* There is just no substitute for hands-on experience, especially with play materials for the developmentally disabled.

Several recent studies have attempted to evaluate specific materials with disabled children, adolescents, and adults. Data have been collected on the amount of time spent with each material, resulting in comparative measures of preference and engagement (Favell and Cannon, 1977; Hamad et al., undated). Even without the systematic collection of data, the basic advantage of a hands-on evaluation of an existing material remains. One can observe, and even measure, many of the variables that are working together to produce the success or failure of that particular product used with that particular client. Evaluation no longer occurs in a vacuum. Instead, the material can be assessed in the environment and with the individual users; in short, "the match" can be focused upon.

Of course, a "free trial" of all interesting materials is not possible, and certainly a hands-on evaluation of possible adaptations or homemade materials cannot be conducted until they have been completed. But all the issues and variables that are at work in a hands-on evaluation are the ones that should be considered, whether selecting, adapting, or creating new materials.

Once again, the emphasis is on evaluating the match, rather than the material in isolation. This means that the recreation programmer will have to consider not only the obvious materials characteristics such as size and price but also any relevant information concerning the individual users and the total program. Some of this information is objective: one can read a diagnostic evaluation of the user's abilities; the play material can be weighed and measured; the program's budget allowed for materials can be determined. On the other hand, much of the information is subjective; frequently a teacher can only get a "feel" for the client's preferences related to materials. In this case the possible uses of a material can best be hypothesized. Finally, many considerations will fall in the realm of "best guesses" and value judgments that attempt to assimilate all the prior information.

In short, a whole spectrum of objective and subjective questions must be asked about any play materials that are considered seriously. Figure 2.1 may help clarify some of the variables that should be addressed—and their relationships—but it certainly does not exhaust the possibilities.

Each of the variables is further described in terms of specific questions related to the issues and items of concern. These variables are pre-

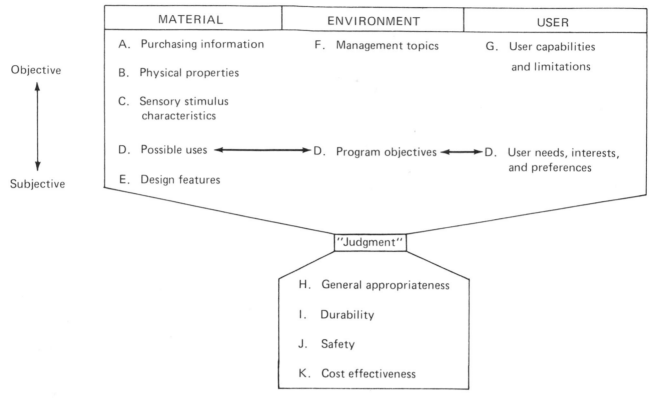

Figure 2.1   Variables for evaluating "the match."

sented as questions for several reasons. We hope this format increases understanding of the uncertainty involved in evaluating materials. Furthermore, we have tried not to imply any particular "value" to whatever answers might be given. For example, consider the questions of size and weight: Is "big and heavy" good? Is "big and lightweight" better? Is "small and medium weight" necessarily bad? Answers to such questions are meaningless, unless they are related to a specific material and its user in pursuit of certain objectives. They do, however, suggest valuable areas for empirical study and data-based evaluation of materials with specific groups of disabilities. We might hypothesize, for example, that lightweight objects are used more easily by arthritics, while heavier objects provide needed resistance to the tremors of cerebral palsied clients. Resulting data would provide concrete suggestions for manufacturers to utilize in product development.

Once teachers are familiar with the questions, it will probably be helpful to abbreviate or exclude some of the considerations that do not pertain to

their population or environment. It is necessary, however, to be aware that each of these questions has relevance and importance to someone involved in "the system" of materials development, evaluation, acquisition, and utilization. Thus, whenever trying to evaluate the match, consider the following variables:

A. *Purchase Information*
1. Cost: retail price? quantity or school discounts? shipping and/or installation included? cost from alternative sources?
2. Source: direct from manufacturer? known distributors? catalog?
3. Availability/delivery time: immediate availability? promised delivery? past performance of supplier?

B. *Physical properties*
1. Size: overall dimensions? size of smallest pieces? of largest pieces?
2. Weight: ounces, pounds, grams? compared to size, is it heavy or lightweight?
3. Materials: paper or cardboard? wood or

plastic? metal? glass or fabric? overall quality?

4. Construction: glued or stapled? sewn or tacked? nailed, screwed, or bolted? overall craftsmanship?
5. Number of pieces: complete, as is? part of a larger set? many small pieces versus few large pieces?

C. *Sensory stimulus characteristics*
1. Primarily neutral or pastel color: eye catching? babyish?
2. Primarily one bright color: distinct? a primary color?
3. Two or more bright colors: contrasting? confusing?
4. Mechanical "noise": attention getting? distracting?
5. Self-contained light source: intensity? battery operated?
6. Reflected light: breakable?
7. Observable moving parts: duration of movement? response required to initiate movement?
8. Primarily smooth, hard surface: interesting to touch?
9. Primarily soft and/or fuzzy: washable? durable?
10. A variety of textures: strong differences for discriminations? still washable and durable?
11. Presents noticeable odor: pleasant? unpleasant?
12. Vestibular stimulation: involves movement in space? spinning? rolling? swinging?
13. Instrumental music sounds: discern instruments? harmonious?
14. Vocal music: recorded singing understandable? childish?
15. Speech (i.e., a "talking toy"): distinct? relevant content?

D. *Possible uses of play material/program objectives/user needs, interests, and preferences*
1. Sensory awareness, exploratory activity?
2. Body awareness, self-concept?
3. Gross motor development, vigorous physical activity, mobility?
4. Manipulation, fine motor development, eye-hand coordination?
5. Self-help skills, prevocational?
6. Speech and language, alternative communication skills?

7. Preacademic skills: reading, writing, math readiness?
8. Creative play?
9. Independent play?
10. Cooperative play?
11. Group play and games?
12. Hobbies and special interests?

E. *Design features*
1. Simplicity: simple required responses? few components? uncluttered design?
2. Complexity: multisensory? numerous pieces? advanced concepts or skills?
3. Realism: relevant to user's needs? accurate in detail?
4. Fantasy: admittedly "just pretend?" confusing or inspiring or frightening?
5. Static or variable: is material completely predictable? does it provide a variety of responses?
6. Malleable: can user change the shape or configuration?
7. Interactive or observable: is it manipulated? or watched?
8. Operation/use: minimum touch, grasp, pressure? easy to do? useful for self-instruction? provides feedback? self-correcting? low frustration level?
9. Special interest: nonethnic? nonsexist? nonviolent? relates to specific use category in D, above?

F. *Management topics*
1. Location for use: indoors—table or floor? carpet or hard surfaced floor? outdoors—grass, sand, hard surface? shade or sun?
2. Additional requirements: batteries or electricity? water for use or cleanup? other appliances, utilities, or supplies needed?
3. Supervision: constant or occasional? structured or unstructured use? instructions available and understandable? replacement parts available? amount of set-up time required? amount of time for dismantling, cleanup or putting away?
4. Storage: require additional storage space? packaging useful for storage? can person use and return to storage independently?
5. Other: portability? require permanent installation?

G. *User's capabilities and limitations*
  1. Sensory awareness: vision? hearing? tactile? oral? olfactory (smell)? kinesthetic? vestibular?
  2. Physical condition: strength? endurance? flexibility? agility? coordination?
  3. Mobility: ambulatory? nonambulatory? wheelchair? braces/walker?
  4. Gross motor: head and trunk control? creeps or crawls? sits? stands and walks? runs, jumps, climbs? catches, throws, kicks?
  5. Fine motor: manipulates small objects? uses eyes and hands in coordinated manner?
  6. Perceptual motor: brings objects to midline? crosses midline? spatial awareness? awareness of body parts? laterality? directionality?
  7. Communication skills: receptive language? expressive language? imitates? verbalizes appropriately?
  8. Social-emotional: responds to adults? to children? plays independently, cooperatively, competitively? engages in creative activity? play characterized as messy? fantasy oriented? passive or active?
  9. Cognitive: attention span? color, shape, size discrimination? problem-solving ability? rule following? uses numbers/letters?
  10. Other behaviors: strong preferences for certain materials or activities? strong dislikes? general behavior toward material and equipment?
H. *General appropriateness*
  1. Play value: potential benefits of use? educational, developmental? social or emotional value? enjoyable?
  2. Adaptable: to various skill levels? to specific disabilities? utilize a sequence of abilities?
  3. General interest and appeal: eye catching? attractive? appealing? provokes curiosity or interest?
I. *Durability of play material:* What would happen if it were
  1. Chewed?
  2. Dropped or thrown?
  3. Stepped or jumped on?
  4. Pounded on?

  5. Cut or torn?
  6. Soaked or wet on?
  7. Subjected to heat or flame?
  8. Subjected to deliberate abuse and/or vandalism?
J. *Safety issues:* If used inappropriately or without supervision, could this play material
  1. Be swallowed?
  2. Be hazardous if chewed?
  3. Generate harmful fumes, dust, or lint?
  4. Cut, burn, strangle?
  5. Carry germs or allergens?
  6. Be a fire hazard?
  7. Be a puncture hazard?
  8. Produce eyestrain?
  9. Produce harmful noise levels?
  10. Produce sustained contraction of muscles?
  11. Produce seizure through overstimulation?
  12. Produce injury if thrown at another?
  13. Be a hazard to step on or climb on?
K. *Cost effectiveness*
  1. Initial overall cost: including shipping? additional requirements and equipment for proper use?
  2. Guarantee available: stated guarantee? past experience with supplier?
  3. Multiple purposes: for a wide range of objectives? for a variety of activities? for one particular child? for many children?
  4. Useful life: consumed with one use? useful for several years? meet durability requirements?

Taken as a whole, these questions may serve several purposes, depending on a teacher's particular needs. For example, they may be used for:

1. Considering and/or selecting materials to be purchased
2. Evaluating the match of existing materials with uses and objectives
3. Providing guidelines for improved adaptations and homemade materials
4. Suggesting needed materials in precise terms
5. Suggesting new materials or activities to try
6. Considering other people's perspectives in the availability problem

However used, remember that these are *questions,* not answers. One should not necessarily believe that a "perfect match" with Product X has been found. Mismatches may develop as children "outgrow" materials; the population of disabilities which is served may change; program emphasis may shift; objectives may be modified drastically; teaching style may change. Any or all of these may lead to a mismatch even where careful selection and evaluation have taken place previously.

OBTAINING "THE MATCH": PURCHASE OPTIONS AND PROCEDURES

It is unfortunate—but generally true—that materials are often the last thing considered in programming activities of any kind. All too often, efforts are concentrated on assessing the client, specifying objectives, developing a "total" program, planning strategies, acquiring adequate facilities, and training personnel in general techniques. While each of these is important to a successful program, it almost seems that staff members "run out of steam" at just the time they need to face the issues of acquiring materials and/ or improving the match of existing materials to their objectives and clients.

In addition the process of acquiring play materials apparently has been viewed as something that "just happens." Perhaps too many people have assumed that the ability to identify appropriate materials is an inherent trait of all teachers and therapists. Actually the converse is more the case, as reported by Foos (1976). In a survey of 101 teachers of the disabled, 98% indicated a need for teacher skills to organize and modify teaching aids and materials.

Part of the problem obviously lies in the failure of most teacher-training programs to include components on selection and acquisition of materials that provide sufficiently practical information to benefit the teacher in the classroom.

Until recently the process of selecting and acquiring materials has received little attention. Acquisition of materials involves an investment of time and energy that often results in disillusionment and disappointment, especially when searching for materials for the disabled. It has been all too common for programs to "do without" or "make do" with less than appropriate materials, simply because the acquisition process has been a negative learning experience. This is a result of not only the limited supply of excellent recreation materials for the developmentally disabled but also the lack of appropriate guidelines and train-

ing for evaluation of the materials that are available.

Perhaps we should enumerate the possible methods of obtaining the match, because too many people think the options are limited.

1. *Purchasing* of materials is the most obvious means of acquisition, or obtaining "the match."
2. *Borrowing* may be utilized for meeting short term objectives, or for a "trial run" prior to purchasing.
3. *Adapting* existing materials or purchasing new materials specifically for their adaptability is often necessary for obtaining "the match" with disabled clients.
4. *Modifying* the environment can also improve "the match."
5. *Assisting* the individual user through prostheses, etc., can help in obtaining a better match.
6. *Changing* program objectives or teaching strategies may also be good alternatives.
7. *Creating* new materials may also be a reasonable alternative in some situations.

Regardless of the method for obtaining "the match," it will be helpful to be fully informed on them all. This allows much greater freedom and flexibility in making careful decisions.

Improved Processes for Gathering Information

Some consumers are completely unnerved by the prospect of initiating the search for appropriate materials. Others have several ideas for possible manufacturers and suppliers; they can access information retrieval systems, and they regard the acquisition process as an interesting challenge. They are adept in the first preliminary process for materials acquisition—that of information gathering. Table 2.1 indicates the spectrum of consumer behavior related to information on available materials.

There are several steps that teachers can take to increase their information about play materials. These steps are especially significant if you are still in training, or are setting up a new program. Such information and procedures will be beneficial whether you are purchasing materials for the first time or as part of your ongoing duties.

The following are suggestions of how to obtain information and develop systems for efficient use.

Table 2.1. Spectrum of consumer behavior: Information gathering

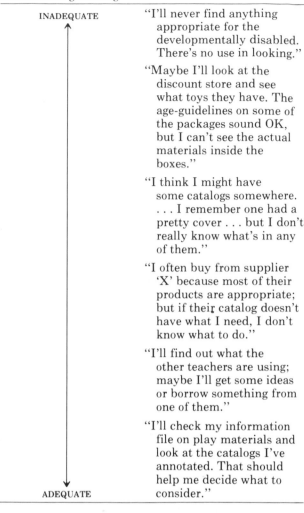

INADEQUATE

"I'll never find anything appropriate for the developmentally disabled. There's no use in looking."

"Maybe I'll look at the discount store and see what toys they have. The age-guidelines on some of the packages sound OK, but I can't see the actual materials inside the boxes."

"I think I might have some catalogs somewhere. . . . I remember one had a pretty cover . . . but I don't really know what's in any of them."

"I often buy from supplier 'X' because most of their products are appropriate; but if their catalog doesn't have what I need, I don't know what to do."

"I'll find out what the other teachers are using; maybe I'll get some ideas or borrow something from one of them."

"I'll check my information file on play materials and look at the catalogs I've annotated. That should help me decide what to consider."

ADEQUATE

They apply primarily to purchased materials, but similar procedures can be followed for adaptations and homemade materials.

1. Create your own file for information concerning play materials:
    a. If someone tells you about a good product they have used, jot down its name, the manufacturer's name, and its use
    b. Include information from workshops, magazines and journals, professional organizations, newspapers, etc.
    c. Include information on Instructional Materials Centers (IMCs), lending libraries, and other sources of borrowed materials
2. Obtain play materials catalogs and brochures from as many different manufacturers and suppliers as possible. Many companies advertise in journals and professional magazines, exhibit at conventions, or are listed in various directories of products and services. Write a postcard asking for current catalogs and to be put on their permanent mailing list. If multiple copies are needed, many manufacturers will be happy to supply them for classes, in-service workshops, etc. Whenever possible, let the supplier know where you learned about them so that they will know how to best provide information to the market. Wasted advertising increases the cost of the materials.
3. Attend conventions. Look for sessions and presentations that apply to your population or your greatest problem area. If the presenters seem knowledgeable, ask questions. Conventions are also a good way to obtain catalogs and to examine available products. Do not hesitate to question the sales representatives critically. If they do not give satisfactory answers, ask for sources of that information within their company. Sign up for future mailings by having labels with your address made prior to the convention. These can be attached easily to any sign-up sheet, will save you a lot of time for inspecting the materials, and will be much more legible for the supplier.
4. Join professional organizations. Conventions are usually good sources for lists of publications and other information. Membership usually includes subscriptions to journals or newsletters that may have articles about play, recreation, materials evaluation, etc. Many organizations sell or rent their mailing lists; this increases the information that may be received directly from manufacturers and distributors.
5. Develop a system for using the play materials file. Before storing the information in a pile at the corner of your desk, develop a system for reviewing and editing. This system need not be elaborate and time consuming—just usable. When looking at a new catalog or brochure, make notes in the margins. If special materials are good for a particular handicapping condition or a specific individual, include this comment in the note. Paper clip important pages for easy access. Consider keeping a separate list by handicapping condition or by individual which lists items that have been located, as well as their sources.

6. Collect information on criteria for selecting and evaluating materials. Revise and modify procedures and criteria so that they fit the child's particular needs.

7. Keep a running "want list" of materials *needed* and one of items that are *desired*. If these are available materials, make a note of the manufacturer's name, catalog location, prices, etc. It will probably help to make another list of ideas you have for something to make or adapt; sketch them, no matter how roughly. Also indicate why any of these materials are needed and the individuals or groups who would benefit from them.

Many of these information-gathering procedures can be started even before beginning a recreation program. They will simplify the job later and save valuable time.

Improved Methods for Stating Needs

Once a recreation program is initiated, work on the second preliminary process necessary to effective materials acquisition can begin: writing specific "needs statements." Each needs statement should clearly define and describe one material that is necessary to the program. The needs statement should mesh with the client evaluations and individualized objectives. In making evaluations and writing objectives, either as an individual or a team member, the format of a needs statement should be obvious. If working in an informal setting where evaluations and objectives are less defined, it is still important to consider them.

For example, the needs statement that is developed must reflect the abilities and limitations of the individual or group with whom the material will be used. At the same time the needs statement must specify the objectives that will be met in using the material. A specific statement will help describe the situation, as well as communicate teachers' materials needs to others. Some examples of both inadequate and adequate needs statements are provided in Table 2.2.

Improved Procedures for Purchasing

The third preliminary process for materials acquisition focuses on considering both the purchase option and the creative options at once. Referring to the six categories of information described earlier, it is necessary to weigh the advantages and disad-

Table 2.2. Spectrum of consumer behavior: Needs statements

INADEQUATE	"I need to spend $200 by the end of this week."
	"I need something to keep Sue busy."
	"I need a material for independent, free-play activities."
	"I need something to use for increasing Rick's fine motor coordination."
	"I need a large ball to use in reflex and recreation activities with a small group of adolescent, multihandicapped clients."
	"I need a durable, self-contained manipulative toy that will fit a wheelchair tray and provide a variety of sensory stimulation experiences for a severely disabled, 4-year-old child with cerebral palsy."
ADEQUATE	

vantages of each alternative. Let us consider the purchase option first. While the details of adaptation and creation are discussed in a later section, much of the following information on purchasing can apply to these two options as well.

Assume that the preliminary processes have been completed:

1. Adequate information on available products
2. A clearly defined needs statement
3. Purchasing is the first choice for acquisition

Up to this point, the teacher has been more or less "in control" of the situation. Now it is necessary to take into account those factors that are either outside his control or are matters of judgment.

Budget and Deadlines

Two aspects of purchasing are usually predetermined by supervisors. One is budget, which is how much money has been allocated for the program. While it may not be possible to modify your current budget, a well organized list of needed materials may carry some weight in obtaining additional funding in the future. Thus, a second aspect of purchasing is the deadline for making selections. This information indicates *when* materials must be ordered to take advantage of available funding. From the teacher's perspective, purchasing deadlines are frequently too short, causing a panic situation to develop. Circumstances creating the need for quick purchasing decisions make the development of a personal file of available materials extremely important. Another issue to consider is the fact that new programs are sometimes funded at much higher levels than existing programs. Purchasing for the first year of any program requires extra caution and effort. Try to maximize the flexibility and adaptability of the materials when there is uncertainty about the exact needs and capabilities of the clients.

Funding Options

If the purchase option appears impossible because available funds have been exhausted, asking civic and charitable groups to donate money or specific materials is one possibility. A word of caution, however; ask the group to give money for a specific item or describe *exactly* the play material that is needed. It is of no benefit for a well meaning organization to give a recreation program items that are inappropriate and/or inadequate. If a charity group offers to make something for the program, do not accept the offer automatically. Share the evaluation criteria and plans for needed adaptations and homemade materials. Check to see that such "free" materials, once completed, are still satisfactory when "the match" is evaluated.

Cost Effectiveness

Once the budget and the purchase deadline are determined, the analysis of what to purchase begins. Because programs operate on limited funds, the cost effectiveness of materials is a major consideration. It is important to identify an approximate "cost per individual," which reflects the multiple uses of the same material by several individuals. Thus a $30 material that addresses the objectives for one client is not as cost effective as another $30 material, or even a $50 material, that can be used with five or six clients. Likewise, a material that is likely to break sooner than a more expensive item may not be a good purchase. Higher initial cost does not, necessarily, mean higher quality; usefulness to a program needs to be considered along with price in order to maximize the cost-effective use of limited funds.

Catalog Purchases

There are several methods for purchasing play materials, but buying from a catalog is probably the most common. Since this can be a confusing task, be sure to refer to the evaluation criteria outlined earlier to assist you in identifying product characteristics. When purchasing from a catalog, be sure to consider the following:

1. Get out all of the catalogs, and compare prices of similar or identical items. Look for the most cost-effective material.
2. Check to see if shipping costs are included in the catalog price. If not, include estimated costs in comparisons.
3. Check the stated delivery time.
4. Critically read and evaluate the text and pictures in relation to specified evaluation criteria.
   a. What are the stated uses of the material? Do they seem accurate? Can you think of additional uses?
   b. Is the material suggested for certain populations? Is it a valid suggestion? How does it compare to your client population?
   c. Age guidelines? Watch out! They are not usually specific enough to be applicable to the disabled.
   d. Determine the actual size of the material by keeping a ruler in front of you. Remember, both photographs and drawings can make the product appear larger than it really is.
   e. Quality and types of materials should be assessed. Avoid "staples," "surface washable," and "pressboard," for example.
5. Evaluate product claims and guarantees.
   a. Is the product returnable if you are dissatisfied?
   b. If the product breaks, who repairs it? How much of a delay will there be?

Remember that the listing in the catalog is an attempt by the supplier to make that material look its best. For example, if the catalog says "giant 10-inch circumference ball," get out a ruler to see how a "giant" 10 inches compares to a "tiny" 10 inches. Then remember that the circumference is really more than three times bigger than the diameter, and you will realize that you could easily hold this "giant" ball between your thumb and forefinger!

Avoiding Pitfalls and Confusion

Whether purchasing direct from local suppliers or through catalogs, there are several additional "traps" that should be avoided. In general they are characterized by impulsiveness, inadequate information, and failure to consider "the match." For example,

> "This item really looks cute. It should be good for something."

> "It's the end of the semester and I don't know who will be in my class next term, but I have to spend $500 by Thursday."

> "This is really a nice package, but I can't see what the actual product is like."

> "This salesperson is so convincing and persuasive. He says his materials are 'just what I need'."

Instead of falling into these traps, remember to consider specific individuals and their needs. Use the needs statements that have been generated for different clients. This ensures that no one will be overlooked. Listen to and discuss recommendations of colleagues. Read available literature on current trends and research in the field of play materials. Develop a set of questions to ask salespeople about materials in relation to the population with whom you work. Also ask salespeople about product testing and research to support their product claims. Remember that "research" to most salespeople means "market research" (how well will this item sell) rather than research into the benefits to be derived by the clients through the use of the product. Do not purchase from a specific company based solely on their reputation. Some manufacturers and distributors provide a mixture of high quality and questionable products, and that mix can change from one year to the next. If limited information is available, it is better to select materials from manufacturers providing good materials in the past. But do not assume that all of their products are good any more than you should assume that all products from other companies will be bad.

It is interesting to note that some companies are now utilizing professional advisory boards and college-based testing facilities in their promotional literature (Cassell, 1975). Do not assume that this qualifies as an endorsement by these professionals for every product in that company's catalog. Usually advisory boards are supervising the format and categorization of products or are en-dorsing the overall approach of the firm. This may contribute nothing to your consideration of a particular material. Another issue to consider is the prevalence of early childhood education materials being labeled as materials for the developmentally disabled. Few of these materials are appropriate for older disabled persons, no matter what their level of functioning. Many of these products are not even useful for young disabled, especially if they have physical handicaps or severe developmental disabilities.

Teachers are less likely to be placed in a "dead-end" or "no-win" position when purchasing materials if they can:

1. Maximize information before making decisions
2. Clearly define or describe the materials needed, i.e., formulate a needs statement
3. Consider the characteristics of "the match" throughout the selection and purchasing procedure

The ability to follow through on these processes may well mean the difference between success and failure.

OBTAINING "THE MATCH": CREATIVE OPTIONS

When a mismatch in materials, environment, and individual user occurs, every effort should be made to "improve the match." Purchasing new materials, as described in the preceding section, is the most obvious option, but not always the most feasible. The greatest barriers to the purchase option are limited funds and limited availability of appropriate materials. While these barriers may be attacked and eventually overcome, the teacher/therapist is usually looking for a more immediate answer to the mismatch. This leads us to the "creative options" that should be explored whenever a match is unsatisfactory.

Creative options include adapting materials, modifying the environment, changing objectives and strategies, assisting the user, and creating new materials. These options are summarized in Table 2.3, with many examples suggested by the recent work of Brackman (1978).

The most significant problem with creative options is that it is too easy to rush into them and pick the quickest, easiest, and cheapest solution that occurs to you. To be perfectly frank, that is a

Table 2.3. Creative options

1. Assist the individual
   a. Positioning
   b. Prostheses/sensory aids
   c. Assistive devices—for mobility, grasping, etc.

2. Modify the environment
   a. Increase lighting
   b. Reduce "background" noise level
   c. Improve floor, table, or ground surface
   d. Change from structured to unstructured environment, or vice versa
   e. Use swimming pool, air mattress, etc.

3. Change program objectives/teaching strategy
   a. Remove extraneous objectives
   b. Add more practice
   c. Program lower steps in developmental process
   d. Program missing steps
   e. Program higher steps
   f. Change required response
   g. Change to another activity or material with the same objectives
   h. Change to another mode of activity
   i. Combine two or more materials
   j. "Teach up" to desired response

4. Adapt the material
   a. Stabilize
   b. Enlarge
   c. Prosthetize for individual
   d. Reduce required response
   e. Make more familiar
   f. Make more concrete
   g. Remove extraneous cues
   h. Remove distracting stimuli
   i. Add more cues or strengthen existing ones
   j. Improve safety/durability

5. Create the material
   a. Use available plans
   b. Use donated labor or materials
   c. Do it all yourself

completely irresponsible approach . . . and it happens all too often. The results range from poorly made, but "cute," manipulative toys to "community-involvement" playgrounds that are well intentioned but inappropriate. And the costs involved in these options, although they are more difficult to see, are just as real as the dollar amounts that are spent for the purchase options.

We are mentioning the negative side of the creative options here, not because these options are unsatisfactory, but because it is critical that they be used only by *informed* personnel. The success of each creative option depends on the clarity of the needs statement and the dimensions of "the match" outlined in Table 2.2 and Figure 2.1. Without this factual, reality-based orientation to

the problem, clever and artistic ideas can rapidly turn into disasters.

Assuming that teachers are sensitive to these pitfalls, let us turn to the positive (and fun!) side of the creative options. Here the greatest asset is flexibility of approach. When a mismatch occurs, it is necessary to juggle the options and look for the possibilities. Whether concentrating on materials, teaching strategies, or the environment, teachers must consider many "What ifs?" and even more "Why nots?" It is important to be flexible in terms of considering all of the options.

Considering the "What Ifs?"

The developmental model of human growth and learning will suggest some of the most likely alternatives and opportunities for creative options. Comprehensive assessment tools present logical categories of skills and, within each category, describe the sequence of normal development (Vort Corporation, 1973; Gross and Cohen, 1975). If one is familiar with developmental sequences, this will facilitate "looking backwards" in many sequences of skills and searching for developmental levels of activities that might lead to a better match, i.e., you can locate basic skills required before your original objectives can be addressed.

Similarly it will be helpful to consider more advanced levels of development for enriching activities, and additional skill categories for combining several activities at once. In addition to the developmental model, the fields of sensori-motor integration, perceptual-motor development, and occupational therapy are rich in the possibility of suggesting creative options (Wilbarger and Kuizenga, undated; Banus et. al., 1971; Pyfer, 1976). There are few yes-or-no answers here . . ., but many challenging and rewarding options are available to those who seek them out.

Looking at the "Why Nots?"

In this section we want to mention the problems and actual dangers that may lie with creative options. Many of them are similar to our concerns with purchased materials. Unfortunately some persons persist in understating the costs and overestimating their own competence in the area of creative options. Their approach certainly fails to improve "the match." Instead, it results in materials that are expensive, poorly constructed, inappropriate, unsafe, and totally dysfunctional.

Once again, when creative options are pursued, it is necessary to consider all the characteristics of the match detailed earlier. If a teacher cannot provide better-than-average durability and excellent safety characteristics, then it is critical to try and improve program plans, raw materials, and teaching skills. Failing that, all other options must be reconsidered. When considering the cost effectiveness of modifications, adaptations, and newly created materials, any "hidden" costs must be examined. Such costs can include greater than anticipated investment of time for planning, locating supplies and raw materials, supervising volunteer labor, and actual creation or construction. There also may be significant costs for the ultimate users, especially if inappropriate materials or improper strategies result in wasted time, confusion, or injury. These factors also must be considered when pursuing creative options.

Another problem that pertains specifically to adapted and created materials is that of product liability. Strictly speaking, if any injury results from the use of the "new product," a client could sue for damages, with the teacher possibly being judged at fault. Large maufacturers can purchase product liability insurance to protect against such claims and pass the expense on to the purchasers of their products. Smaller companies find it difficult to afford the premiums for such insurance and may, in fact, be forced to "self-insure." Teachers, as the professional providers of services, may be able to obtain coverage with some types of professional insurance. Ultimately, court cases will settle the questions of the rights of the clients and the rights of those providing materials to them. In any event, safety of the material is of paramount importance.

Before examining two of the creative options more closely, examine Table 2.3 for suggestions concerning assistive devices, prostheses, and environmental modifications. These should be utilized in a program only with the advice and support of registered occupational or physical therapists and/or the approval of medical staff and related clinicians. Additional sources of information on positioning and environmental modifications (Finnie, 1975; Campbell, Green, and Carlson, 1977; Living Environments Group and Western Carolina Center, undated) are included in references in the Appendix.

Changing Objectives and Strategies

Creative teaching is a challenging topic that relies on flexibility in objectives and strategies. Too many teachers and therapists are given materials and told that they should be able to "do something" with them. But they do not have the basic information and they have not been taught the dimensions from which to work. Conversely, too many teachers and therapists are told that they must use only the specified materials, and use them only in the specified manner—without exception. Both of these approaches are incredible hindrances to creative programming and to obtaining "the match" as well. Teachers must learn to see both the possibilities and the realities of recreation materials. Those who are well informed can then be clever and creative. Readily available materials can be used in novel ways, just as occupational therapists use everyday objects in therapeutic activities and parents use household items for teaching. Another strategy might be to experiment with "incidental teaching," in which the adult requires more and more complex verbal responses from a child before giving the desired response (Hart and Risley, 1974). Similar strategies might be built around gross motor skills, such as requiring closer and closer approximations of correct ball throwing before allowing free play with the ball (Wehman et al., 1976.)

Other examples of creative programming include using recreation materials, playgrounds, and physical education equipment for activities emphasizing language development, social skills, or math concepts. It is basically a matter of "seeing beyond the obvious" and looking carefully at all the dimensions of "the match."

Adapting Recreation Materials

The number and variety of handicapping conditions virtually *require* some adaptations of materials. No producer of materials can anticipate and adequately provide for all possible combinations of your clients' capabilities and limitations. Instead, most producers design their products for the mass market of so-called "average" or "normal" users. As mentioned in the introductory section of this chapter, we believe that it is much more useful to design products with the severely developmentally disabled in mind. It is much easier, then, to adapt the preliminary design (or the finished product) for use with higher functioning populations. The common procedures for adaptation are directly counter to this; usually a product must be made more durable. The required responses may have to be reduced. Fewer adaptations (and simpler adaptations) would be necessary if producers offered materials that are simple to understand, easy to use, and durable to begin with!

Basic suggestions for adapting materials, and several examples for each of these processes, are described below:

1. *Stabilize:* For medium-sized objects, consider suction-cup feet or "octopus" soap holders; clay, or the malleable substance for attaching posters to walls, can stabilize small objects on a table; paper for drawing or painting can be attached to a clipboard, using additional bulldog or spring clips for the loose edges.

2. *Enlarge:* For games of skill, enlarge the target; for arts and crafts, use large sheets of paper on the wall for painting and large scrap items for collages, etc.; also use large brushes and containers for painting, or gluing activities (painting the sidewalk with water is good practice and especially fun on a hot day); try many different sizes of balls, bats, racquets, etc.

3. *Prosthetize:* Modify material so it is appropriate for the individual using a headstick; add handles or straps so that the object can be grasped or picked up by a person with a hand disability.

4. *Reduce required response:* Shorten the distance the individual must move, e.g., across the room; reduce the range of motion required; reduce complexity of responses, i.e., from multiple to single movement, from following several instructions to a single one.

5. *Make more familiar:* Change objects, drawings, instructions or rules to relate to individual's self-concept, environment, etc; relate to successful experiences in individual's history.

6. *Make more concrete:* Reduce abstract quality of material or instructions; demonstrate activity, proper use of material, desired end product, etc.

7. *Remove extraneous cues:* For example, if your objective is to teach shape recognition in a game, be sure that the objects or drawings are not color coded at the same time.

8. *Remove distracting stimuli:* Simplify "busy" backgrounds on puzzles, on areas behind targets, etc.

9. *Add more cues or strengthen existing cues:* Consider increasing sensory stimulus characteristics—bright, contrasting colors may help; increase tactile characteristics with glue-on sandpaper, fabric, etc.

10. *Improve safety/durability:* Paper and cardboard materials, such as cards, books, table games, etc., may be improved with clear contact paper or heat-laminated plastic covers; nonwashable filler in stuffed toys may be replaced with polyester fiber or cut-up nylon hosiery; staples or nails should be replaced by screws, bolts, or high quality glue; sharp corners or edges should be rounded off or padded; coats of urethane-based varnish may improve durability and washability of wooden equipment and materials; be very careful of toxicity of paints—lead-free paints are not necessarily nontoxic, since the pigments used in some red and green paints can be poisonous.

For additional information regarding these adaptations and other possibilities, refer to ICTA (1972), Gerson (1975), Griswold and Allshouse (1976), Capper Foundation (1977), and other souces mentioned in the Appendix.

Creating New Materials

The careful reader, by now, will arrive at the option of creating new materials with some skepticism. All of the previously mentioned "Why nots?" are especially applicable here. Nevertheless, creating and personally designing materials may be the only way available to obtaining "the match."

The skilled and informed teacher may be able to design and construct exactly the materials needed. Otherwise it may be necessary to rely on the skills of co-workers, family members of clients, etc.

Plans for both homemade and adapted materials are becoming more available. Some of these plans and suggestions may be useful for your clients and your objectives. However, many of their creators have failed to consider safety and durability. It is critical to evaluate each plan on its own merits and its potential value in helping obtain the match. Creating materials can be especially rewarding, but it also places the ultimate responsibility on the teacher.

CONCLUSION

In this chapter we have presented information and issues relevant to materials selection for careful

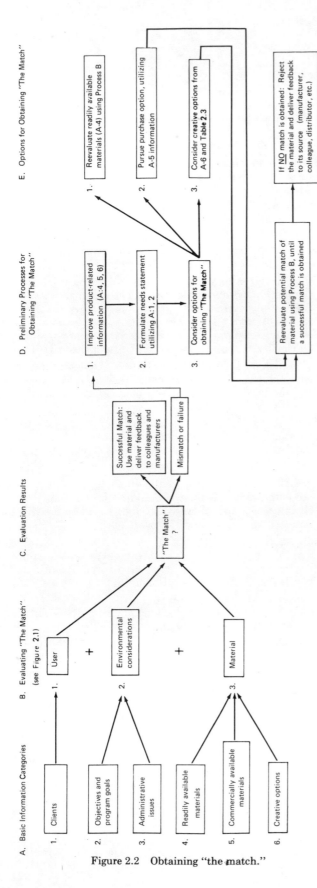

A. Basic Information Categories

1. Clients
2. Objectives and program goals
3. Administrative issues
4. Readily available materials
5. Commercially available materials
6. Creative options

B. Evaluating "The Match"

1. User
2. Environmental considerations
3. Material

"The Match"?

C. Evaluation Results

Successful Match: Use material and deliver feedback to colleagues and manufacturers

Mismatch or failure

D. Preliminary Processes for Obtaining "The Match"

1. Improve product-related information (A:4, 5, 6)
2. Formulate needs statement utilizing A:1, 2
3. Consider options for obtaining "The Match"

Reevaluate potential match of material using Process B, until a successful match is obtained

E. Options for Obtaining "The Match"

1. Reevaluate readily available materials (A-4) using Process B
2. Pursue purchase option, utilizing A-5 information
3. Consider creative options from A-6 and Table 2.3

If NO match is obtained: Reject the material and deliver feedback to its source (manufacturer, colleague, distributor, etc.)

Figure 2.2   Obtaining "the match."

consideration. Procedures for improving teachers' skills in materials evaluation, adaptation, and selection have been explored, as well as the problem areas that must be avoided. Figure 2.2 summarizes much of this information and depicts the variety of processes that are involved.

Reading from left to right, the six basic categories of information should be recognized. Section A:1–6 will assist in the initial selection process of recreation materials. The relationship of this information to the processes for evaluating "the match" is indicated by the arrows leading to B:1–3. Refer to Figure 2.1 for a more complete analysis of the evaluation process.

Section C summarizes results of the evaluation. If a match is determined, be sure to fulfill the feedback requirement. Sharing results with others will increase *their* basic information—A:4, 5, and 6. Let the manufacturer know, and/or express your appreciation to whoever was helpful in adapting or creating a new material.

When evaluation has resulted in a mismatch at Section C, it is necessary to proceed to Section D. There you will see the preliminary processes to initiate when trying to acquire new materials or obtain "the match." Section E summarizes the options that must be considered. Remember that each option cycles back to Section B for reevaluation.

If only mismatches and failures continue to occur after cycling through Sections D and E several times, there is another type of feedback to deliver. It, too, can be quite valuable. Write to the manufacturers. Make your information as specific as possible. And do not forget to talk to colleagues; they will be interested in the results of these evaluation efforts as well.

This process-oriented approach also lends itself to understanding the availability problem. Each of the five sections, A through E, of the flowchart is susceptible to insufficient information, lack of feedback, uncertain priorities, and failure to consider the options. We challenge teachers/therapists to:

1. Improve these processes for obtaining "the match"
2. Join efforts to resolve the availability problem
3. Maximize your own effectiveness in programming recreation materials for the developmentally disabled

The benefits are worth the effort.

REFERENCES

Audette, R. H. 1973. Trick or treat: A call for advertising standards and product evaluation. Except. Parent 3(3):19–20.

Banus, B. S., et al. (eds.). 1971. The Developmental Therapist: A Prototype of the Pediatric Occupational Therapist. Charles B. Slack, Inc., Thorofare, N.J.

Bartholomew, R., and Meyer, B. 1976. Developing and evaluating learning devices for exceptional children. Paper presented at meeting of the Council for Exceptional Children, Chicago.

Bleil, G. 1975. Evaluating educational materials. J. Learn. Disabil. 8(1):19–26.

Boland, S. 1976. Instructional materialism—or How to select the things you need. Teach. Except. Child. Summer:156–158.

Brackman, B. 1978. Materials modification. Department of Special Education, University of Kansas, Lawrence. Unpublished paper.

Campbell, P., Green, K., and Carlson, L. 1977. Approximating the norm through environmental and child-centered prosthetics and adaptive equipment. In E. Sontag (ed.), Educational Programming for the Severely and Profoundly Handicapped, Council for Exceptional Children, Reston, Va.

Capper Foundation. 1977. It Takes All Parts: An Activity Book To Develop Self-Concept in Young Children. Topeka, Kan.

Cassell, J. T. 1975. Introduction to Suggested Aids for Educating the Exceptional Child: Materials for Use in Developmental Learning Programs. Milton Bradley Co., Springfield, Mass.

Consumer Product Safety Commission. 1976. Assorted reprints and brochures. Washington, D.C.

Favell, J. E., and Cannon, P. R. 1977. Evaluation of entertainment materials for severely retarded persons. Am. J. Ment. Defic. 81(4):357–361.

Finnie, N. R. 1975. Handling the Young Cerebral Palsied Child at Home. 2nd ed. E. P. Dutton, New York.

Foos, R. 1976. A survey of competencies of teachers of trainable mentally retarded. Educ. Train. Ment. Retard. 11(3):269–272.

Gerson, D. 1975. Be Big Somewhere: A Structured Playroom for the Severely and Profoundly Retarded. Rainier School, Buckley, Wash.

Gips, C. D. 1950. A study of toys for hospitalized children. Child Dev. 21(3):149–161.

Griswold, P., and Allshouse, C. 1976. Application of adaptive materials and equipment to meet the needs of preschool physically handicapped children. Paper presented at a meeting of the Council for Exceptional Children, Chicago.

Gross, P., and Cohen, M. 1975. Developmental Pinpoints. 1st ed. University of Washington Child Development and Mental Retardation Center, Seattle.

Hamad, C., Herbert-Jackson, E., and Risley, T. 1975. The selection of toys as the basis for maximizing appropriate play behaviors in children. Paper presented at meeting of the American Psychological Association, Chicago.

Hamad, C., Watkins, B., Hope, L., and Risley, T. The evaluation of play materials for deaf-blind children. Department of Human Development, Living Environments Group, University of Kansas, Lawrence. Unpublished paper.

Hart, B., and Risley, T. 1974. Using preschool materials to modify the language of disadvantaged children. J. Appl. Behav. Anal. 7(2):243–256.

ICTA. 1972. Technical aids for physically handicapped children. ICTA Information Centre, Bromma, Sweden.

Langdon, G. 1948. A study of the uses of toys in a hospital. Child Dev. 19(4):197–212.

Living Environments Group and Western Carolina Center. Roadrunner procedures: The organization of a residential environment for non-ambulatory severely and profoundly retarded persons. Department of Human Development, Living Environments Group, University of Kansas, Lawrence. Unpublished paper.

McClannahan, L., and Risley, T. 1976. Design of living environments for nursing home residents: Activities and materials for severely disabled geriatric patients. Mod. Nurs. Home 24:10–13.

Murn, T. 1977. Consumers and consumerists—still a relevant issue. Playthings June:41.

Public Action Coalition on Toys. 1976. Assorted pamphlets and reprints. Providence, Utah.

Pyfer, J. 1976. The role of theory in practice. Paper presented at a meeting of the American Alliance of Health, Physical Education, and Recreation, Milwaukee.

Quilitch, H. R., and Risley, T. R. 1972. The organization of group care environments: Toy evaluation. Paper presented at a meeting of the American Psychological Association, Honolulu.

Thompson, M. 1977. Britain's Toy Libraries Association: Adapting toys for disabled children. Rehabilitation/WORLD Spring:31–32.

Twardosz, S., Cataldo, M. F., and Risley, T. R. 1974. Infants' use of crib toys. Young Child. July:271–276.

Vort Corporation. 1973. Behavioral Characteristics Progression. Palo Alto, Cal.

Wehman, P. 1976. Selection of play materials for the severely handicapped: A continuing dilemma. Educ. Train. Ment. Retard. 11(1):46–50.

Wehman, P., Renzaglia, A., Schutz, R., and Karan, O. 1976. Training leisure skills in severely and profoundly handicapped adolescents and adults. In O. Karan, P. Wehman, A. Renzaglia, and R. Schutz (eds.), Habilitation Practices with the Severely Developmentally Disabled, Vol. I. University of Wisconsin, Madison.

White, J. 1976. Stimulus box for the profoundly mentally retarded. Amer. J. Occup. Ther. 30(3):167.

Wilbarger, P., and Kuizenga, J. Undated. Activities for the Remediation of Sensorimotor Dysfunction in Primary School Children. Goleta Union School District, Goleta, Cal.

Wolinsky, G. F., and Koehler, N. 1973. A cooperative program in materials development for very young hospitalized children. Rehabil. Lit. 34(2):34–46.

3 TOY PLAY

Paul Wehman

Teaching developmentally disabled children appropriate play skills with toys is an important instructional goal. Constructive interactions with objects in the child's environment may facilitate fine motor development (Friedlander, Kamin, and Hesse, 1974). Second, a qualitative analysis of toy play may provide the teacher with an assessment of the child's cognitive functioning level (Uzgiris and Hunt, 1975). A third reason, perhaps of greatest importance, is that many developmentally delayed children have an abundance of free time (Gozali and Charney, 1972; Stanfield, 1973; Wehman, 1977a). This is reflected in evenings, weekends, and holidays when the child is at home, and during most of the summer months. If handicapped children are unable to interact with toys and other play materials appropriately, and require constant supervision, many families will feel the need to institutionalize the child.

The purpose of this chapter is to describe the developmental sequence of toy play as it occurs in nonhandicapped and handicapped children, discuss viable assessment and intervention strategies for development and implementation of a play program, and outline specific methods for overcoming instructional problems. A final section, relevant to parents' perceptions of handicapped children's play activity at home, is included as well, to expand the focus of this chapter beyond the classroom.

PROGRESSION OF TOY PLAY SKILLS

Before the development and implementation of a toy play program, it is necessary to understand the general developmental sequence in which play behavior occurs in children. Table 3.1 provides the horizontal sequence of toy play, which was presented earlier as part of the curriculum in Chapter 1. This sequence is an adaptation of the work of earlier researchers who worked with nonhandicapped children (Parten, 1932; Barnes, 1971).

Exploratory Play

Exploratory play is characterized by four basic stages of development. Orientational responses are at the lowest level, that of responding to gross stimulus changes in the environment. Unfamiliar and unusual stimuli tend to evoke orientational responses. At this level duration of attending behavior is very short. Once an individual has become aware of the eliciting stimulus and the uncertainty and novelty have been removed, the individual returns to his previous cognitive state. When working with the profoundly retarded, this may mean complete withdrawal and lack of social responsiveness.

At the next level is locomotor exploration. As an individal begins to move about the environment, his visual, auditory, and tactile senses give him sensory and affective feedback about the surroundings. An empty or barren room, or an area with age-inappropriate play materials, elicits little sustained exploratory behavior from severely handicapped persons.

Ellis (1973) conceptualizes locomotor exploration in the following way: When an individual is placed in an area with novel stimuli, he begins to explore cautiously, not knowing whether the stimuli may be noxious or pleasurable. Hence, he is in a state of conflict as he determines whether he must approach or avoid the stimulus. Continued presentation of the same or similar stimuli reduces the arousal level of the person in that situation, thus enabling him to move on to a next phase. Ellis (1973) provides the following definition of locomotor exploration:

> Locomotor exploration does not involve interaction with the object or situation but when sufficient exploration by the distance receptors has been done so that approach/avoidance conflicts are resolved, the animal begins to employ the peripheral sensors to gain more information (pp. 97–98).

Borrowing from Hutt (1970), Ellis divides exploratory activity into specific exploration and

Table 3.1. The horizontal sequence of toy play within a recreation curriculum

Level I: Toy play

Exploratory play	Independent play	Parallel play
1. Acts on toy or play objects. 2. *Representative activities:* Reaches for objects; bats at objects; grasps and squeezes toys; makes regular oral contact with toys; shakes objects; throws toys; engages in high rate self-stimulatory actions with toys.	1. Plays appropriately alone with wide range of materials. 2. *Representative activities:* Uses playground equipment. Uses following toys: blocks, puzzles, dolls, stacking rings, top, snap beads, play phone, pull toys, ball, musical instruments, tricycle, Lincoln Logs, books, water colors, hula hoop.	1. Plays independently with wide range of materials in close proximity to others. 2. *Representative activities:* Swings on swing next to peer; builds block tower near peer; bounces ball near peers; colors at table with peers.

Level I: Toy play
(continued)

Associative play	Cooperative play	Symbolic play
1. Initiates interaction with peers in play situations for short periods of time. 2. *Representative activities:* Approaches peer with a toy; makes brief physical contact with peer during play; makes regular eye contact with peer during play.	1. Exhibits mutual participation and peer interaction during play. 2. *Representative activities:* Rolls a ball; builds with blocks; pulls a peer in a wagon; uses a toy phone; pushes a peer on a swing or down a slide; takes turns hitting Bop Bag.	1. Engages in dramatization and imaginative/pretend play. 2. *Representative activities:* Plays domestic make-believe with dolls, cars, trucks, blocks, house, and dishes; engages in dress-up activities; uses puppets, paper dolls; plays cowboys/Indians, doctor/nurse, cops/robbers.

diversive exploration. Specific exploration refers to responses made as an organism seeks information about a specific object or situation. Diversive exploration occurs in an effort to elevate arousal level through seeking novel stimuli in the environment.

Once an individual has explored the environment sufficiently, he may choose to interact with one or more of the stimuli in an investigatory manner. Ellis (1973) states:

Investigation is a process whereby the animal tests the object, employing the peripheral sensors to determine the contingencies associated with it. The animal investigates the outcomes of its interactions with the object or situation. The object is repeatedly felt, sniffed, tested, hefted, shoved, pulled, turned, etc., and its various components are treated similarly (p. 98).

If most developmentally disabled children did act on their physical surroundings in the way described by Ellis, the development of play be-

haviors and movement out of exploratory behavior stages would be inevitable. Unfortunately this does not usually occur. Handicapped children at this functioning level rarely explore in such detail and duration. This is behavior that must be trained.

Searching behavior represents the logical termination of exploratory play. As the individual tires of stimuli in the area through extensive manipulation and investigation, the search for new stimuli and situations begins with the exploratory behavior cycle starting over. Nunnally and Lemond (1973) suggest that only certain objects in the environment induce exploratory behaviors (e.g., sound potential, configural complexity), and that

. . . the amount of time spent in each of the successive phases and the probability of moving from one phase to the next depend upon the nature of the stimulus, the other stimulus impingements in the environment, organismic states, maturity of the animal, and possibly many other factors (p. 66).

Independent Play

Independent play, also termed isolate play by some, refers to appropriate play actions with objects. More specifically, appropriate play should refer to constructive and purposeful action directed toward play materials by the child. Usually this should occur for a sustained period of time.

By developing through exploratory stages of play, the child is now prepared to investigate, in greater depth, objects in the environment. The representative activities associated with independent play are diverse and span many different fine motor skills.

Although much research has been directed toward encouraging delayed children to socially interact more (e.g., Strain, Cooke, and Apolloni, 1976), in addition to play independently, this level of play is important for the child to acquire. One of the more critical factors in keeping the child at home and not institutionalizing him is whether he can fit into home life. If the child requires continual care and cannot use leisure time appropriately and *independently,* then parents must reevaluate the child's long term living situation.

Teaching independent play is also a necessary prerequisite to moving to more advanced types of leisure instruction. Marchant and Wehman (1978) found that table game instruction with nonverbal, severely retarded children was not effective unless the participants had already acquired at least a limited degree of toy play proficiency. Later sections of this chapter describe specific assessment and intervention techniques for facilitating independent toy play in developmentally disabled children.

Parallel and Associative Play

These levels of toy play are excellent indicators of social development. In parallel play the child plays independently with objects but in close physical proximity to peers; in associative play the child will exhibit a limited amount of approach responses to peers. Parallel and associative play have also been termed onlooker play (Knapczyk and Yoppi, 1975) and attempted interaction play (Paloutzian et al., 1971).

When the child begins to exhibit this type of social development, introduction of higher functioning or nonretarded peers into the play session may be a useful facilitator for encouraging social interaction. Previous to this point in social development, the individual may not be attending, and hence models would be of limited value. Knapczyk and Peterson (1977) have shown that nonretarded children can influence the play and social responses of trainable level mentally retarded children through imitation.

Keeping this developmental sequence in mind, the teacher optimally would arrange for the gradually extended involvement of a withdrawn peer with other children. As Strain and Hill have demonstrated, interactions with nonhandicapped peers can be an efficient means of increasing social behavior (see Chapter 4).

Cooperative Play

In social or cooperative play the child engages regularly in approach responses to other peers and adults. Usually mutual participation and peer interaction are exhibited during free-play situations.

Typical activities include ball play between two or more peers, taking turns with games or toys, and cooperative play on the playground.

When delayed children interact cooperatively with each other and with nonhandicapped children, they are viewed in a more positive light by adults, as well as by peers. There is research to document the role of competence, rather than labels, as a factor in social acceptance of educable mentally retarded children (Strichart, 1974). If handicapped children are able to get along with others, and still not be taken advantage of, their chances of being "mainstreamed" into regular classes and regular schools are heightened considerably.

One goal of a free-play program for developmentally disabled children is to develop *self-initiated* social behavior. Although many children will play with toys appropriately, or receive interactions in an acceptable manner, self-initiated social interactions frequently must be trained (Strain, Cooke, and Apolloni, 1976).

Symbolic Play

The development of symbolic and creative play actions is a more advanced level of play. Singer (1973) has published an excellent text on the child's world of make-believe. Symbolic play involves the use of puppets (Domnie, 1974), dress-up, doll play, and other types of pretend situations.

There are few reports in the literature that describe creative play and make-believe with developmentally disabled children. However, the work of Smilansky (1968), Biblow (1973), Gottlieb (1973), and Pulaski (1973) certainly provides fertile ground for adaptations with handicapped children.

Teaching children to engage in dramatization and imaginative activities is an excellent means of facilitating concept development. Furthermore, relatively few objects are needed and, instead, the child must be taught to imagine. The child's emotional growth and development are enhanced in this way.

Although it is not clear, at least with handicapped children, whether each preceding substage is a necessary condition for learning the next substage in toy play, it seems that following this developmental sequence is necessary. If the child does not exhibit certain prerequisite skills, then learning social play or symbolic play would be very difficult and would probably be learned in a rote fashion.

The balance of this chapter is concerned with assessing toy play actions of handicapped children and how to utilize that data for purposes of implementing a program. Problem-solving strategies also are suggested.

RELEVANT PLAY VARIABLES FOR INITIAL ASSESSMENT

When beginning a play program, the specific instructional objectives of the program must be determined and the child's play behavior should be assessed. These factors directly affect each other; that is, the play variable(s) selected for assessment will depend on the purpose of the program.

As an illustration, consider the child who plays with the same two or three toys and fails to explore with other toys. The purpose of a play program for this child would be to increase the amount of appropriate exploratory actions with different toys. An instructional objective for this program might be:

Given 10 toys in the play area, the child will play with at least 6 different toys over a 2-week period.

The logical variable to assess would be the number of toys the child played with each session. To make the assessment more reliable, a second observer could record independently the number of toys the child played with as well. For a valid observation it would be advisable to identify, from the outset of the program, the minimum length of time the child should play with the toy. Definitions of appropriate versus inappropriate toy play also must be established.

Proficiency of Toy Play: Task Analytic Assessment

Although there are a number of variables that can be assessed in the play environment, an initial consideration must be: *Does the child know how to play with the toy?* Stated another way, when given a toy, can the child play with it appropriately? If not, then basic instruction is required. The specific training techniques necessary are discussed in a later section.

What is required for evaluating toy play proficiency is task analytic assessment (Knapczyk, 1975). An instructional objective must be written for a given toy. The objective should reflect the specific skill that the teacher wants the child to learn. An example of a task analytic assessment for playing with a spinning top is provided in Table 3.2. This table contains an instructional objective, a task analysis for playing with a top, and the verbal cue provided during the assessment.

Table 3.2. Task analytic assessment for playing with a top. Cue: "John, play with the top."

Step	M	T	W	Th	F
1. Student(s) approaches top.	+	+	+	+	+
2. Student(s) places hands on top.	+	+	+	+	+
3. Student(s) finds handle of top.	+	+	−	+	+
4. Student(s) pushes handle down on top once.	−	−	−	+	+
5. Student(s) brings handle up.	−	−	−	−	−
6. Student(s) brings handle down on top twice.					−
7. Student(s) brings handle up each time.					−
8. Student(s) brings handle down on top three times.					−
9. Student(s) brings handle up each time.					−
10. Student(s) brings handle down on top four times.					−
11. Student(s) brings handle up each time.					−
12. Student(s) brings handle down on top five times.					−
13. Student(s) brings handle up each time.					−
14. Student(s) stops top from spinning.					−
15. Student(s) puts top away.	−	−	−	−	−

The recording form indicates that for the first 5 days of assessment (baseline) the child performed a total of three, three, two, four, and four steps independently. This indicates that instruction should begin at Step 3 in the task analysis.

There are multiple advantages to this type of observational assessment. First, the information collected about the child on this particular play skill helps the teacher to identify the exact point where instruction should begin. In this way the child does not receive instruction on skills in which he is already proficient. Second, this facilitates step-by-step individualized instruction for children with complex learning problems. Evaluation of the child's proficiency with different toys over an extended period of time will also be more objective and precise, and will be less subject to teacher bias.

Duration of Toy Play

If the child has some degree of proficiency with toys, then the instructional variable of interest may be the duration or length of time the child engages in toy play. This is assessed by recording the amount of time the child plays with the toys during the play session.

Because this may be an extremely time-consuming measure to use with several children, the teacher may elect to observe only half the children one day and the other half the next. Another option would be to record play duration only twice a week instead of daily.

The length of independent toy play is a particularly important variable to assess because of its relevance to most home situations, where parents cannot constantly spend time with their handicapped child. A frequent request heard from many parents is to teach the child to play independently, thereby relieving the family of continual supervision. A careful assessment of the child's duration of play before instruction will help the teacher and parents set realistic independent play goals for the child. The final section of this chapter addresses parental perceptions of the handicapped child's leisure activity at home.

Frequency of Toy Play: Interval Recording

Another method of assessing amount of play behavior is interval recording. Behavior is recorded during short time periods and not for the total time performed, as in duration recording. In this assessment strategy the child's play is observed during designated time blocks. Typically a time block of 20 minutes might be divided into 20 10-second intervals in which behavior would be recorded.

In interval recording behavior is recorded as occurring or not occurring, with a plus indicating a behavior occurrence and a minus signifying no occurrence of behavior. Table 3.3 provides an illustration of interval recording. Using an example of a child acting on toys, observation of action on toys is measured through a different assessment strategy. Observations are made for 20 10-second periods. If the target behavior occurs, a plus is recorded. No action on play materials results in a minus for that observation period. If there are 20 observation cells and the target behavior is observed 16 times, then physical action on toys would be charted as occurring 80% of the time ($16/20 \times 100 = 80\%$).

The economical features of an interval recording strategy should be apparent. Behaviors that are difficult to record, such as continuous behaviors, may be reliably recorded with this approach. Also, it is a relatively easy task to convert results into percentages, thus facilitating communication about program efficacy. Interval recording is a widely used assessment method in many applied settings and is most suitable for play programs in institutions, special education classrooms, work

Table 3.3. Interval recording

10-Second observation cell	1	+
10-Second observation cell	2	+
10-Second observation cell	3	+
10-Second observation cell	4	+
10-Second observation cell	5	+
10-Second observation cell	6	+
10-Second observation cell	7	0
10-Second observation cell	8	0
10-Second observation cell	9	+
10-Second observation cell	10	+
10-Second observation cell	11	0
10-Second observation cell	12	+
10-Second observation cell	13	+
10-Second observation cell	14	+
10-Second observation cell	15	+
10-Second observation cell	16	+
10-Second observation cell	17	+
10-Second observation cell	18	+
10-Second observation cell	19	0
10-Second observation cell	20	+

+ = Physical action on toys occurred during 10-second interval.

0 = Physical action on toys did not occur during 10-second interval.

centers, and other settings where mentally retarded persons are present (Fredericks et al., 1978).

Discriminating Between Appropriate and Inappropriate Play

Another assessment issue faced by teachers and researchers is differentiating appropriate play with toys from actions that would not be considered appropriate. Several play studies have failed to address this issue (Burney, Russell, and Shores, 1977; Favell and Cannon, 1977; Wehman, 1977b). Inappropriate play actions have typically been considered those behaviors that are harmful or destructive to the child, peers, or materials. However, many profoundly retarded and autistic children will exhibit high rates of repetitive self-stimulatory behavior with toys, e.g., banging, pounding, slamming, which are not necessarily harmful or destructive, yet are still inappropriate. Furthermore, the problem is compounded because with certain toys banging or slamming actions may be appropriate. Many children will do unusual things with toys which *might* be considered appropriate by other observers (Goetz and Baer, 1973).

Hence teachers are faced with how to assess the qualitative nature of the toy play. There are several ways of coping with this difficulty. The first one involves using two to three observers periodically and having these observers rate the appropriateness of the play. Objective judging provides a checks-and-balances system for the teacher.

A second method of assessing appropriateness of play is to identify the principal actions that a nonhandicapped child of comparable mental age might do with each toy (Fredericks et al., 1978). These actions may serve as guidelines for appropriateness of play.

Identifying a number of motor categories for toy play is yet another means of coding the qualitative nature of responses. This requires generating a fine motor classification system, which observers can use as a basis for recording toy play actions. Tilton and Ottinger (1964) provide nine categories, which are self-explanatory, and which were identified after extensive observational analysis of normal, trainable retarded, and autistic children. These are listed below:

1. Repetitive manual manipulation
2. Oral contacts
3. Pounding
4. Throwing
5. Pushing or pulling
6. Personalized toy use
7. Manipulation of movable parts
8. Separation of parts of toys
9. Combinational uses of toys

Toy Preference Evaluation

Assessing favorite toys of each child is an important step in initiating a toy play program. The goal in this process is to identify which, if any, toys are preferred by the child. This is a fairly easy task. By employing duration assessment, the number of minutes spent with each toy can be recorded for each child. This observation and recording should take place for at least a week.

A second means of assessing toy preference is through presenting a small number of toys and determining the amount of time before the child responds to different toys. This is referred to as a *latency* measure of behavior.

McCall (1974) has used latency as a measure of the length of time that elapsed before infants acted on a variety of play objects that were presented. Each of the objects possessed different stimulus attributes, such as configural complexity or sound potential. Through measuring passage of time until a response, teachers may be able to evaluate the relative attractiveness of, and preferences for, certain play materials with developmentally disabled children.

Frequency of Interactions

For many developmentally delayed children an important instructional goal is to initiate and sustain interactions with peers more frequently. A relatively common occurrence may be the presence of several delayed children all playing in isolation of each other during free play (Fredericks et al., 1978). When this happens the potential benefits of social interaction are not accrued.

One way of assessing social interaction is a simple count of the number of times one child 1) initiates an interaction, 2) receives an interaction, and 3) terminates interaction. Duration assessment may be used to measure the length of the interaction between peers and also between the child and adults in the room.

A second means of gathering more information on social interactions is the coding of specific types of interactions. Carney and her associates

(1977) have detailed the following social interaction skills:

Social Interaction

A. Receives interaction
   1. Receives hug
   2. Returns smile
   3. Gives object to other who has requested it
   4. Returns a greeting
   5. "Receives" cooperative play
   6. Answers questions
   7. Recognizes peers, teachers by name
   8. Shows approval
   9. Discriminates appropriate time, place, situation before receiving
B. Initiates interaction
   1. Greets another person
   2. Requests objects from another person
   3. Initiates cooperative play
   4. Seeks approval
   5. Seeks affiliation with familiar person
   6. Helps one who has difficulty manipulating environment
   7. Initiates conversation
C. Sustains interactions
   1. Attends to ongoing cooperative activity
   2. Sustains conversation
D. Terminates interactions
   1. Terminates cooperative play activity
   2. Terminates conversation

This sequence provides an important step toward detailing the specific skills that teachers should be attempting to elicit in delayed children. In addition to providing sequence, these skills may be task analyzed and the child's proficiency on selected behaviors assessed. These four categories of interaction can be employed to code the qualitative nature of the interaction (Hamre-Nietupski and Williams, 1977).

Direction of Interaction

Analyzing to whom interactions are directed may also be helpful in assessing which individuals in the play environment are reinforcing to the child. As Beveridge, Spencer, and Mittler (1978) have observed, child-teacher interactions occur more frequently than child-child interactions, especially with severely delayed children. Structured intervention by an adult usually is required to increase child-child interactions (Shores, Hester, and Strain, 1976).

When making home visits and observing the child playing at home with siblings or with neighborhood children, the direction of interactions should be assessed. This should be done not just with the handicapped child but also with nonhandicapped peers. This type of behavioral analysis can be revealing since most nonhandicapped children do not include handicapped children in play unless prompted and reinforced by adults (Apolloni, Cooke, and Cooke, 1977; Synder, Apolloni, and Cooke, 1977; Cooke, Apolloni and Cooke, 1978; Cooke, Cooke, and Apolloni, in press).

In conducting a behavioral assessment of social interactions, the checklist below might be used as a means of coding a number of interactions:

	Initiated interaction	Received interaction
Robert		
Wendy		
Martha		
James		

This form, however, would not allow for analyzing the direction of interactions. The checklist below would facilitate assessing which peers or adults the child interacted with:

	Robert	Wendy	Martha	James	Teacher
Robert	×				
Wendy		×			
Martha			×		
James				×	

Free-Play Assessment

In some cases there may be little interest or time to collect the specific types of information discussed above. Some teachers may want to consider using a simpler method of assessing the level of free play at which the child is functioning (Wehman and Marchant, 1978).

With this strategy the teacher clearly defines the types of behaviors that are characteristic of the different developmental levels of play. In the recreation curriculum presented in Chapter 1, the toy play level provides the sequence and operational definitions for each stage in the toy play area. For example, in the autistic play stage, characteristic behaviors might include not touching or physically acting on any play materials during free-play periods or nonfunctional repetitive actions for long periods of time. Independent play might be considered as any appropriate play behaviors that were exhibited alone or away from other peers. Cooperative or social play would be another skill level in the basic developmental sequence and would include such skills as physical or verbal interaction with other peers and teachers (Paloutzian et al., 1971; Fredericks et al., 1978).

This assessment strategy is convenient and economical in terms of time expended; it can allow for ease in collecting fairly accurate information, provided the categories are clearly defined and, therefore, easy to discriminate. This type of behavioral assessment, however, does not capture many of the collateral skills that are clearly associated with play skill development, such as fine motor skills, changes in emotionality, and social behavior.

Determining Reliability of Assessment

Thus far, assessment has been discussed primarily as observation of behavior by one person. To achieve reliability of agreement that the target behavior is actually occurring at a given rate, however, two or more independent observers must simultaneously view the target behavior. In this way an index of the consistency of agreement may be established. Reliable recording of behavior is the foundation of a good behavioral program. Inconsistent agreement between observers casts serious doubt on the credibility of program results.

Reliability may be determined two ways, depending on the assessment method employed. With a frequency measure of responding the smaller frequency is divided by the larger frequency and multiplied by 100; that is, if Observer A notes a child acting on 20 different toys, and Observer B counts only 18, then the reliability index would be 90% ($18/20 \times 100 = 90\%$). The same procedure is used in duration or latency recording, with the smaller measure being divided by the larger measure and then multiplied by 100.

A slightly different formula is used in finding reliability of agreement with interval recording. Reliability is calculated in the following way:

$$\frac{\text{Total agreements}}{\text{Total agreements} + \text{Total disagreements}} \times 100$$

Only intervals or cells in which behavior occurred are counted with both agreements plus total disagreements. An examination of the display below reveals how reliability for interval recording would be determined. During 7 of the 10 intervals

Observer A and Observer B agreed on the occurrence of the target behavior. In the other three intervals, Nos. 4, 6, and 10, there was disagreement. Therefore, a reliability index of 70% was established.

Determining Reliability for Interval Recording

+ = Behavior occurred
− = Behavior did not occur

Observer A	Cell	1	2	3	4	5	6	7	8	9	10
	No.	+	+	+	+	+	−	+	−	−	+

Observer B	Cell	1	2	3	4	5	6	7	8	9	10
	No.	+	+	+	−	+	+	+	−	−	−

$$\frac{\text{Total agreements} = 7}{\substack{\text{Total agreements} + \\ \text{Total disagreements} = 10}} \times 100 = 70\% \text{ Agreement}$$

It is generally accepted that reliability less than 80% is suspect, and program results may be questionable. The importance of initially gaining high reliability in a behavioral program and then maintaining it through periodic spot checks cannot be overemphasized. Findings in many behavioral studies are suspect because of the failure to report high reliability coefficients.

DEVELOPING A TOY PLAY PROGRAM

Implementation of a toy play program for developmentally disabled children can occur after sufficient initial assessment data have been collected. In the previous section different categories of data that might be collected were described. It should be apparent that several of the play variables, i.e., proficiency of toy play, duration, and frequency, would be more appropriate for lower functioning children who exhibit severe physical, emotional, and learning handicaps. Social interaction variables reflect toy play objectives for higher functioning handicapped children.

The purpose of this section is to describe how to implement play programs for developmentally disabled children. A program development sequence that teachers and other practitioners can follow when setting up a toy play program is outlined.

Systematic Instruction of Play Skills

With many developmentally delayed children there is a need to provide systematic instruction in how to use different toys. It is necessary to get on the floor with the child and directly teach the different functions of the toy. There is an instructional sequence of events that should be followed in implementing the program. These events are illustrated in Figure 3.1.

Informal Observation Through an extended period of observation and consultative services of occupational and physical therapists, it may be determined which children display the physical prerequisites necessary for acquisition of selected fine motor skills. An effort should be made to select skills that require the use of a variety of fine motor actions, and that are thought to be within the child's capabilities. An occupational therapist will be able to assess which goals are realistic, help in the planning of sequence, identify important stimulus characteristics in toys, and usually can help adapt toys for children.

Toy Selection The purchase or development of toys is a critical factor in the success of any play program. Since the previous chapter provided a discussion of the variables involved in selecting toys, this process is not discussed further here. However, it may be helpful to evaluate the information contained in Table 3.4. This table describes a list of selected toys and their functions. The topical area is life skill toys. At the end of this chapter is a more complete listing of toys and their functions (Sied-Schlaw, 1976). Topical areas include motor skills, sensory skills, concepts, and math readiness.

Instructional Objectives Selection of relevant toy play objectives is the next step in the program development process. One objective can be written for each toy, or three or four objectives can be written for one toy. As Goetz and Baer (1973) demonstrated with preschoolers in block play, there are a variety of actions that a child can learn with only one or two toys. Three sample objectives are provided below:

1. Given a set of different size blocks, the child will identify and arrange at least 10 different formations within a 30-day period.
2. Given a dollhouse, the child will demonstrate how to open and close the doors of the house and how to place different dolls in the rooms of the dollhouse for 4 out of 5 consecutive days.
3. Given a jack-in-the-box, the child will wind it frequently enough so that the jack pops up for 4 out of 5 consecutive days.

It is usually optimal to identify toy play objectives that allow the child several different correct responses. Objectives 1 and 2 allow for some creativity, whereas the third objective does not.

Task Analysis Development There is a growing body of research to support training mentally retarded persons through use of task analysis (Williams, 1975; Wehman, 1977a). Task analysis is the breaking down of a skill into small behaviors. These behaviors are taught individually and then chained together as the individual becomes more proficient at the skill. This allows for part learning instead of whole learning; learning in small chunks reduces strain on the learner's memory and facilitates acquisition of new material.

Numerous other advantages are present with a task analytic format of instruction (Knapczyk, 1975). For example, determining the optimal point at which to begin instruction is facilitated by assessing the number of steps in the response chain that the child demonstrates independently. Selection of the appropriate entry skill for training is important because it minimizes the likelihood of teaching skills that are either too simplistic or too advanced. Task analysis also provides a more systematic means of evaluating the effectiveness of a program because it allows for an objective measure of how many steps are taught and learned after instruction has commenced.

Task analysis can be developed in a number of ways. Before attempting to break down a behavior into smaller components, it is essential to review

Do informal assessment of child's play skills

↓

Select toys

↓

Write instructional objective for target skill(s)

↓

Do task analysis of target skill(s)

↓

Do task analytic assessment to determine child's exact proficiency level

↓

Implement instructional procedures

↓

Evaluate and monitor results

↓

Plan for transfer and retention of skill(s)

Figure 3.1. Instructional sequence for developing toy play program for low functioning children.

Table 3.4. Life skill toys and their function

Farm Lotto (Ed-U-Cards)
Preparation for community living for child with special needs. Game is suitable for ages 3–8.

Fuzzy-Wuzzy Lacing Cards (Whitman)
Six hole-punched lacing cards and six plastic laces. Various objects and designs can be outlined with laces. Teaches idea of basic sewing stitches and utilizes motor skill.

Go-Together Lotto (Ed-U-Cards)
Especially adapted to observing relationships between familiar objects. Six cardboard pieces ($\frac{7}{8}$″ $\times$ 6½″) each showing six pictures of identifiable objects. Matched by 3½″ $\times$ 2¼″ cardboard pieces showing persons or things that fit to the picture. Can be played by one or more.

Inside Story Puzzles (Childcraft)
Lift the bus and see the people, lift the bakery and see the cakes. Three puzzles are perfect for storytelling and learning about community occupations.

Jet Plane (Fisher Price)
Manipulative pull toy is made of tough plastic. Makes a whirring sound, and the door lowers allowing small wooden people to be removed from the plane. For ages 2–6.

Mechanics Bench (NASCO)
Colorful plastic bench, screws, nuts, bolts, and wrenches. Teaches color association and manual dexterity. For ages 3–7.

Mother's Helper (MB)
A game for two to four players, ages 5–10. Object is to race through the house helping mother with her chores.

Occupation Puzzles (Childcraft)
Six realistic puzzles portray men and women in working situations. 9″ $\times$ 12″ wooden puzzles.

Pounding Bench (Playskool)
Tight pegs challenge the child to develop eye-hand coordination and afford him an emotional outlet. 12″ $\times$ 6¾″ $\times$ 5½″.

Princess Phone (ETA)
This child's version of a modern telephone has realistic movable dial and strong nylon cord. Used for housekeeping play.

School Bus (Fisher Price)
Seven toy children color match seats in bus. Engine makes sound when bus is pulled. Strong wood body and plastic roof. Bus is 13″ long. Ideal for teaching safe school bus procedures.

Sculptured Rubber Animals (Creative Playthings)
Accurately scaled, realistic reproduction of familiar animals with particular attention to coloring and natural features. Contoured rubber and proportioned bodies make them particularly valuable for the visually handicapped.

Sewing Cards (MB)
Cardboard cards, 6″ $\times$ 8″, with punched outline of animals. Plastic tipped laces are used to sew around the pictures. Improves coordination and concentration.

Simplex Wooden Play Board (Childcraft)
Scenes of zoo animals, classrooms, etc. Cutouts can be lifted from the puzzle board by small knobs and used as stand-up figures in slots on the puzzle board. 11½″ $\times$ 8¼″.

What's Missing Lotto (Ed-U-Cards)
Skills in observation and classification are increased. Pictures of farmyard, street scene, store, and playground are mounted on heavy cardboard. (6½″ $\times$ 9¼″). Items missing in the picture are shown on 1½″ $\times$ 1½″ pieces and matched to the pictures. 24 matching squares and 4 playing boards.

Table 3.4.   (continued)

Which Room Lotto (ETA)
> Wooden frame, 23'' × 5½'' × ½'', divided into three recessed sections. Six 2¼'' × 2¼'' wooden squares for each section contain pictures of items that can be found in one of the pictures within the recessed section. Each picture is of a different room in the house.

Work Bench (Playskool)
> Wooden bench equipped with nuts, bolts, screwdriver—to develop coordination skills. Child learns to handle tools, threading and replacement of screws, nuts, bolts, and nails. 11½'' × 5¼'' × 5¼''.

World Around Us Lotto (Ed-U-Cards)
> Children learn through play to relate to the home and community. Child matches pictures on playing cards to same pictures shown on the playing board.

Zoo Animals (Dick Blick)
> Six wooden animals realistically painted (elephant, giraffe, lion, zebra, tiger, and polar bear). Range in size from 1¾'' high to 6¼''.

related program literature to evaluate whether task analyses have been developed previously (e.g., Williams, 1975). If no information is available, then consulting curriculum guides and child development texts for basic sequences in the relevant areas many be helpful. Many recreation activity texts for handicapped persons are available and can be used by those familiar with a task analysis format of instruction.

Brown and his associates (e.g., Brown, Bellamy, and Sontag, 1971) specified six steps to follow in generating a task analysis. This methodology is valid across disciplines and is recommended when developing recreation programs for the mentally retarded. The steps include:

1. The teacher must specify terminal objectives in behaviorial terms; that is, he must convert the required criterion performance into observable responses.

2. The teacher must analyze the criterion responses and divide them into a series of less complex responses.

3. The teacher must arrange the responses he decides are necessary for completion of the terminal response into a series.

4. The teacher must teach or verify the existence of the student's ability to perform each response in the series.

5. The teacher must teach the students to perform each response in the sequence in *serial* order.

6. In an attempt to delineate successes and failures the teacher must record student performance during each training phase so that adjustments can be made during the teaching process (Brown, Bellamy, and Sontag, p. 3.).

As an illustration of how task analysis is applied to toy play instruction, Tables 3.5 and 3.6 outline two task analysis sequences of play skills that might be relevant for low functioning children.

Task Analytic Assessment   The next step is to assess the child's skill level on each task analysis. This procedure can be done as follows. The teacher gives the general instruction: "Phil, show me how you spin the top," or "Jean, show me how you play with Raggedy Ann." Each student may be assessed on the number of steps in each task analysis that he could perform independently, i.e., with no physical or modeling assistance. From this assessment, the appropriate entry level skill for instruction may be determined.

Data may be collected at the middle or end of each assessment or instructional period. The student is asked to perform the given skill and

Table 3.5.   Task analysis for a string toy

1.	Student(s) approaches toy.
2.	Student(s) turns front knob.
3.	Student(s) inserts finger in ring.
4.	Student(s) pulls string ½ way out.
5.	Student(s) pulls string all way out.
6.	Student(s) releases string.
7.	Student(s) resets front knob.
8.	Student(s) inserts finger in ring again.
9.	Student(s) pulls string ½ way out.
10.	Student(s) pulls string all the way out.
11.	Student(s) places toy back on rug.

Table 3.6.   Task analysis for hammer toy

1. Student(s) approaches toy.
2. Student(s) picks up hammer.
3. Student(s) pushes one ball down with hammer or finger.
4. Student(s) pushes two balls down with hammer or finger.
5. Student(s) pushes three balls down with hammer or finger.
6. Student(s) puts hammer on rug.
7. Student(s) picks up one ball.
8. Student(s) places ball back in top slot.
9. Student(s) picks up second ball.
10. Student(s) places second ball back in top slot.
11. Student(s) picks up third ball.
12. Student(s) places third ball back in top slot.

receives a plus for each step completed independently and a minus for no response or for one in which assistance is required.

These figures may be expressed in percentages by dividing the total number of steps in the task analysis by the total number of steps performed independently and multiplying by 100. For a more detailed discussion of data collection methods, the reader is referred to an excellent article by Hanson and Bellamy (1977).

Instructional Procedures   The instructional model that may be employed involves a basic sequence or continuum of teacher assistance. Initially verbal instructions should be given to the student to perform the designated target step in the task analysis. If the student responds correctly, positive reinforcement is given immediately. If not, the target behavior is then modeled or demonstrated by the teacher. If this level of instruction still does not result in correct responding, manual guidance may be provided.

Although systematic instruction has been successful in teaching situations with severely handicapped students, there are a number of possible "pitfalls" that can lead to breakdowns in learning or programming problems. Several of these points are listed below as guidelines for those involved in implementing instructional procedures:

1. Do *all* staff understand how to implement program?
2. Are *all* staff consistent in instruction?
3. Is an effective reinforcer(s) being employed?
4. Is the reinforcer given immediately? Is praise *expressive*?
5. Does the student have an opportunity to consume reinforcer before next trial begins?

6. Do you have a student's attention before starting next trial?
7. Is the student attending to the relevant part of the task or skill that you are teaching?
8. Are your language cues consistent and are they kept short, i.e., be careful not to give irrelevant (and distracting) language cues?
9. Are you giving instructions head-on to student and facing him directly as you give instruction?
10. Have you broken skill into smallest behavioral components?
11. Have you provided physical guidance too long and not begun to fade assistance appropriately?
12. Have you considered using extra cues to help the student learn, i.e., colors to help attending to relevant part of task?
13. Have you developed an easy-to-hard sequence of instruction?

Monitoring and Evaluation   The daily collection of data enables the careful monitoring of the progress being made or the identification of where difficulties may be occurring in the instructional situation. Ongoing evaluation of data facilitates the immediate modification of program procedures and subsequent alterations in teacher behaviors if necessary. Child evaluation should take place daily, weekly, or at least on a regular basis.

Planning for Transfer and Retention   Although many developmentally disabled children can learn appropriate play with toys fairly quickly, there is usually a limited amount of skill generalization to the home or other settings in the community. Unfortunately it cannot be assumed that the child will transfer training beyond the original instructional situation unless specific teaching procedures are provided (Wehman, Abramson, and Norman, 1977).

Several strategies are available, however, in generalizing and maintaining results of leisure time programs. One study that demonstrates how trainer instruction can be gradually faded was performed by Hopper and Wambold (1978). In this program four profoundly retarded children were trained to increase independent play actions and to decrease inappropriate self-abusive behaviors. The study was performed in a school classroom by three practicum students under the supervision of the teacher.

Once successful increase were gained in appropriate play actions, the number of trainers was reduced gradually from three to two to one, and finally no trainers were present. At this time the children were still able to maintain independent play skills.

Fading in peers is another method of programming generalization, and this has been demonstrated in the development of ball-rolling skills in severely retarded children (Whitman, Mercurio, and Caponigri, 1970). Another strategy, which has not been attempted, but might also be effective, would be that of fading in higher functioning peers who already have a well developed play repertoire. These peers might then serve as multiple models for generalization.

One technique that has not been documented, and that also might prove worthwhile in developing maintenance of leisure time skills, would be gradually decreasing the amount of time that a trainer spends with students. Presumably continual supervision and assistance would be required initially when training social play to a dyad of children. As the children become more spontaneous and acquire a greater number of appropriate play skills, the trainer can systematically reduce the training time and involvement.

Situation-specific learning is a common problem with severely handicapped individuals and refers to the limited ability to display newly acquired behaviors in settings other than the original training environment. One way of overcoming this deficit is to practice play skills in different places, such as the home, the playground, and school. Play materials, games, and toys should become cues for play to occur, not different types of buildings and environments.

Another method of achieving play skills across environments is through continued involvement of parents, relatives, and siblings. By including the child's family in leisure time programming, greater maintenance and generalization may be attained. This also may have positive effects on the way other family members view the severely handicapped child.

Leisure time skills that are performed only in gym class, in the classroom, or during Saturday morning recreation have limited value. There must be ample opportunity for the severely handicapped to participate in leisure time activities in community facilities, such as parks, camps, clubs, and other local recreation centers. Leisure time programming should be community based, with a major direction toward integration with nonhandicapped individuals. The frequent use of segregated recreation settings in the community should be discouraged.

ANALYZING PLAY PROBLEMS OF DEVELOPMENTALLY DISABLED CHILDREN

Most of this chapter has described assessment and intervention strategies as they relate to toy play in developmentally disabled children. There has been relatively little discussion concerning what to do if and when the program *does not* work or fails to be effective with the child. Because this is a constant source of frustration to teachers, this section is devoted to identifying typical problems encountered in implementing toy play programs and to delineating different strategies that may be employed to overcome these problems. Inasmuch as severely delayed children usually present the greatest learning problems, a special emphasis is placed on how to work with these children.

Refusal to Play

Problem #1. When provided with several toys, the child refuses to act on any of the toys.

In many profoundly retarded and autistic children, the presence of toys elicits little or no response except for continued high rates of physical or verbal self-stimulation. This type of problem prohibits constructive free-play actions on different toys and necessitates immediate intervention.

The three strategies listed below may be employed in overcoming the refusal to play problem.

Strategy 1: It may be helpful, initially, to increase the number of toys in the area. Also, the total play area should be reduced in size and enclosed. If the child interacts with any of the toys appropriately, then immediate attention and praise should be provided. In some situations proximity to materials (Wehman, 1978b) and number of toys (Quilitch and Delongchamps, 1974) will facilitate action on toys.

Strategy 2: In other cases demonstrating the use of different toys directly in front of the child will provide a sufficient stimulus for the child to copy the teacher's behavior. Therefore, before moving to direct manual guidance, a verbal instruction plus demonstration should be provided (Morris and Dolker, 1974; Wehman, Karan, and Rettie, 1976).

Strategy 3: In the majority of cases, however, the above strategies will not prove totally effective, and physical prompting and guidance will be required. Once several play materials have been selected, a task analysis of the target skill(s) should be developed. Each skill should then be task analyzed (Williams, 1975; Wehman, 1978a). To teach these skills, a *backward chaining* method of instruction is optimal. With this strategy the teacher gets on the floor next to the child, places her hands around the child's hands on the toys, and physically guides the child through the skill until the final step in the sequence. At this point the child is encouraged to complete the action. Praise and edible reinforcement usually should be provided for each correct response.

As the child becomes increasingly proficient in the sequence, the amount of teacher assistance may be reduced gradually. Backward chaining techniques can then be employed with a second and eventually a third toy. Research supports the effectiveness of this intervention in decreasing self-stimulation in autistic (Koegel et al., 1974) and profoundly retarded individuals (Flavell, 1973; Wehman, Karan, and Rettie, 1976; Kissel and Whitman, 1977).

Although this type of behavior-shaping procedure is not considered play by many researchers (e.g., Piaget, 1962; Piers, 1972), the development of appropriate motor actions with play objects appears to be a necessary prerequisite to more sophisticated types of exploratory action.

Inappropriate Play

Problem #2. When presented with several toys, the child repeatedly beats on them in a nonfunctional, unconstructive way.

Differentiating between what is "appropriate" and "inappropriate" play has never been an easy task for researchers or teachers. Because the very nature of toy play may involve creative actions (Goetz and Baer, 1973), it often is difficult to code right from wrong. One possible solution to this problem is to classify toy play responses as negative and non-negative, with negative being defined as physically harmful or destructive actions directed on the toys or toward peers. On the other hand, constant banging of a top on the floor, al-

though not necessarily destructive is certainly not appropriate. This response measurement problem is one which must be solved by the teacher. While the optimal way would be to record the specific actions on the toys and then make objective judgments from these records, this can be quite time consuming.

After a teacher sorts through these difficulties of coding appropriate versus inappropriate responses, there are several strategies that may be attempted to improve play skills. These are listed below:

Strategy 1: Select toys that are novel (new) to the child, demonstrate how to use them, and then let the child practice using them under supervision. Possible reasons for inappropriate play are that the child is bored with the same toys or the toys are broken, thus inhibiting appropriate play actions.

Strategy 2: Demonstrate the correct use of the toy in front of the child. Interrupt inappropriate responses immediately, and model a constructive way to use the toy. If the child does it correctly, respond immediately with praise. If not, provide corrective feedback to the child by saying, "No, Bob, you don't bang the top, you spin it like this . . ."

Strategy 3: In situations in which the child is continually acting inappropriately with the toys, an assessment must be made of how many of the toys are being played with inappropriately. If most of the materials are being "abused," it will be necessary to limit the number of toys in the area and teach the child appropriate actions through physical prompting and manual guidance. The backward chaining strategy may be applied with this problem as well.

Lack of Sustained Play

Problem #3. When presented with several toys, the child plays with each for only a few seconds and then withdraws.

This is a common problem experienced with many severely and profoundly handicapped children. It is usually a problem that can be remediated through more frequent and structured reinforcement of appropriate play.

Consider the following illustration. Robert is presented with a play workbench and hammer. One set of appropriate responses might be to hammer three different shape pegs. Earlier observations indicate that Robert has these responses in his repertoire but he does not usually emit them. The correct teaching strategy for this problem would be to:

1. Identify an effective reinforcer for Robert.
2. Identify how long Robert must play before receiving reinforcement.
3. Establish a continuous schedule where Robert receives the reinforcement for meeting the time criterion.
4. Gradually increase the time criterion as Robert plays for longer periods.
5. Introduce either a second response with the toy *or* a new response with a different toy.

Limited Range of Play Materials

Problem #4. When presented with a variety of toys on different days, the child always plays with the same one or two toys.

Many severely handicapped children will only interact with the same toy. Unfortunately this may lead to satiation with the toy and restrict the range of fine motor actions that develops.

Strategy 1: Briefly remove the preferred toys, and encourage use of other materials. If the child acts on other toys, then for a short period of time (2 minutes) allow use of a preferred toy. This strategy, also known as the Premack Principle, will strengthen weak play activity.

Strategy 2: Identify toys that have similar stimulus characteristics to the favored toys. After removing the preferred toys, introduce similar materials into the area. Similar stimulus characteristics may include color, shape, size, same cause-effect relationship, and same type of motor skill required to operate toy.

Strategy 3: If these strategies do not work, it may be necessary to provide totally new toys and to demonstrate the reinforcing attributes of these toys. The favored toys should be removed completely from the play area during this instructional time.

Isolate Play

Problem #5. When presented with several toys and one or more peers, the child plays in isolation.

Isolate play is a normal stage of play in child development (Parten, 1932; Barnes, 1971). However, when it persists over several years, to the total exclusion of other children, it becomes a problem. There are times when it may clearly be appropriate for the child to play alone, particularly when creating materials (Rubin, Maioni, and Hornung, 1976); frequently, however, continued social withdrawal during play time is viewed as abnormal and is unacceptable.

There are numerous strategies that can be employed to overcome this problem. They range from material selection to ways of arranging instructional environment.

Strategy 1: By teaching table games (Marchant and Wehman, 1978) and using materials that require interaction by two or more individuals (Quilitch and Risley, 1973), isolate play can be reduced and social play encouraged. Before implementing different teaching methods, the types of materials available should be evaluated.

Strategy 2: A severely handicapped child can be integrated with two or more nonhandicapped peers (Knapczyk and Peterson, 1977). The optimal ratio of nonhandicapped to handicapped children is not clear (Strain, Cooke, and Apolloni, 1976). However, mixing several nonhandicapped children with one handicapped child may be effective. There is one caution with this or any stategy requiring modeling: be sure the child has developed imitation skills. If he has not, it may be presumptuous to assume the child will copy appropriate responses.

Strategy 3: A child can be paired with a higher functioning, although still retarded, peer who engages in appropriate play (Morris and Dolker, 1974). Similarly, "confederate" peers may be integrated into the play session and trained by the teacher to initiate social interactions with the child (Strain, Shores, and Timm, 1977).

Strategy 4: Two equivalent (low functioning) peers can be paired and trained by one or more adults (Wehman, Karan, and Rettie, 1976). Implementing this strategy may be difficult if one child is extremely active, runs away, or has a very short attention span. If this difficulty is not encountered, however, this situation will be a more natural training mode because it allows the teacher to "fade out" while the children play together (Whitman, Mercurio, and Caponigri, 1970).

Strategy 5: A child can be paired with an adult. With more difficult children, the teacher can provide one-to-one instruction to the child in taking turns (Wehman and Marchant, 1978).

Refusal To Initiate Social Interaction

Problem #6. When playing with a group of peers, the child fails to initiate social interactions with a peer.

Many young children are withdrawn and reluctant to enter into social play actively (Strain, Cooke, and Apolloni, 1976); this problem is not always limited to developmentally disabled children. Unfortunately this is a critical shortcoming with regard to the acquisition of play skills and leads to the child becoming dependent upon others to initiate responses.

There are few documented efforts that describe successful interventions for improving self-directed behavior, let alone *self-initiated* social interactions. However, there are several techniques that may be attempted.

Strategy 1: In a fashion similar to that discussed above, it may be helpful to set up task interdependent situations (Hake and Vukelich, 1972; Mithaug and Wolfe, 1976). The reciprocally reinforcing consequences that occur in leisure activities, such as table games, set a natural cue for prompting the child to take turns and initiate an interaction.

Strategy 2: If this does not work, it may be necessary for the teacher to play with the withdrawn child and verbally prompt him to initiate an interaction (Beveridge, Spencer, and Mittler, 1978). It will be helpful in these situations to set up social interactions that are easy for the child and that he can already perform. An example of this might be the teacher saying, "Roberta, take the ball over to Larry." Pointing or gesturing to Larry may be necessary. When the child completes the interaction, reinforcement must be provided immediately.

Strategy 3: Sociodramatic activity and role playing appropriate social play can be used as other means of effectively modeling social interaction (Domnie, 1974; Strain, 1975). By having the teacher model the way "good" children play, severely handicapped students who have adequate attention spans and imitative skills may be able to copy this behavior if a play session immediately follows.

Toy Throwing

Problem #7. When presented with several toys, the child engages in a high frequency of toy-throwing behavior.

Unlike the other problems described, this is an excessive play skill, not a play skill deficit. Al-

though this is not a common problem, it can be highly frustrating to teachers attempting to improve the qualitative nature of the child's toy play.

Strategy 1: The initial management strategy should be one of ignoring the inappropriate response and looking to another child. For example:

1. Larry throws the toy piano across the room.
2. Teacher immediately looks away.
3. Teacher goes to Ronnie and says, "Ronnie, I like the way you're playing so nicely!"
4. When Larry engages in at least 10 seconds of appropriate play, teacher looks to Larry and reinforces in a similar way.

This combination of ignoring and differential reinforcement is highly potent, provided it is applied consistently.

Strategy 2: Assuming the problem persists and high rates of throwing continue, the type of play materials available should be manipulated. It will be considerably more difficult to throw heavy objects or objects that are difficult to grasp easily. This, of course, assumes that the child is young.

Strategy 3: A third possibility that can be attempted is the use of a combination verbal reprimand and differential reinforcement for playing appropriately. Although research literature is mixed on the efficacy of reprimands (Madsen et al., 1970; Schutz et al., 1978), they can be effective, especially if reinforcement is employed as well. This strategy has the danger, however, of strengthening the throwing response, thereby serving as a positive reinforcer instead of punisher.

Strategy 4: If none of these methods is effective, a brief 30-second removal from the play area may be necessary, contingent on the throwing response. Timeout from a reinforcing play area should be an effective means of suppressing the inappropriate play response.

The issue of having the child pick up the toy after it has been thrown is one which is undoubtedly of concern to most teachers, and it may be the correct thing to do no matter what management strategy is employed. Caution should be taken, however. After all, is it really important who wins the battle of picking up the toy if a prolonging of the confrontation thereby becomes a possibility? Or is it better to ignore the incident and resume playing with the rest of the toys? This is a difficult decision, requiring the careful judgment of the teacher.

In this section an effort has been made to identify typical play problems of severely handicapped children and to suggest several instructional strategies that may be employed to overcome these difficulties. As teachers and parents struggle with the complex problems exhibited by children with severe behavioral handicaps, the development and maintenance of appropriate social and leisure skills is one instructional area that requires greater attention (Hamre-Nietupski and Williams, 1977; Wehman, 1978c). To prevent institutionalization and to facilitate acceptance of the child by other family members and neighborhood children, instructional strategies like those described in this chapter must be implemented. Finally, it should be recognized that these are only suggestions. Every child is unique and has a different learning history, which makes it difficult to prescribe solutions to all problems.

PARENTAL PERCEPTIONS OF THE HANDICAPPED CHILD'S LEISURE ACTIVITY

Through most of this chapter there has been an implicit understanding that toy play takes place in the school classroom. Yet children are in school, at the most, 30 hours per week and spend by far the majority of their time at home. It is important, therefore, to understand how the developmentally disabled child plays at home.

A review of relevant literature reveals little or no information indicating specific information about handicapped children's toy play behavior at home. Although some workers have investigated the mother-child interaction relationship in the context of play and social skills (e.g., Seitz and Hoekenga, 1974), little direct observational data relevant to child's toy play at home are available. In the absence of this information, a survey is the next best vehicle for asssessing handicapped children's play behavior.

This final section is directed toward describing the results of a questionnaire sent to the parents of 45 severely and profoundly retarded children. The survey was designed to ascertain parent's perceptions of their child's leisure activity. Specifically, questions were asked that would hopefully reveal information about the child's toy preferences, which toys were most durable and most fragile, the child's level of interaction with other peers, the

necessity for parental supervision, and how much parents valued play as a part of the educational curriculum. Each child's parents received a cover letter and a copy of the survey from the school administrator. The cover letter indicated that there was a need for parents to provide information concerning their child's leisure activity at home. Thirty-three of the 45 surveys were returned.

Favorite Leisure Activity

Passive leisure activity was rated as being the category of activities in which children engaged the most. Listening to the radio, watching TV, and looking at magazines were named most frequently. Table 3.7 lists all the activities identified by parents.

Child's Playmates

An effort was also made to assess with whom the child played and how independent the child was in his play activity. Of the children who had siblings, 10 played with a brother or sister regularly; 15 did not. The absence of playing with neighborhood children was more pronounced. Twenty-seven children did not play with neighborhood peers. Table 3.8 indicates the totals for each category.

Table 3.7. Favorite leisure activity of children as perceived by parents

Activity	No. of Times Listed
Watching TV	10
Turning pages in books	9
Listening to the radio	7
Playing with trucks	5
Playing with cars	4
Dancing	2
Using a musical toy	2
Lying around	2
Playing with airplanes	0
Pushing/catching ball	0
Pulling out pots/pans	0
Going up stairs	0
Going into cabinet	0
Playing with train with whistle	0
Walking around house	0
Walking outside	0
Sleeping	0
Playing in sandbox	0
Playing with Barbie dolls	0
Swinging	0

Table 3.8. Parent perceptions of child play patterns

	"Yes" responses	"No" responses
Child regularly plays with siblings	10	15
Child regularly plays with neighborhood children	6	27
Child regularly plays independently at home	15	18

Durability of Toys

Another question asked parents to identify the most durable toys and the most easily damaged toys. No consistent pattern of toy stability was found whatsoever. Books, stuffed animals, and crayons were among those items that were considered fragile. Table 3.9 lists all toys that were reported on the survey.

Parents were also asked how important play skill training was in the educational curriculum. One said it was not important, 10 indicated that it was important, and 21 responded that it was very important. At least in this sample, leisure skill instruction was viewed as being a high priority in the educational curriculum.

Results from this survey must be viewed with caution because they were limited to parents of a population of severely and profoundly handicapped children. However, they are indicative of the types of problems and deficits that characterize play activity of children with severe handicaps.

Table 3.9. Parental perceptions of durable versus fragile toys

Durable toys	
Blocks	Puzzles
Wagon	Rubber dog
Ball	Pinball machine
Bouncing buggy	Cards
Books	Big-wheeled cars
Plastic cereal bowls	Playschool basketball
Plastic doll	Busy Bee
Doll bed	Trampoline
Trucks	
Toy mailbox	

Easily damaged materials	
Stuffed bears	Stuffed toys
Record player	Books
Comic books	Magazines
Crayons	Slinky dog
Pocketbooks	

SUMMARY

This chapter has provided information relevant to helping developmentally disabled children acquire play skills. Interacting with toys and other play materials is an important aspect of a child's development, and there is a need for systematic instruction in this area by teachers. The normal progression of play skills, assessement techniques, and program development were discussed in detail. Also presented, primarily for those who work with more severely handicapped children, was a section describing typical play problems and offering suggested strategies for overcoming these problems. The role of the family and their expectations was discussed in the final section, with results from a leisure skill needs survey presented.

TOYS ACCORDING TO CATEGORY AND FUNCTION

Motor Skills

Animal and Bird Stencils (Kenworthy) Twelve cardboard stencils of animals and birds familiar to children. Can be traced and identified.

Animal Learning Shapes (Ideal) Eight rubber squares in assorted colors, each with an animal cutout which can be removed and replaced.

Animal Wooden Playboard (Simplex Toys) Fourteen stand-up pieces shaped like animals, each with easy-lift knobs. Can be used to aid in identifying shapes.

Baby Cherche (ETA) Hardwood squares with 17 vari-sized circles and half-circles that fit into recessed spaces. $\frac{1}{2}'' \times 7\frac{1}{2}'' \times 7\frac{1}{2}''$.

Beaded Pegs and Peg Board (Ideal) Eye-hand coordination and concrete demonstrations of number problems and color sorting and pattern building. 100-hole pegboard and small beaded pegs in six colors. Board $6'' \times 6''$.

Bingo Game (MB) Fifty-card set with plastic embossed numbered pieces. Player must coordinate eye-hand concept to play the game.

Bird Fun (Built-Rite Toys) Bird pictures are on $6\frac{3}{4}'' \times 6\frac{3}{4}''$ cards. Cutout heads of birds and identifying titles may be removed and then matched by a player to correct bird body and shape-opening of the title.

Casper the Friendly Ghost Game (MB) For two, three, or four players. Simple but exciting.

Object to be the first to move four ghosts into haunted house. For ages 5–12.

Cello Build Counting Game (ETA) Fifty rectangular wooden pieces, five wooden playing boards (5″ × 9″), counting book and discs. Numbered pictures on small pieces fit corresponding pictures on boards. Stored in 10½″ × 12″ wooden box.

Discovery Ball (DLM) A plastic ball (6″-diameter) composed of sections that may be removed by unscrewing the top. Teaches coordination of eye-hand muscles.

Double-Deck Peg Board (ETA) To give child with a visual handicap excellent practice in depth perception and eye-hand coordination on two levels. Pegs are painted in two colors. Top deck is clear plexiglas. Bottom deck is wood. Each deck has twenty-one holes in vertical alignment (twelve red and nine green pegs).

Drop-In Box (ETA) A well built wooden box with five different shapes to be inserted into proper slots for coordination exercises with handicapped older children. 6½″ × 6½″ × 5″.

Easy-Grip Pegs and Jumbo Peg Board (Ideal) Large plastic pegs (1″ knob) in six colors. Easy for spastic or handicapped to handle. Useful to develop motor skill and eye-hand coordination.

Eye-Hand Coordination Game (ETA) Hand-sized pegs in five colors are inserted into boards drilled to receive them. Degree of difficulty of task can be increased by using fewer boards. Boards are painted, allowing color training by matching pegs to boards. Twelve pegs, four boards, and housing.

Farm (Fisher Price) Barn, silo, farm animals, and figures assist child in relating to community life. Parts can be manipulated into correct positions in barn and barnyard.

Flip-Chex (Educational Concepts) Twelve puzzles in one kit. Pictures, shapes, colors, and numbers painted on each side of the eight pieces in each puzzle. Parts can be used to aid in matching, word discrimination, rhyming, and number concept and employs eye-hand control.

Form Board (ETA) Large handles allow children to improve eye-hand coordination and practice in grasping. More severely involved children can indicate by pointing or telling which color block goes in which place. Four primary colors are used.

Form Puzzle (DLM) A colorful exercise in shape matching. The sturdy plastic base has twelve recesses in which different colored geometric shapes are placed. Each insert may be used as a trace-around stencil in introducing the student to the drawing of geometric figures or to encourage hand control. The underside of each insert is a vertical-sided dish approximately ¼″ deep that may be used as a mold for the production of solid forms from clay.

Four-Way Blocks (Creative Playthings) Set of six wooden blocks 1¼″ × 1¼″ × 7½″. Turn blocks until parts fit together to form four different animals painted on the sides of the blocks.

Fuzzy-Wuzzy Lacing Cards (Whitman) Eye-hand coordination used to thread plastic laces into the six holes which outline objects and designs on the card.

Geometric Cabinet (Montessori) Child learns to visually discriminate geometric forms and to use eye-hand control. Sixteen geometric colored figures, each in its own 4″ × 4″ template are stored in a solid hardwood cabinet.

Geometric Learning Shapes (Ideal) Geometrically cut rubber pieces in primary colors are assembled in hard-rubber trays. Twelve shapes in a set. 5½″ × 5½″ forms.

Geometric Sorting Board (Childcraft) A self-corrective sorting exercise. Each piece has to fit over the correct group of pegs. Polished wooden base, 7″ × 7″. Shapes are brightly colored and include circles, triangles, and squares (16 pieces).

Hand-Eye Square Pegboard (ETA) Natural finished wooden board and twenty colored pegs. Pegs fit into notched slots, cannot roll out of reach, and are easily controlled.

Hundred Peg Board (Judy) Wooden pegs (red, blue, green, and yellow) help children understand number relationships, color arrangements, and shapes. 16″-board (1″ thick) and 100-colored pegs (3″ in diameter, 1¼″ long).

Jet Plane (Fisher Price) Manipulative pull toy (13½″ × 6¼″ × 11¾″) makes a whirring sound when pulled. Door lowers to enable small figures to be placed into plane.

Jumbo Wood Beads (Playskool) Provide opportunities for learning colors and shapes and stimulate use of eye-hand control. Two strings with plastic tips and 30 extra large wooden beads in five shapes and colors.

Keys of Learning (NASCO) Plastic box with six shapes to fit into corresponding slots and six keys to fit keyholes to eject the shapes. Develops coordination and manual control.

Lace Boot (Playskool) Lacing boot, drop box combined. Six figures match three shapes in show for shape training. Unlacing the boot releases the figures. 8¹¹/₁₆″ × 6¹/₁₆″ × 7¹¹/₁₆″.

Lacing Animals (ETA) Four wooden animals in colors, each with three laces. Subjects add interest and excitement to routine threading.

Large Parquetry Designs and Blocks (DLM) The set of blocks and the set of designs are designated to be used in conjunction with each other (22 designs, four 2″ red squares, four 2″ green squares, four diamond shapes in each of yellow, blue, orange, and purple, and four each of yellow and blue isosceles triangles). Used in teaching of children with minimal brain dysfunction whose visuomotor skills are undeveloped.

Large Pegboard and Pegs (Childcraft) Pegs can be grouped according to color, create designs, and form geometric shapes. Used to explore spatial relationships and count to 100. 2″-pegs come in different colors. 10″ × 10″ board.

Learning Tower (Childcraft) Twelve six-sided polyethylene nesting cups in bright colors to provide challenge to stack or nest according to size and shape.

Lego Systems (Educational Aids) Interlocking bricks snap together and pull apart. A combination of sizes and shapes designed for maximum range of creative possibilities (402 pieces).

Lincoln Logs (Playskool) Ideal for individual or group activity. Eye-hand coordination employed to form shapes from wood pieces.

Locking Box (Creative Playthings) Smooth wooden box with four sections, each section having a door and a different type of lock. Teaches dexterity in handling different locks.

Mechanics Bench (NASCO) Colorful plastic bench, screws, nuts, bolts, and wrenches can be used to teach manual dexterity.

Mini-Peg Board (Judy) Twenty-five-hole hardboard pegboard mounted on a wooden frame. Forty pegs in four basic colors.

Multivariant Sequencing Bead and Patterns

(DLM) Wooden beads in three sizes, four shapes, and five basic colors (total of 120). Can be used to identify size, shape, and color matching.

Number Learner (Childcraft) Fifteen colored foam squares that must be fitted over pegs that stand for each number. Excellent for blind children, youngsters with learning disabilities, and other handicapped children. Wood base 4″ × 16″.

Occupational Puzzles (Childcraft) Realistic puzzles portray men and women in working situations. 9″ × 1″ wooden puzzles with pieces large enough to make handling by spastic or handicapped easier for the individual.

Outdoor Puzzles (Childcraft) Four colorful beginning puzzles (few pieces per puzzle) with simple cutouts.

Peg Activity Box (NYT) Durable plastic pegboard and pegs, excellent for creating freeform and geometric designs and visuo-motor skills. Can also be used to teach numbers. 6″ × 16″ board.

Picture Dominos (Ed-U-Cards) Identifiable objects and shapes shown on 1⅝″ × 3¾″ cardboard pieces which are matched as in regular dominos. No reading or number concept needed.

Picture Matching Boards (ETA) Encourages eye-hand coordination in matching identical pictures (on blocks) with those on the board. Boards have four or eight recesses with matching blocks.

Play Chips (Playskool) Helps the child discriminate between various shapes, colors, designs, and quantities. Forty hardwood chips (four basic shapes) in different colors in a carrying case. Holder 5½″ × 6⅞″. Wood chips approximately 2″ overall and ⁵/₁₆″ thick.

Playskool Puzzle Plaques (Playskool) All pieces of each puzzle are specifically cut to represent some identifiable part of the subject picture. Nontoxic colors on top quality woodboard.

Pounding Bench (Playskool) Tight pegs challenge the child to develop eye-hand coordination and afford him an emotional outlet. 12″ × 6¾″ × 5½″.

Puzzle Box (Montessori) Nine shapes—two boxes. Teaches visuo-manual coordination.

Puzzle Inset Board—Assortment A (DLM) Wooden form, 11¾″ × 8½″, holds 15 cutout shapes that can be lifted from the tray by knobs and placed into a recessed slot beside its proper space in the form. Aids in identification, visual perception, and motor control.

Puzzles with Knobs (Childcraft) Brightly colored wood plaque puzzles—excellent for the handicapped child for each piece has its own easy-to-grasp knob. Assorted shapes and pictures. Sharply defined borders make these puzzles excellent for blind and other exceptional children.

Puzzling Dozen (Childcraft) Set of 12 colorful puzzles, each with nine plywood pieces. Subjects are familiar objects. Teaches eye-hand coordination.

Reels and Wheels (DLM) Eighteen vari-shaped colored plastic discs to fit over different sized stems. Teaches visual discrimination and eye-hand coordination.

Rig-A-Jig (Landfield) Construction parts (430) and 16-page idea book. For ages 3–11. Colored plastic parts can be used to form shapes and objects. To encourage motor skill.

Ring Tops (MB) Two sturdy wooden stakes and four heavy rope rings. For two, three, or four players. Rings are tossed over stakes and points allowed. Good for coordinating eye-hand control.

Rubber Puzzles (Childcraft) Six colorful subjects are depicted in this puzzle set. Easy-to-handle rubber pieces are useful for manually handicapped. 8½″ × 11¾″.

Select-A-Block—Automatic dispensing machine (Montessori) Color-coordinated pull levers drop one block at a time. Match blocks to same opening and levers. For ages 2–6.

Sewing Cards (MB) 6″ × 8″ cardboard cards with punched outline of animals. Plastic-tipped laces are used to sew around picture. Improves coordination and concentration.

Shape Concept Forms (Childcraft) Set of cutout forms representing eight common geometric shapes. For each cutout there is a corresponding colored inset with a knob to facilitate handling. Cutouts and insets can be traced or fitted together to permit comparisons.

Shapes/Forms Boards (Ideal) Rubber strips in colors each with cutout geometric shapes or pictures which can be removed and rearranged.

Sensory Skills

Animal Learning Shapes (Ideal) Rubber squares in assorted colors (5½″ × 5½″) each with an animal cutout that can be removed and re-placed. Useful in identifying colors and shapes.

Animal Wooden Playboard (Simplex Toys) Fourteen stand-up animal shapes with easy-lift knobs. Pieces can be handled and moved about by child.

Baby Cherche (ETA) Hardwood squares with 17 vari-sized circles and half-circles in bright colors that fit into recessed spaces. ½″ × 7½″ × 7½″. Child learns concept of size and color.

Beaded Pegs and Peg Board (Ideal) Eye-hand coordination and concrete demonstrations of number problems and color sorting and pattern building. 100-hole pegboard and small beaded pegs in six colors.

Build-A-Shape (Philograph) Twenty-four cards which, when paired, form 12 simple and easily recognized shapes.

Cage with Animals (Dick Blick) Colored plastic cage with assorted colored plastic animals which may be handled and identified.

Circle Board (ETA) Teaches the child size perception without the factor of shape. The circle forms are raised on the board and painted different colors. Each has a large knob that is easy to grasp. There is a ½″ difference in diameter between any of the five circles.

Clothespin Circle (ETA) A pegboard variation which will hold pegs forming four distinct circles. Pegs are easily removed even by most severely handicapped child. board is 13″ in diameter and has 30 holes. Pegs are in four colors.

Color Cubes (Playskool) Parquetry design blocks. Educational play game for school and home, to encourage creative play and teach color recognition and simple counting. For ages 3–8.

Color Matching Board (ETA) This board has one object: to teach color matching. Four cutouts on the board are painted red, blue, yellow, and green to match blocks which fit into them. Each block has a large handle for easier handling.

Color Stacking Discs (Playskool) A large spindle upon which brightly colored wooden discs of graduated sizes may be arranged. Nine discs varying in diameter stack to a 9″ cone. Each hardwood piece has different nontoxic colors in spectrum sequence.

Coordination Board (Childcraft) Raised geometric forms are matched for color and shape to corresponding cutouts in the puzzle board.

Useful in challenging manipulation, color and form recognition. 12″ × 8¾″.

Deluxe Pegboard Set (Ideal) Gray plastic pegboard, 10″ × 10″, with 25 plastic pegs each of six colors. Develops awareness of geometric shapes and a strong realization of numbers.

Double-Deck Peg Board (ETA) To give the child with a visual handicap excellent practice in depth perception and eye-hand coordination on two levels. Pegs are painted in two colors. Top deck is clear plexiglas. Bottom deck is wood. Each deck has 21 holes in vertical alignment (12 red and 9 green pegs).

Eye-Hand Coordination Game (ETA) Hand-sized pegs in five colors are inserted into boards drilled to receive them. Degree of difficulty of task can be increased by using fewer boards. Boards are painted, allowing color training by matching pegs to boards (12 pegs, 4 boards, and housing).

Form Board (ETA) For perception of geometric shapes. Large handles allow children to improve eye-hand control and practice in grasping. More severely involved children can indicate by pointing or telling which color block goes into which place. Four primary colors are used.

Form Puzzle (DLM) A colorful exercise in shape matching. The sturdy plastic base has 12 recesses in which different colored geometric shapes are placed. Each insert may be used as a trace-around stencil.

Four-Way Blocks (Creative Playthings) Set of six wooden blocks on which pictures of four animals are painted. Turn blocks until parts fit together for form and animal. 1¼″ × 1¼″ × 7½″.

Geometric Cabinet (Montessori) Child learns to visually discriminate geometric forms and to use eye-hand control. Sixteen geometric colored figures, each in its own 4″ × 4″ template, are stored in a solid hardwood cabinet.

Geometric Learning Shapes (Ideal) Geometrically cut rubber pieces in primary colors are assembled in a hard-rubber tray. Twelve shapes in a set. 5½″ × 5½″ forms.

Geometric Sorting Board (Childcraft) A self-correcting sorting exercise. Each piece has to fit over the correct group of pegs. Polished wooden base, 7″ × 7″. Shapes are brightly colored and include circles, triangles, and squares (16 pieces).

Hundred Peg Board (Judy) Wooden pegs (red, blue, green, and yellow) help children understand number relationships, color arrangements, and shapes. 16″-board (1″ thick) and 100 pegs (3″ in diameter, 1¼″ long).

Jumbo Wood Beads (Playskool) Provide opportunities for learning colors and shapes. Two strings with plastic tips and 30 extra large wooden beads in five shapes and colors.

Large Parquetry Designs and Blocks (DLM) Thirty-two wooden blocks in three shapes and six colors to be used with *Design Cards* (22 cards). Teaches form relationship, visual sequencing, and form and color matching.

Learning Tower (Childcraft) Twelve six-sided polyethylene nesting cups in bright colors to provide challenge to stack or nest according to size and shape.

Merry-Go-Round Music Box (Fisher Price) Wooden and plastic merry-go-round plays tune and rotates. Small wooden figures can be placed on and removed from the toy. Utilizes eye-hand coordination and appreciation of musical tunes.

Multivariant Sequencing Bead and Patterns (DLM) Wooden beads in three sizes, four shapes, and five basic colors (total of 120). Can be used to teach simple size, shape, or color matching.

Music Box Tic-Tock Clock (Fisher Price) Plays "Grandfather's Clock" when wound. Instructive and interesting. Teaches time by approved association method. Wood case construction, 10½″ high.

Number Puzzle (ETA) This puzzle is a basic one in which children become acquainted with numbers by handling them. The wooden puzzle tray gives the child something to do with the brightly painted numbers which can fit into recessed spots on the board.

Peg Activity Box (NYT) Durable plastic pegboard and pegs, excellent for creating free-form and geometric designs and visuo-motor skills. Can also be used to teach numbers.

Picture Matching Boards (ETA) Encourages eye-hand coordination in matching identical pictures (on blocks) with those in the board. Boards have four or eight recesses with matching blocks.

Play Chips (Playskool) Helps the child discriminate between various shapes, colors, designs, and quantities. Forty hardwood chips (four basic shapes) in different colors in a carrying case.

Puzzles with Knobs (Childcraft) Brightly colored wood plaque puzzles, excellent for the handicapped child because each piece has its own easy-to-grasp knob. Assorted shapes and pictures. Sharply defined borders make these puzzles excellent for blind and other exceptional children.

Select-A-Block—Automatic dispensing machine (Montessori) Color coordinated pull levers drop one block at a time. Match blocks to same opening and levers.

Shake-And-Match Sounds (Teaching Resources) Eight pairs of identical plastic cylinders, in each of which is sealed an item or items that produce sound when the cylinder is manipulated. Can be used to develop and sharpen auditory perception skills relating to nonspeech sounds.

Shapes, Colors, and Forms (Childcraft) Three basic shapes in primary colors—for learning sizes, shapes, and colors. Fit into a tray which is part of the wood box with sliding cover.

Shapes/Forms Boards (Ideal) 10½″ × 2½″ × ¼″ rubber strips in colors, each with a cutout geometric shape of a picture that can be removed and rearranged.

Size Board (ETA) Give the child practice in very elementary size perception. May also be used for color matching and color identification.

Size and Shape Puzzles (Childcraft) Similar to *Animal Puzzles* but emphasize size and shape discrimination. In four to nine pieces they enable the child to start with simple construction and progress to more difficult perceptual tasks. 14″ × 12″ × ½″.

Stringing Rings (Childcraft) Flat wooden discs have large holes and the string has an extra-long tip at each end. Forty enameled rings in bright primary colors. Helpful for eye-hand coordination for more severely handicapped.

Talking Toys (Mattel) Circular plastic "talking boxes" (10″ diameter) with pictures on the face and a dial which, when pointed to the picture and the string is pulled, gives sound corresponding to the picture. Valuable in increasing attention span, picture-word association, and motor coordination.

Tell-By-Touch (Childcraft) Feel the textured knob and place it in the matching textured hole. This wooden put-together develops tactile discrimination.

Concepts

Bird Fun (Built-Rite Toys) Eight carboard bird pictures (3¾″ × 6¼″) with removable heads and identifying titles that must be matched to correspond with empty areas on the card. Titles are in various shapes, heads of birds are on circles.

Candyland (Ed-U-Cards) Game for ages 1–4. Promotes beginning concepts in reading.

Dimensional Puzzle (Creative Playthings) Fit-in geometric shapes in primary and secondary colors. Each of the 12 colorful shapes in this puzzle has a raised center piece over which fits the same shape in another color, making a three-dimensional puzzle.

Flip-Chex (Educational Aids) A kit containing 12 puzzles (eight pieces each) with colored pictures or shapes on each side. Can be used to assist in teaching sequencing, matching, work discrimination, rhyming, and number concept.

Giant Floor Puzzle (Child Guidance) Twelve giant jigsaw pieces make a giant puzzle (38″ × 28″). Completed puzzle tells a funny story and teaches counting and number concepts. For ages 3–7.

Graduated Cylinders (NYT) A set of graduated wooden cylinders comprised of 10 each of four colors: orange, purple, green, and yellow. The height and diameter of the cylinders vary. Materials are designed to help students acquire the basic perceptual, motor, and cognitive skills.

Headache (Kohner) Chase game for two to four players. Plastic game board.

Lego Systems (Educational Aids) An aid that stimulates the growth of natural creativity. Interlocking bricks snap together and pull apart. A combination of sizes, shapes, and colors designed for maximum range of creative possibilities (402 pieces).

Number Learner (Childcraft) Fifteen colored foam squares representing numbers from 1–5 must be fitted over wooden pegs that stand for each number. Teaches simple number concepts. Excellent for blind children, youngsters with learning disabilities, and other handicapped children.

Perception Puzzles (DLM) These colorful

wooden puzzles offer an interesting approach to perceptual learning. Five pigs (or chickens), differing in size, present an exercise in graduation, demonstrating concepts of biggest, smallest, in-between, bigger-than, and smaller-than. Each 10½'' × 3¼'' puzzle includes a clear wood field in an attractive box.

Raggedy Ann (MB) For two, three, or four players, ages 4–8. Players build pictures of Raggedy Ann and Witch Wiggle using cards obtained by matching the spin of the spinner with characters on the board. No reading required.

Shape Concept Forms (Childcraft) Set of cutout forms representing eight common geometric shapes. For each cutout there is a corresponding colored inset with a knob to facilitate handling. Cutouts and insets can be traced or fitted together to permit comparisons.

Shapes/Forms Boards (Ideal) Rubber strips, 10½'' × 2½'' × ¼'', in color, each with cutout geometric shapes or pictures that can be removed and rearranged.

Sorry (Parker Bros.) A slide-pursuit game for ages 8 to adult. For two to four players.

Sorting Tray (NYT) The tray provides six individual plastic compartments or bins. Label cards, showing numbers, letters, and shapes, can be used to develop concepts and determine the essential similarity between two or more different things as the cards are sorted into the trays. Trays can also be used with blocks, beads, cubes, cylinders, pegs, etc.

Spirograph (Kenner) Eighteen transparent plastic wheels, two rings, two racks, four ball point pens (colored). Baseboard and paper patterns book in a fitted storage tray. A simple way for all ages to learn to draw patterns.

Talking Toys (Mattel) Circular plastic "talking boxes," 10''-diameter with pictures on the face and a dial which, when pointed to individual pictures and the string is pulled, gives sound corresponding to picture. Topics include "The Bee Says," "The Farmer Says," and "Mother Goose Says." Valuable in increasing attention span, picture-word association, and motor coordination.

Three Bears Puzzle (ETA) This puzzle has been used with blind children of kindergarten age. The bear forms are raised. Gives the child practice in recognizing size differences with the factor of shape involved.

Zoo Lotto (Ed-U-Cards) An effective aid for children with special learning needs in school or home. For ages 3–8.

Math Readiness Skills

Form Puzzle (DLM) A colorful exercise in shape matching. The sturdy plastic base has 12 recesses in which different colored geometric shapes are placed. Each insert may be used as a trace-around stencil in introducing the student to the drawing of geometric figures or to encourage hand control. The underside of each insert is a vertical-sided dish approximately ¼'' deep, which may be used as a mold for the production of solid forms in clay.

Fraction Discs (MB) Seven colored cardboard discs (9½''-diameter) plus pie-shaped pieces in ½, ⅙, ⅕, ¼, ⅓, ½, and 1 segments to be placed on circles. Useful in teaching comprehension of fractions to grades 3 through 8.

Fractions Are Easy As Pie (MB) Spinner board shows kinds of pies and sizes of pie pieces (½, ¼, ⅓, ⅛, and ⅙). Players have board cutouts of pies into which they place sizes of pieces as indicated by spinner. Aids in teaching addition of fractions as well as understanding different sizes. For grades 2 through 7.

Geo-Form Boards (Childcraft) Set of two geometric puzzles. Each puzzle has 12 divisions. Shapes are in high relief and easy to grasp. 7¾'' × 9¾''.

Geometric Cabinet (Montessori) Child learns to visually discriminate geometric forms and to use eye-hand control. Sixteen geometric colored figures, each in its own 4'' × 4'' template, are stored in a solid hardwood cabinet.

Geometric Sorting Board (Childcraft) A self-corrective sorting exercise. Each piece has to fit over the correct group of pegs. Polished wooden base, 7'' × 7''. Shapes are brightly colored and include circles, triangles, rectangles, and squares (16 pieces).

Giant Floor Puzzle (Child Guidance) Twelve giant jigsaw pieces makes a giant puzzle (38'' × 28''). Completed puzzle tells a funny story and teaches counting and number concepts. For ages 3–7.

Hundred Peg Board (Judy) Wooden pegs (red, blue, green, and yellow) help children understand number relationships, color arrangements, and shapes. 16"-board (1" thick) and 100 colored pegs (3" in diameter, 1¼" long).

Instructo-Magnetic Numerals (Instructo) Kit includes numerals, number names, and symbols. (Numerals 0 through 10, names one through ten, strips of blocks of various lengths to correspond with numerals 1 to 10, and signs +, −, and =). Used to teach counting and give practice in counting objects in groups. *Magnetic Ten Frame*—to be used with magnetic numerals.

Instructo Pupil-Pack: Money (Instructo) Five packs for five children. Cutouts include coins, bills, operation signs, and illustrations of things to buy. Each pack has combination lid and individual flannel board, over 100 cutouts, and partitioned plastic storage tray. Children learn to identify coins and bills and develop a beginning understanding of equivalents.

Instructo Pupil-Pack: Numerals and Counting Shapes (Instructo) Set contains six pupil-packs for six children: combination lid and individual flannel board, 99 felt cutout, and partitioned plastic storage tray. Flannel numbers, objects, and shapes to be placed on corresponding spaces on flannel boards.

Large Pegboard and Pegs (Childcraft) Pegs can be grouped according to color, create designs, and form geometric shapes. Used to explore spatial relationships and count to 100. 2"-pegs come in different colors. 10" × 10" board.

Locking Numbers (Ideal) Rubber forms, 4" × 8", cut into two jig-saw pieces—to match numerals with corresponding shape on second piece.

Math Mates (Creative Playthings) Ten number-learning puzzles for 3- to 6-year-olds. Learn to associate numerals and quantities.

Number Learner (Childcraft) Fifteen colored foam squares representing numbers from 1–5 must be fitted over wooden pegs that stand for each number. Teaches simple number concepts. Excellent for blind children, youngsters with learning disabilities, and other handicapped children. Wooden base 4" × 16".

Number Puzzle (ETA) This puzzle is a basic one in which children become acquainted with numbers by handling them. The wooden puzzle tray gives the child something to do with

the brightly painted numbers which can fit into recessed spots on the board.

Number Recognition and Conservation (NYT) Kit contains three decks of 30 cards, each containing various configurations of shapes, objects, and forms, and one strip book with pages divided into three separate sections. Used as a game to emphasize the recognition and meaning of numbers and quantity.

Peek-Peabody Early Experiences Kit (American Guidance Service) Daily, spontaneous play-like learning experience for children of prekindergarten age. Kit includes teacher's manual; lesson manuals; four puppets; rope sections; six minidecks of cards to teach actions, singular and plurals; tools, objects that go together, whole objects, missing parts and opposites; beads; shape pictures; scenic pictures; cassettes to teach sound identification and associations; 30 small easily identified objects; 27 song cards; sound makers; story cards and story pictures; six tumblers to teach full/empty, hot/cold; two cloth textured balls; and four cloth bags to teach colors and to conceal objects the children identify by touch. All materials contained in a large plastic carrying case.

Peg Activity Box (NYT) Durable plastic pegboard and pegs, excellent for creating free-form and geometric designs and visuo-motor skills. Can also be used to teach numbers. 6" × 16" board.

Perception Puzzles (DLM) These colorful wooden puzzles offer an interesting approach to perceptual learning. Five pigs (or chickens) different in size, present an exercise in graduation, demonstrating concepts of biggest, smallest, in between, bigger than, and smaller than. Each 10½" × 3¼" puzzle includes a clear wood field in an attractive box.

Play Chips (Playskool) Helps the child discriminate between various shapes, colors, designs, quantities. Forty hardwood chips (four basic shapes) in different colors in a carrying case. Holder 5¼" × 6⅞". Wood chips approximately 2" overall and 5/16" thick.

Size Board (ETA) Gives the child practice in very elementary size perception. May also be used for color matching and color identification.

Size and Shape Puzzles (Childcraft) Similar to *Animal Puzzles* but emphasize size and shape discrimination. In four to nine pieces they enable the child to start with simple construction and progress to more difficult perceptual tasks. 14″ × 12″ × ½″.

Teaching Clock Music Box (Fisher Price) A musical clock teaches time by approved association method. Develops child's interest in music and provides fun-filled method to teach time.

Teddy Bear Counters (MB) One hundred teddy bear counters in three colors (red, blue, yellow). A multisensory introduction to numbers.

Telling Time Flash Cards (Ed-U-Cards) Cards, 3½″ × 5¾″, show time in 15-minute intervals; answer clock with movable hands. Can be utilized in game form to teach time. For ages 5-9.

Three Bears Puzzle (ETA) Gives the child practice in recognizing the size differences with the factor of shape involved. This puzzle has large, cutout pieces of the three bears—the bear forms are raise from the board. The puzzle has been used with blind children of kindergarten age to aid in determining relative sizes and shapes.

Toss and Total Ice Cream Cone Game (DLM) A target game in which lightweight balls are used in place of darts. The board and balls are velcro covered so when the balls hit the board they adhere to it on impact. Scoring areas are indicated on the board. 12″ circular board. Useful for eye-hand integration exercises. Also may be useful as a high interest math game.

Trouble Game (Kohner) Plastic playing board and 16 "men" (four each of four colors). Player moves four men around circular playing track to "finish" line.

REFERENCES

Apolloni, T., Cooke, S., and Cooke, T. 1977. Establishing a normal peer as a behavioral model for delayed toddlers. Percept. Mot. Skills 44:231–241.

Apolloni, T., and Cooke, T. 1978. Integrated programming at the infant, toddler, and preschool levels. In M. Guralnick (ed.), Early Intervention and the Integration of Handicapped and Nonhandicapped Children. University Park Press, Baltimore.

Barnes, L. 1971. Preschool play norms: A replication. Dev. Psychol. 5:99–103.

Beveridge, M., Spencer, J., and Mittler, P. 1978. Language and social behavior in severely educationally subnormal children. Br. J. Soc. Clin. Psychol. 17(1):75–83.

Biblow, E. 1973. Imaginative play and the control of aggressive behavior. In J. Singer (ed.), The Child's World of Make Believe, Academic Press, New York.

Brown, L., Bellamy, T., and Sontag, E. 1971. The Development and Implementation of a Public School Prevocational Training Program for Trainable Retarded and Severely Emotionally Disturbed Children. Madison Public Schools, Madison, Wis.

Burney, J., Russell, B., and Shores, R. 1977. Developing social responses in two profoundly retarded children. AAESPH Rev. 2(2):53–63.

Carney, I., et al. 1977. Social interaction in several handicapped students: Training basic social skills and social acceptability. In The Severely and Profoundly Handicapped Child. State Department of Public Instruction, Springfield, Ill.

Cooke, S., Cooke, T., and Apolloni, T. Developing nonretarded toddlers as verbal models for retarded classmates. Child Study J. In press.

Domnie, M. 1974. Teaching severely handicapped students to enact an imaginary event. Unpublished manuscript. Madison Public Schools, Madison, Wis.

Ellis, M. J. 1973. Why People Play. Prentice-Hall, Englewood Cliffs, N.J.

Favell, J. E., and Cannon, P. R. 1977. Evaluation of entertainment materials for severely retarded persons. Am. J. Ment. Defic. 81(4):357–361.

Flavell, J. 1973. Reduction of stereotypes by reinforcement of toy play. Ment. Retard. 11(4):24–27.

Fredericks, H. D., Baldwin, V., Grove, D., Moore, W., Riggs, C., and Lyons, B. 1978. Integrating the moderately and severely handicapped preschool child into a normal day care setting. In M. Guralnick (ed.), Early Intervention and the Integration of Handicapped and Nonhandicapped Children. University Park Press, Baltimore.

Friedlander, B., Kamin, P., and Hesse, G. 1974. Operant therapy for prehension disabilities in moderately and severely retarded young children. Train. School Bull. 71:101–108.

Goetz, E., and Baer, D. 1973. Social control of form diversity and the emergence of new forms in children's blockbuilding. J. Appl. Behav. Anal. 6:209–217.

Gottlieb, S. 1973. Modeling effects upon fantasy. In J. Singer (ed.), The Child's World of Make Believe. Academic Press, New York.

Gozali, J., and Charney, B. 1972. Agenda for the '70's: Full social integration of the retarded. Ment. Retard. 10:20–21.

Hake, D., and Vukelich, R. 1972. A classification and review of cooperation procedures. J. Exp. Anal. Behav. 18:333–343.

Hamre-Nietupski, S., and Williams, W. W. 1977. Implementation of selected sex education and social skills programs with severely handicapped students. Educ. Train. Ment. Retard. 12(4):364–372.

Hanson, M., and Bellamy, G. T. 1977. Continuous measurement of progress in infant intervention programs. Educ. Train. Ment. Retard. 12(1):52–58.

Hopper, C., and Wambold, C. 1978. Improving the independent play of severely mentally retarded children. Educ. Train. Ment. Retard. 13(1):42–46.

Hutt, C. 1970. Specific and diversive exploration. In H. W. Reese and P. L. Lawton (eds.), Advances in Child Development and Behavior, Academic Press, Vol. V. New York.

Kissel, R., and Whitman, T. L. 1977. An examination of the direct and generalized effects of a play training and overcorrection procedure upon the self-stimulatory behavior of a profoundly retarded boy. AAESPH Rev. 3:131–146.

Knapczyk, D. 1975. Task analytic assessment of severe learning problems. Educ. Train. Ment. Retard. 16:24–27.

Knapczyk, D., and Peterson, N. L. 1977. Social play interaction of retarded children in an integrated classroom environment. Res. Retard. 3:104–112.

Knapczyk, D., and Yoppi, J. 1975. Development of cooperative and competition play responses in developmentally disabled children. Am. J. Ment. Defic. 80(3):245–255.

Koegel, R., Firestone, P., Kramme, K., and Dunlap, A. 1974. Increasing spontaneous play by suppressing self-stimulation in autistic children. J. Appl. Behav. Anal. 7(4):521–528.

McCall, R. 1974. Exploratory manipulation and play in the human infant. Monogr. Soc. Res. Hum. Dev. University of Chicago Press, Chicago.

Madsen, C., Becker, W., Thomas, D., Koser, D., and Plager, E. 1970. An analysis of the reinforcing function of "sit down" commands. In R. K Parker (ed.), Readings in Educational Psychology. Allyn and Bacon, Boston.

Marchant, J., and Wehman, P. (March) 1978. Teaching table games to severely retarded children. Paper presented at Virginia Council on Exceptional Children, Richmond.

Mithaug, D., and Wolfe, M. 1976. Employing task arrangements and verbal contingencies to promote verbalizations between retarded children. J. Appl. Behav. Anal. 9:301–314.

Morris, R., and Dolker, M. 1974. Developing cooperative play in socially withdrawn retarded children. Ment. Retard. 12(6):24–27.

Nunnally, J. C., and Lemond, L. 1973. Exploratory behavior and human development. In H. W. Reese (ed.), Advances in Child Development and Behavior, Vol. 8. Academic Press, New York.

Paloutzian, R., Hasazi, J., Streifel, J., and Edgar, C. 1971. Promotion of positive social interaction in severely retarded young children. Am. J. Ment. Defic. 75(4):519–524.

Parten, M. 1932. Social play among school children. J. Abnorm. Psychol. 28:136–147.

Piaget, J. 1962. Play, Dreams and Imitation in Childhood. W. W. Norton, New York.

Piers, M. 1972. Play and Development: A Symposium. W. W. Norton, New York.

Pulaski, M. 1973. Toys and imaginative play. In J. Singer (ed.), The Child's World of Make Believe. Academic Press, New York.

Quilitch, H., and Delongchamps, G. D. 1974. Increasing recreational participation of institutional neuro-psychiatric residents. Ther. Recreat. J. 8:56–57.

Quilitch, H., and Risley, T. 1973. The effects of play materials on social play. J. Appl. Behav. Anal. 6:573–578.

Rubin, K., Maioni, T., and Hornung, M. 1976. Free play behaviors in middle and lowerclass preschoolers: Parten and Piaget revisited. Child Dev. 47:414–419.

Schutz, R., Wehman, P., Renzaglia, A., and Karan, O. 1978. Efficacy of contingent social disapproval on inappropriate verbalizations of two severely retarded males. Behav. Ther.

Seitz, S., and Hoekenga, R. 1974. Modeling as a training tool for retarded children and their parents. Ment. Retard. 12(2):28–31.

Shores, R., Hester, P., and Strain, P. S. 1976. The effects of amount and type of teacher-child interaction on child-child interaction during free play. Psychol. Schools 13:171–175.

Sied-Schlaw, B. 1976. Toys and their function. Annotated educational materials list. University of South Dakota,Vermillion.

Singer, J. 1973. The Child's World of Make Believe. Academic Press, New York.

Smilansky, S. 1968. The Effects of Sociodramatic Play on Disadvantaged Preschool Children. John Wiley & Sons, New York.

Snyder, L., Apolloni, T., and Cooke, T. 1977. Integrated settings at the early childhood level: The role of nonretarded peers. Except. Child. 43:262–266.

Stanfield, J. 1973. Graduation: What happens to the retarded child when he grows up? Except. Child. 6:1–11.

Strain, P. S. 1975. Increasing social play of severely retarded preschoolers through socio-dramatic activities. Ment. Retard. 13:7–9.

Strain, P. S., Cooke, T., and Apolloni, T. 1976. Teaching Exceptional Children: Assessing and Modifying Social Behavior. Academic Press, New York.

Strain, P. S., Shores, R., and Timm, M. 1977. Effects of peer social initiations on the behaviour of withdrawn preschool children. J. Appl. Beh. Anal. 10(2):289–298.

Strichart, S. 1974. Effects of competence and nurturance on imitation of non-retarded peers by retarded adolescents. Am. J. Ment. Defic. 78:665–673.

Tilton, J., and Ottinger, D. P. 1964. Comparison of toy play behavior of autistic, retarded, and normal children. Psycholog. Rep. 15:967–975.

Uzgiris, I., and Hunt, J. 1975. Assessment in Infancy. University of Illinois Press, Urbana, Ill.

Wehman, P. 1976. Selection of play materials for the severely handicapped: A continuing dilemma. Educ. Train. Ment. Retard. 11(1):46–51.

Wehman, P. 1977a. Helping the Mentally Retarded Acquire Play Skills: A Behavioral Approach. Charles C Thomas, Springfield, Ill.

Wehman, P. 1977b. Research on leisure time and the severely developmentally disabled. Rehab. Lit. 38(4):98–105.

Wehman, P. 1978a. Teaching recreational skills to severely and profoundly handicapped persons. In E.

Edgar and R. York (eds.), Teaching Severely Handicapped Persons, Vol. IV. AAESPH, Seattle.

Wehman, P. 1978b. Effects of different environmental conditions on leisure activity of the severely and profoundly handicapped. J. Spec. Educ. 12(2).

Wehman, P. 1978. Leisure skill programming for severely and profoundly handicapped persons: State of the art. Br. J. Soc. Clin. Psychol. 17(4).

Wehman, P., Abramson, M., and Norman, C. 1977. Transfer of training in behavior modification programs: An evaluative review. J. Spec. Educ. 11(2):217–231.

Wehman, P., Karan, O. C., and Rettie, C. 1976. Develop-

ing independent play in three severely retarded women. Psycholog. Rep. 39:995–998.

Wehman, P., and Marchant, J. 1978. Improving free play skills of severely retarded children. Am. J. Occup. Ther. 32(2):100–104.

Whitman, T., Mercurio, J., and Caponigri, V. 1970. Development of social responses in two severely retarded children. J. Appl. Behav. Anal. 3(2):133–138.

Williams, W. W. 1975. Procedures of task analysis as related to developing instructional programs for the severely handicapped. In L. Brown, T. Crowner, W. Williams, and R. York (eds.), Madison's Alternative for Zero Exclusion: A Book of Readings. University of Wisconsin, Madison.

4 SOCIAL INTERACTION

Phillip S. Strain and Ada D. Hill

The development of recreational or play skills has become a major curricular concern to educators of the developmentally disabled. Indeed, a wide variety of teaching tactics has been demonstrated to be effective in improving the social and play repertoire of individuals categorized as mentally retarded (Wehman, 1977), behaviorally disordered (Strain and Shores, 1977), learning disabled (Cooke and Apolloni, 1976), multihandicapped (Gable, Hendrickson, and Strain, in press), and autistic (Ragland, Kerr, and Strain, in press).

In terms of broad educational applicability, it should be pointed out that the vast majority of tactics described in these studies requires a "one-to-one" instructional format. When teachers are responsible for several handicapped children simultaneously, such direct tutorial situations are extremely limited. Teachers must look, therefore, to other available resources if systematic, individual instruction is desired.

Probably the most readily available (and most appropriate) resources for social and play skill programming are classroom peers. In this chapter are outlined the many natural interaction processes among children that can be programmed to enhance the social and play repertoires of handicapped youngsters. Specifically, peer influence, as mediated by social reciprocity, social reinforcement, and modeling, is discussed in detail. Particular attention is paid to the importance of developmentally integrated settings in enhancing social development. The vast majority of educational research on peer influences conducted to date has involved preschool-age children, and this review reflects that bias.

BEHAVIORAL PROCESSES OF PEER INFLUENCE

Interactions among preschool children are remarkably regularized. They are not random, but rather quite predictable with respect to timing and content (Hartup, 1977). The observed reciprocity that characterizes preschool children's interactions can be traced to the newborn's first social encounters. A considerable body of naturalistic and experimental data points to the human newborn's "predisposition" to respond to social stimuli. For example, social consequences operate as powerful reinforcers for infants' vocal behavior (Rheingold, Gewirtz, and Ross, 1959); interaction patterns within visual and vocal modes are quite reciprocal between infants and caregivers (Strain, 1975); and infants clearly prefer the human voice and face over inanimate stimuli (Stone, Smith, and Murphy, 1973). It is most likely that the same behavioral processes that maintain the reciprocity of interaction among adults also function at the infant, toddler, and preschool levels (Hartup, 1977; Nordquist, 1977). These processes include the reciprocal exchange of positive social bids, social reinforcement of peers' behavior, and peer modeling. Each of these processes is considered below in terms of their applicability as social behavior intervention procedures in educational settings.

Reciprocity of Interaction and Peer Behavior Change

Considerable observational research has been conducted on the reciprocal quality of child-child interaction. Lee (1973) observed that babies who responded contingently to their peers' social bids were sought out more frequently than babies who did not. A series of observational studies by Hartup and his colleagues highlights the reciprocal exchange of positive social behaviors between preschool children (Charlesworth and Hartup, 1967; Hartup and Coates, 1967; Hartup, Glazer, and Charlesworth, 1967). These investigators observed four categories of behavior: 1) giving positive attention and approval, 2) giving affection and personal acceptance, 3) submission, and 4) token giving. Although these categories are identical to those described by Skinner (1953) as potentially reinforcing, no assessment was made in these investigations of the functional relationship between these events and other child behaviors. In each study it was noted that the amount of reinforcement emitted toward peers was positively related to the amount of reinforcement received from peers. Specifically, there was a 0.79 correlation between the frequency with which a child gave and received positive reinforcement events. One limitation of these studies is the use of time-sampling recording methods that obviate the measurement of reciprocity as an ongoing, temporally bound exchange of behaviors (Strain and Shores, 1977).

In a recent, large scale study by Greenwood et al. (1976) continuous recording procedures were employed to assess the social contacts of preschool children. Results indicated a 0.90 correlation between initiated positive behaviors and positive behaviors emitted in response to these overtures.

The results of these observational studies indicate that preschool children create their own social environment. Children's behavior patterns tend to set the occasion for that kind of social reaction by peers that validates their own approach to peers. For example, the withdrawn child is seldom the recipient of positive social behavior from peers, whereas the child who actively initiates social bids toward peers tends to receive many positive social responses from age-mates. It seems reasonable to suspect that positive social initiations by normal or less handicapped children could be employed to increase the positive social behavior of withdrawn, handicapped classmates. Recent behavioral research confirms this proposition (Strain, 1977; Strain, Shores, and Timm, 1977; Ragland, Kerr, and Strain, in press).

Functional Analysis
Research on Reciprocity

In the first in a series of studies, Strain, Shores, and Timm (1977) trained two nonhandicapped preschool boys to initiate positive social contact with two triads of withdrawn, behaviorally disordered age-peers. The six handicapped children, all males, were enrolled in an integrated preschool program. It is important to note that all subjects were selected on the bases of observational data that indicated they rarely interacted with any other children, handicapped or not, in the setting. Both nonhandicapped children were given four 20-minute training sessions in which they were taught specific behaviors that they were

to use to initiate social play with their handicapped peers. Verbal behaviors such as "Come play," "Let's play school," and "Throw the ball," and gestures such as passing a toy, were taught. A role-playing format was employed whereby the trainer assumed the typical social behavior pattern of the handicapped children. Every other appropriate social initiation by a peer "therapist" was either praised by the trainer or ignored. After 5 seconds of ignoring, the trainer explained to the children that many approaches to play probably would be ignored by the handicapped children, but they were to keep trying to initiate play. This procedure of "training to expect rejection" seems essential to ensure that the social behaviors of nonhandicapped children will not be punished and eventually extinguished by initial peer opposition and rejection. Employing a withdrawal of treatment design, the peer "therapists" made few social approaches to handicapped peers during the initial baseline phase. Peers greatly increased their rate of initiations during intervention, reduced initiations during a second baseline phase, and again increased their rate of initiations in a final intervention phase. During no point in the study did adults prompt or reinforce any positive social behavior. For each of the six subjects positive social behavior greatly increased in response to accelerating levels of initiations. For five of the subjects an increase was observed in their social initiations toward each other and their nonhandicapped peers. The magnitude of behavior change resulting from the peer-initiation tactic was directly related to the subjects' initial social repertoire; that is, children who engaged in the most social activity during the initial baseline phase were most responsive to this intervention.

A second study in this series, Strain (1977) examined the replicability of this peer-initiation tactic and the generalization of behavior change across time and settings. One triad of behaviorally disordered preschool boys and one nonhandicapped age-peer participated. These subjects were located in the same integrated setting as that described previously. The peer "therapist" participated in training sessions identical to those employed in the study by Strain, Shores, and Timm (1977). All experimental sessions during the withdrawal of treatment design took place in a small playroom equipped with gross and fine motor toys, dress-up clothes, and kitchen area items. The genralization sessions took place in the subjects' classroom. On 25 of the 40 days of the study generalization assessment took place shortly after training. On the other days there was a 23-hour time lapse between training and generalization sessions. Training data from this study closely replicated results reported by Strain, Shores, and Timm (1977). For one handicapped child, whose baseline of interaction was nearly zero, the intervention tactic was not effective. Generalization data indicated that behavior change exhibited during training persisted across time and settings. It is important to note, however, that positive behavior during the generalization sessions was approximately one-half the level observed during training.

The results of these two studies on preschool handicapped children and their nonhandicapped peers indicate that the reciprocity, or occasion-setting function of social stimuli may be employed to enhance the social repertoire of withdrawn children. Additionally, the peer "therapists" were remarkably consistent in their adherence to initial training and instructions across phase changes. Data on children with extremely limited repertoires suggest that more intensive training tactics, i.e., prompting and reinforcement, are required to produce positive social interaction.

The most recent study in this series, Ragland, Kerr, and Strain (in press) was concerned with promoting positive social behavior in school-age autistic children. The subjects were observed to engage in active social withdrawal and physical aggression toward peers, whereas previously studied children were more "passive" in their social withdrawal. Again, an age-peer was trained to emit specific social inititations toward handicapped children (see Strain, Shores, and Timm, 1977, Table 1). Prebaseline observations on the target subjects indicated that they would isolate physically themselves during free-play periods and engage in brief tantrums if approached by a peer. The experimental sessions in the withdrawal of treatment design were conducted in a playroom equipped with toys that promote cooperative play (e.g., telephones, balls, trucks, cooking utensils, puppets). Unlike prior studies, the peer "therapist" began intervention at different points in time for each subject. This multiple baseline procedure was employed to determine whether increased social initiations directed toward one child would result in increased positive behavior by children not under intervention procedures.

One might suspect that intervention applied to one subject would afford other handicapped children the opportunity to imitate appropriate social behavior being modeled by the peer "therapist" and handicapped child. Increases in peer initiations resulted in an immediate acceleration in the frequency of all subjects' positive social behaviors. For two of the subjects, who were most oppositional to social bids, negative behaviors also showed a slight increase during intervention conditions. In no case did intervention applied to one child result in a "spillover" of treatment effect on the behavior of children not under intervention at that time.

Clinical Application Issues

In summary, research on peer-initiation tactics offers a promising strategy by which to promote constructive interaction and play skills. The successful implementation of such a strategy requires that a number of issues be addressed by the practitioner. First, research to date seems to indicate that children must have some positive social behaviors in their repertoire if the tactic is to be successful. Exactly what behaviors, and their frequency of occurrence, are yet to be determined (Strain and Carr, 1975). It would seem that some appropriate language behavior is central to reciprocal interaction (Hester and Hendrickson, 1976). In those studies conducted by Strain and his colleagues, most successful initiations (those followed by a positive peer response) were vocal-verbal. Unfortunately the data collection system employed did not provide an assessment of the precise verbal topographies involved. Since vocal-verbal behaviors do not occur frequently between handicapped preschool children (Guralnick and Paul-Brown, 1977), some stimulus novelty effect may account for the responsiveness of the handicapped subjects to vocal-verbal bids to play (Cantor and Cantor, 1964; King, 1966; Strain and Cooke, 1976). In a related study Mueller (1972) identified particular behavioral parameters that were predictive of successful social initiations between 3½- to 5½-year-old children. Data indicated that 62% of all utterances were successful in that they obtained a verbal response from the partners. Another 23% were followed by visual orientation by the partner to the speaker. The most robust predictor was visual attention of the partner before an utterance. Failure to gain reciprocal responding was most frequently associated with grammatically poor speech.

Other behaviors may also set the occasion for reciprocal responding. For example, Cooke and Apolloni (1976) taught school-age, mildly handicapped children to smile at each other, share toys, make appropriate physical contacts, and engage in complimentary comments. Using a modeling strategy, these behaviors were taught successfully in a classroom setting. In a free-play period that immediately followed training, the target subjects and other mildly handicapped children were observed. Not only did the positive behaviors of target subjects maintain, but untrained subjects also began to engage in these same behaviors. One might suspect that the target responses set the occasion for reciprocal responding by peers; however, the data collection system did not permit an analysis of reciprocal behavior patterns. What seems needed at this point is a thorough delineation of the response topographies that have a high probability of setting the occasion for, and maintaining, interaction.

Another issue related to the successful implementation of the peer-initiated tactic concerns the generalization or maintenance of positive social behavior in less contrived settings. Research evidence to date indicates that positive social behaviors developed by this tactic do generalize to a nontreatment setting. However, the magnitude of behavior change was considerably less than that observed during training sessions.

The precise level of behavior generalization observed at any one time is doubtless a product of complex interactions between a number of factors. The first factor concerns the level of behavioral handicap exhibited by target children. In peer- and adult-mediated studies, the level of generalization appears, in part, to be a function of subjects' overall behavioral development (Gable, Hendrickson, and Strain, in press). For example, studies employing severely or profoundly retarded and autistic children have met with minimal success in promoting generalized behavior change. Recent research on the mechanisms of behavior generalization indicate that severely handicapped children's lack of behavior change across time and settings may be a function of their responding (simultaneously) to the presence of irrelevant as well as relevant stimuli (Rincover and Koegel, 1975).

A second factor related to generalized behavior change relates to the difference between behavior generalization and the maintenance of behavior in the generalization setting(s) (Koegel and Rincover, 1977). Behavior generalization refers to the initial level of responding in the nontreatment environment(s). Maintenance of behavior, on the other hand, refers to the level of posttreatment responding over time or trials. In efforts involving peer-initiation tactics, it appears that generalization, as defined above, can be expected to occur. However, the maintenance of behavior, which is controlled by a separate set of variables, is less certain. Research by Koegel and Rincover (1977) indicates that maintenance of treatment effects can be enhanced by reducing the discrepancy between training and generalization settings. For example, practitioners might consider the systematic, response-dependent leaning of social initiations, training across settings and peer "therapists," and/or controlling the social behaviors of nontrained peers in the generalization setting(s). Regrettably the data base for these suggestions is severely limited.

PEER REINFORCEMENT AND SOCIAL BEHAVIOR CHANGE

A primary, although seldom expressed, operating principle of peer reinforcement research is that liking, interpersonal attraction, and friendships are determined by an individual's history of reward in the presence of particular individuals. Accordingly there are several conditions by which the conditions of reward in the presence of another person can be met (Lott and Lott, 1974). First, by the quality of one's characteristics (e.g., beauty, family relationship) another person may be provided with pleasure simply by being in the same place at the same time. Second, an individual can provide direct consequences to another in the form of smiles, positive personal comments, or offers of valued items. Third, a person may be instrumental in providing another with access to primary or secondary reinforcers. For example, a person's skillful behavior may ensure success in a game or access to favored items. Finally, a person may become liked or attractive through a pairing process with events totally independent of that person's behavior. For example, Lott and Lott (1974) maintain that an individual's association with such potentially reinforcing settings as a holiday party or vacation can lead to an increased level of attraction. In any educational, integrated preschool setting, any or all of these processes may be employed to increase the likelihood of social interaction between handicapped and nonhandicapped classmates.

Correlational Studies of Peer Reinforcement

As noted earlier, Charlesworth and Hartup (1967) have observed that preschool children exchange, on an equitable basis, behaviors that are potentially reinforcing. Other correlational data are also available that support this view of preschool children's social encounters (Marshall and McCandless, 1957; Kohn, 1966; Hartup, Glazer, and Charlesworth, 1967).

A number of investigators have sought to correlate the occurrence of particular child behaviors (potential reinforcing or punishing events) with the behavior of interacting peers. For example, Patterson, Littman, and Bricker (1967) examined the consequences of aggressive behavior in two nursery school settings. Six categories of children's responses to peer aggression were examined: "passive actions," "cries," "defensive postures," "telling the teacher," "recovering property," and "retaliation." Short term, temporal analyses revealed that crying, passivity, and defensive behaviors were the most frequent consequences of aggression. When these behaviors occurred, additional acts of aggression toward the original victim escalated. Patterson, Littman, and Bricker (1967) suggest that aggressive acts are reinforced by these behaviors. When the original aggressor was met with threats of, or actual, aggression by the intended victim, subsequent acts of aggression toward these victims rarely occurred. Thus, aggressive acts may also be punished successfully by victims' responses. Longitudinal data revealed similar reinforcement-punishment processes in operation. Children who were initially nonaggressive, but who successfully punished aggressive initiations by peers, became more active aggressors across time. It was also noted that children who were not victims or who did not punish aggression from peers successfully showed no escalation in aggressive behavior across time.

Kopstein (1972) employed a similar methodology to examine the effects of aggressive, negative reactions to both positive and negative social bids. Data were obtained during free-play periods in which two groups of elementary-age, trainable mentally retarded children were engaged in self-selected activities. Results discordant with a strict reinforcement-punishment interpretation of interaction were obtained. Aggressive responses to positive social bids reduced the probability of later instances of prosocial activity. However, aggressive responses to aggressive overtures resulted in an accelerated level of aggressive interaction. It would seem that some of the negative responses by peers operated as "punishers" of prosocial activity, while others served to set the occasion for additional hostile interaction. The conflict in results between this study and that of Patterson, Littman, and Bricker (1967) may have been caused by unspecified differences in the topography, temporal relationship, intensity, and/or duration of specific behaviors labeled as "aggression." On a related, conceptual issue, it is important to recall that behavior categories such as prosocial activity or aggression only represent a *description* of behavior. They should not imply or be interpreted as functional categories of behavior that have predictable reinforcing or punishing effects on activity that precedes them. The functional properties of behaviors can be determined only by their systematic manipulation across time. Even then, the functional effects of specific behaviors will vary across time and individuals (Bijou and Baer, 1963).

Experimental Analyses of Peer Reinforcement

Expanding upon observational research, a number of investigators have provided an experimental analysis of peer contingencies in preschool settings. In his now classic study Wahler (1967) collected baseline data on a number of social behaviors exhibited by five preschool children. For three subjects, behaviors associated with frequent positive consequences by peers were established. For the other two children, behaviors associated with only occasional positive consequences by peers were identified. In an initial intervention condition, Wahler instructed peers who had reinforced certain behaviors frequently to now ignore their three classmates when they engaged in these designated behaviors. Moreover, the peers were instructed to reinforce their two classmates' behaviors that previously were ignored. Results indicated that members of the peer group responded in strict compliance to the experimenter's instructions. In addition, behaviors that were reinforced by peers increased dramatically and behaviors that were ignored decreased accordingly. These effects were replicated during a subsequent reinstatement of baseline and intervention contingencies.

Johnston and Johnston (1972) provide evidence that peer—as opposed to adult—mediated reinforcement is associated with greater treatment generalization effects. The contingency arrangements for producing correct articulation were evaluated in treatment and free-play settings. The first arrangement involved the application of contingent teacher attention and tokens for correct responding. The second procedure required both correct responding and the self-recording of these behaviors before attention and tokens were administered. In the final procedure two children were taught to attend to each other's correct responses and ignore incorrects. All procedures resulted in increased levels of correct responding, but only the peer-contingency resulted in behavior change in the free-play environment.

In a study of peer-reinforcement effects in an integrated setting, Guralnick (1976) further demonstrated the influence of classmates' behavior on social interaction. Using a role-playing tactic, Guralnick trained nonhandicapped preschool children to model, prompt, and reinforce social behaviors by their handicapped peers. Baseline data indicated that few positive interactions occurred between handicapped and nonhandicapped children. When handicapped children were given the opportunity to observe two nonhandicapped peers playing cooperatively, no behavior change was noted. However, a peer-modeling, prompting, and reinforcement strategy produced a substantial change in the social play and verbal interaction between handicapped and nonhandicapped children. The results of this study are quite encouraging, although it is not possible to determine which or what combination of intervention procedures (modeling, prompting, reinforcement) was responsible for the improvement in handicapped children's social behavior.

A number of studies have shown that friendships between preschool and school-age children are determined by exchange of rewarding events (Karen, 1965; Kirby and Toler, 1970; Drabman, Spitalnick, and Spitalnik, 1974). For example, Kirby and Toler employed a stimulus-pairing technique whereby a 5-year-old isolate boy offered choices of candies to his playmates just before a daily free-play period. The child was instructed to ask each peer which of several kinds

of candy he would like. Prior to this procedure the subject was observed to engage in positive interaction during 13% of the free-play time. As long as the subject engaged in the candy-offering activity, his level of positive interaction was above 60%.

In further work on the relationship between experience with positive consequences and positive social interaction, Strain (1978) attempted to alter the behavioral rejection of three mildly handicapped, school-age boys enrolled in regular classroom. During a 5-day baseline period the three target subjects engaged in only four episodes of positive interaction with nonhandicapped peers during a 20-minute free-play period. In each of these instances, the target subjects had initiated the interaction. During the first intervention phase each of the target subjects was assigned by the experimenter to one of three teams of children. The teams participated in a 15-minute competition game before the daily free-play time. On each day members of the teams took turns at a beanbag toss game. All members of a team would earn a reward if the team's total point score exceeded a set criterion. The game was physically arranged such that children tossed across a large barrier, and were thus unable to see the actual score they earned. After each toss the experimenter would call out a score. On each team the target subject had the last toss on each day, and the experimenter would always announce a score sufficient for the team members to earn their reward. Observational data collected during free-play indicated that the intervention procedure resulted in approximately 20 times the amount of positive social interaction as that observed during baseline. Moreover, target subjects and their peers initiated episodes of interaction on an equal basis.

Haskett (1974) provided particularly convincing data regarding the relationship between children's social responsiveness and the maintenance of social encounters. More than 20 infants and preschool children were introduced, individually, into a play setting with two age-peer confederates and familiar toys. Four social behaviors were examined: verbalizations, visual regard, onlooking, and mutual play. The confederates alternated being either verbally responsive or nonresponsive to subjects' play initiations. Subjects invariably directed most of their social overtures toward the verbally responsive confederate.

Research on the delivery of peer reinforcement indicates that events can be programmed successfully to increase the positive social behavior of withdrawn handicapped children. Although minimal data are available, it is possible that peer-mediated reinforcement may lead to more generalized responding than adult-mediated reinforcement (Johnston and Johnston, 1972). In fact, there is some evidence that adults' behavior may distract children from ongoing interaction (O'Connor, 1972). For example, Shores, Hester, and Strain (1976) measured social interaction among preschool behaviorally disordered children under three experimental conditions: 1) active teacher prompting and reinforcement, 2) no teacher involvement, and 3) teacher structured free-play with no active prompting and reinforcement. When teachers initially structured play by suggesting activities for children, then withdrew from the setting, the amount of social interaction among subjects increased significantly over baseline, no teacher involvement, and active prompting and reinforcement conditions. Because programmed generalization to natural environmental contingencies should be the terminal goal of all intervention efforts, it is probably more efficient to utilize peers at the beginning of training (Guralnick, 1978).

More complex programming of peer reinforcement has been reported by Hill and Strain (1978). In this study two mentally retarded teenagers implemented a shaping procedure designed to increase the ball-throwing behavior of a 12-year-old mentally retarded class peer. Individual steps in the shaping process included: 1) holding a ball with both hands, 2) holding a ball at chest level and pushing it toward a peer, 3) holding a ball overhead and throwing it toward a peer, and 4) holding a ball behind head and throwing it toward a peer. Once appropriate ball throwing was established, the frequency of this social response was increased dramatically when the peer trainers delivered contingent social praise for instances of ball throwing. In this study the increased ball-throwing response of the subject naturally led to a greater level of positive interaction between the target subject and his peers. It should be pointed out, however, that training in less specific play skills also may lead to increased social interaction. For example, Hill and Strain (1978) reported collateral increases in the social interaction between a 16-year-old mentally retarded boy and his class peers following training on gross motor movements.

Numerous important theoretical and applied questions concerning peer reinforcement of social interaction remain unanswered. For example, who are the most powerful reinforcers? There is some naturalistic evidence to suggest that same-sex children are more effective reinforcing agents than opposite-sex youngsters (Fagot and Patterson, 1969). It is certainly possible that some handicapped preschool children would not be reinforced by attention from peers (or adults). In such cases the stimulus-pairing technique, as applied by Kirby and Toler (1970) and Strain (1978), to increase interaction between handicapped and nonhandicapped children might be applied to enhance the reinforcement value of social attention.

Another important question concerns the long term effects of peer reinforcement. What modifications, if any, occur in the interaction patterns between agents of reinforcement and nontarget children? Do handicapped children come to interact more positively with nonhandicapped peers with whom they have no reinforcement history? What, if any, collateral behavior changes are observed for nonhandicapped and handicapped children during and following peer reinforcement? It would be particularly beneficial if, for example, nonhandicapped children become more effective behavioral models as a result of their reinforcement history with handicapped peers (Hartup and Coates, 1967). These and many other issues demand thorough experimental study.

PEER MODELING
AND SOCIAL BEHAVIOR CHANGE

An extensive body of research points to the importance of modeling processes during early childhood (Bandura and Walters, 1963). Observational learning includes both incidental and controlled interactions among children whereby new behaviors are acquired and existing response patterns undergo modification as a direct result of observing another's behaviors and consequences for them.

Film-Mediated Models

O'Connor (1969; 1972) has employed film-mediated models to increase positive interaction between preschool children. In his initial effort, one group of children saw a film depicting peer interaction. A comparison group saw a nature film of equal length. Social interaction among members within each of the two groups was assessed in a free-play class period that followed their viewing of the film. Statistical analyses revealed that positive interaction among experimental subjects significantly surpassed the level observed before viewing the film and the postviewing level demonstrated by comparison subjects. Strain, Cooke, and Apolloni (1976) have noted, however, that two of the six experimental subjects primarily were responsible for the changes observed. Those subjects who were most isolate during the pretreatment observation were least responsive to the intervention. Although no specific data are provided, it is possible that the most isolate of subjects demonstrated other behavioral deficits, including the lack of a generalized imitative repertoire.

O'Connor (1972) replicated and expanded these earlier findings in a comparative study of observational versus direct shaping procedures on social interaction. In summary, the results indicated that subjects who had received the observational learning experience were more socially active than children who had been exposed to direct shaping alone. The largest maintenance effect was demonstrated by subjects who had received both observational and direct shaping of positive social behavior.

Walker and Hops (1973) further tested the effects of film-mediated models on withdrawn children's social behavior. Two subjects were shown the same training film used by O'Conner (1969), and they were reinforced for positive interaction with peers. A third withdrawn subject's peers were shown the film, but the target child was not. Reinforcement procedures also were imposed. Although the treatment "package" approach used here does not readily lend itself to a clear, separate analysis of modeling and reinforcement effects, the data do suggest that the film viewing had a minimal impact on the documented behavior change. First, both laboratory (Bandura, Ross, and Ross, 1963) and applied studies (O'Connor, 1969, 1972) of observational learning demonstrate immediate (although likely short term) behavior change following treatment. In this study, however, it was not until the contingencies had been imposed for several days that substantial behavior change was noted. It seems likely that Walker and Hop's stringent procedures for selecting *severely* withdrawn children yielded a group of youngsters whose behavior repertoire resembled that of the more isolate subjects employed by O'Connor (1969).

More precise information on the interaction between initial behavior repertoire and observa-

tional learning effects has been provided by Keller and Carlson (1974). These authors monitored the effects of film-mediated models on five categories of positive social behavior: verbalizations, imitation, smiling, token giving, and affection. The categories of verbalizations, imitation, and smiling, which had the highest previewing rate, were also the only categories to show statistically significant postviewing change. Across-subject comparisons revealed that the least behavior change was demonstrated by the most isolate of the 19 preschool-age subjects.

Language Models

Research has been conducted also on the effects of modeled linguistic structures on the verbal behavior of handicapped children in an integrated setting (Guralnick, 1976). In this study a nonhandicapped age-peer was prompted to use correct syntactic structures, which were reinforced by an adult. The observing, handicapped child was encouraged to attend to the particular language forms being used by the nonhandicapped peer. The procedure resulted in increased use of appropriate language forms by the target child. It is likely, however, that the use of correct language forms by the handicapped child would not maintain in the absence of direct consequences. Kazdin (1973) proposes that such vicarious learning as that demonstrated by Guralnick may be a result, in part, of the cue properties of reinforcement delivery; that is, observing children come to emit reinforced behaviors by others with the expectation that these behaviors will bring about similar consequences for them. The importance of reinforcement delivery to observing children has been highlighted by Strain and Pierce (1977). In their study one retarded preschool child from each of two dyads was given social reinforcement contingent upon attention to task behavior. The other two retarded children never received any reinforcement for their on-task activity. Intervention applied to the designated child in each dyad produced an immediate increase in the attending behavior of both subjects. However, after a number of days (approximately 10), the attending behavior of observing subjects began to decline, and at the end of 20 days their attending behavior paralleled that observed during nonreinforcement conditions.

In a related area of language research, Guralnick and Paul-Brown (1977) have reported that nonhandicapped preschool children regulate the length and complexity of verbalizations toward handicapped classmates. Nonhandicapped children were observed in verbal interaction with other nonhandicapped, mildly handicapped, moderately handicapped, and severely handicapped peers during instructional and free-play sessions. Data from both setting conditions indicated that nonhandicapped and mildly handicapped peers received a similar length and complexity of directed verbal behavior. Moderately and severely handicapped children, however, were exposed to much briefer and less complex utterances from nonhandicapped peers. Although data on children's verbal interactions are extremely limited, these and other reports (Shatz and Gelman, 1973; Bates, 1975) indicate a remarkable similarity to the speech regularization of parents with their children (Broen, 1972; Snow, 1972). It is important to note that many authors (e.g., Mahoney and Seely, 1976; Moerk, 1976) have proposed that parents' speech adjustments to their children's comprehension abilities serve to stimulate language development.

Establishing Imitative Behavior

Although the imitation process offers a significant contribution to the array of behavior change tactics available in educational settings, many handicapped children display minimal levels of generalized imitation. In such cases direct training is required to establish peer imitation of appropriate behaviors. In an initial series of studies, Apolloni, Cooke, and Cooke (1977) trained developmentally delayed toddlers to imitate motor, material use, and verbalizations modeled by nondelayed peers. Training tactics included the use of physical and verbal prompts by an adult to initiate imitation. Reinforcement also was provided to the handicapped children contingent upon correct imitation. Physical and verbal prompts were removed systematically as imitative responding became more reliable. Results indicated that each subject's level of imitative behavior increased during the training setting. With the exception of verbalizations, the subjects also exhibited an increased level of the modeled behaviors in a free-play situation that followed training.

In a replication effort (Peck et al., 1976), this imitation-training paradigm was applied directly in free-play settings. Here, developmentally delayed preschool children were prompted and rein-

forced for imitating the ongoing free-play behavior of nonhandicapped classmates. The adult trainer was not present during generalization assessment. Again, the procedure resulted in a substantial increase in peer imitation. Increases in imitative responding were noted also during generalization sessions. Finally, social interaction between delayed and nondelayed children increased concomitant with the initiation of training procedures. In a follow-up study, however, Cooke, Apolloni, and Cooke (1976) showed that imitation training did not result in increased interaction between handicapped and nonhandicapped children when nonhandicapped children had the option to play with either a normal or a handicapped peer.

Variables Affecting Imitative Behavior

Given that a child possesses the behavioral prerequisites to reproduce a modeled response, a number of variables can affect the performance of imitative behavior in a given situation. Relevant variables include those concerned with the discriminative properties of the modeled response and various personality characteristics of the individual modeling the response.

The discriminative properties of the modeled response seem to be affected primarily by the observation of reinforcement or punishment, contingent upon the designated response (Bandura, 1971). Specifically such consequences function as a discriminative stimulus for observing children because it often precedes (in the natural classroom environment) the delivery of reinforcement or punishment to these subjects. The cue properties of reinforcement or punishment can be made more salient by the delivery of consequences that designate the behavior(s) of concern. For example, Kazdin, Silverman, and Sittler (1975) examined the differential effects of nonverbal approval (patting a child), nonverbal approval paired with a verbal prompt to the nonreinforced child ("Dave, look at Timmy"), and nonverbal approval paired with verbal approval ("That's really good") on the attentive behavior of target subjects and adjacent peers. The results indicated that nonverbal approval in the form of patting a child altered the attentive behavior of reinforced subjects only. Vicarious effects were noted when either a prompt or verbal approval accompanied nonverbal reinforcement.

In additional work Christy (1975) demonstrated that highly specific, contingency contracts with individual children resulted in vicarious effects on the in-seat behavior of several classmates. Following a baseline period, the teacher addressed the group as follows: "Everybody listen. I'm going to make a deal with (*child's*) name. (*Child's*) name, if you are sitting in your seat when the whistle blows, you'll get a goody. A goody is a piece of candy, or raisin, or nut, or marshmallow. The whistle blows from this box. Every time you're sitting in your seat—all the way down and facing front—when the whistle blows, you get a goody." All target and observing children either increased in the desired behavior or decreased variability by the end of the study. Particularly dramatic changes were noted for children with relatively low rates of sitting during baseline.

Similar results have been obtained in studies involving problem-solving situations. Geshuri (1972), for example, found that imitation of correct responses was demonstrated more often by children who observed reinforcement for specific behaviors as opposed to those who observed more generalized reinforcement for correct performance.

The effects of vicarious punishment on imitative behavior has also received considerable attention (Walters, Parke, and Cone, 1965; Bandura, 1971; Morris, Marshall, and Miller, 1973). For example, Morris, Marshall, and Miller (1973) exposed 120 first- and second-grade students to one of the following filmed sequences: 1) baseline, confederate child plays with toys while adult reads a book, 2) nonsharing, no outcome, confederate refuses to share candy with a fictitious peer and no consequences are given, 3) nonsharing, punished, confederate refuses to share candy and adult says she cannot play any longer and asks her to leave the room, 4) punishment only, confederate does not model nonsharing, but adult delivers the same punishments as described above. Following this viewing, each subject was given a bag of candy and told that there would not be enough candy for all the children who were to come and that perhaps the subject would want to leave some candy. Results indicated that merely observing selfish behavior did not affect sharing behavior. Both punishment conditions, however, provided a significant increase in sharing over baseline.

It may also be possible to increase the attention of observing children by providing novel stimuli to imitate. Parton (1976) reported that infants' imi-

tative behavior was elicited more often by novel rather than familiar stimuli. Furthermore, novel stimuli also may function to set the occasion for interaction between model and observer. In a naturalistic study of social encounters between school-age autistic children, Strain and Cooke (1976) observed the vocal-verbal, motor-gestural, and initiated-responded dimensions of interaction. Novel social initiations (i.e., those vocal-verbal behaviors that rarely occurred) were followed by a peer response significantly more often than frequently occurring, motor-gestural initiations. Haskett (1974) also reported that novel stimuli (toys in this case) may lead to increased peer contact between normal preschool-age children. Target subjects were observed interacting with two confederate children who played with the same materials during baseline. When one of the confederates introduced a new toy, interaction with that child increased dramatically over the baseline level.

Another set of factors affecting the likelihood of imitative behavior centers on the characteristics of the model. Generally research indicates that perceived similarity on various dimensions of personality yields greater peer imitation. For example, imitation has been observed to occur more readily when model and observer are of the same sex (e.g., Bandura, Ross, and Ross, 1963), when they have shared similar emotional experiences (Aronfreed, 1968), and when they are of similar social status (Rosenkrans, 1967). Of particular importance to educational programming, Strichart (1974) has noted that children are more likely to imitate models who perform responses effectively. Thus, it appears unlikely that normal preschool children would readily imitate less sophisticated behaviors emitted by handicapped peers.

SUMMARY AND CONCLUSIONS

Literature reviewed in this chapter documents the critical importance of positive, early peer encounters on children's behavioral development. Both naturalistic and manipulative research indicate that linguistic, cognitive, and social skills are facilitated by peer interaction. Indeed, limited peer interaction most certainly places young children "at risk" for developmental delay and later appearing adjustment problems.

Given the instructional opportunities for peer-mediated intervention, a number of behavioral processes may be employed to improve the functioning of handicapped children. Peer social initiations, contingent social reinforcement, and the modeling of appropriate behaviors are intervention procedures with consistently demonstrated effectiveness in producing a wide variety of behaviors. Moreover, there is increasing evidence that these peer-mediated strategies produce more rapid and durable behavior change than adult-mediated tactics.

REFERENCES

Apolloni, T., Cooke, S. A., and Cooke, T. P. 1977. Establishing a normal peer as a behavioral model for delayed toddlers. Percept. Mot. Skills 1968. 44:231–241.

Aronfreed, J. 1968. Conduct and Conscience: The Socialization of Internalized Control Over Behavior. Academic Press, New York.

Bandura, A. 1971. Principles of Behavior Modification. Holt, New York.

Bandura, A., Ross, D., and Ross, S. A. 1963, Imitation of film-mediated aggressive models. J. Abnorm. Soc. Psychol. 66:3–11.

Bandura, A., and Walters, R. H. 1963. Social Learning and Personality Development. Holt, New York.

Bates, E. 1975. Peer relations and the acquisition of language. In M. Lewis and L. A. Rosenblum (eds.), Friendship and Peer Relations. John Wiley & Sons, New York.

Bijou, S. W., and Baer, D. M. 1963. Some methodological contributions from a functional analysis of child development. In L. P. Lipsitt and C. C. Spiker (eds.), Advances in Child Development and Behavior, Vol. 1, pp. 197–231. Academic Press, New York.

Broen, P. A. 1972. The verbal environment of the language-learning child. ASHA Monogr. 17.

Cantor, J., and Cantor, G. 1964. Observing behavior in children as a function of stimulus novelty. Child Dev. 35:110–128.

Charlesworth, R., and Hartup, W. W. 1967. Positive social reinforcement in the nursery school peer group. Child Dev. 38:993–1002.

Christy, P. R. 1975. Does use of tangible rewards with individual children affect peer observers? J. Appl. Behav. Anal. 8:187–196.

Cooke, T. P., and Apolloni, T. 1976. Developing positive emotional behaviors: A study in training and generalization effects. J. Appl. Behav. Anal. 9:65–78.

Cooke, T. P., Apolloni, T., and Cooke, S. A. 1976. The effects of a second non-delayed playmate on the free-play imitation and interaction of delayed and nondelayed children. Unpublished manuscript. Sonoma State College. Sonoma, Ariz.

Cooke, S. A., Cooke, T. P., and Apolloni, T. 1977. Developing nonretarded toddlers as verbal models for retarded classmates. Child Study J.

Drabman, R. S., Spitalnik, R., and Spitalnik, K. 1974.

Sociometric and disruptive behavior as a function of four types of token reinforcement programs. J. Appl. Behav. Anal. 7:93–101.

Fagot, B. I., and Patterson, G. R. 1969. An in vivo analysis of reinforcing contingencies for sex-role behaviors in the preschool child. Dev. Psychol. 1:563–568.

Gable, R. A., Hendrickson, J. M., and Strain, P. S. Assessment, modification, and generalization of social interaction among severely retarded, multi-handicapped children. Educ. Train. Ment. Retard. In press.

Geshuri, Y. 1972. Observational learning: Effects of observed reward and response patterns. J. Educ. Psychol. 63:374–380.

Greenwood, C. R., Walker, H. M., Todd, N. M., and Hops, H. 1976. Preschool teachers' assessments of student social interaction: Predictive success and normative data (Report No. 26). Center at Oregon for Research in the Behavioral Education of the Handicapped, Eugene, Ore.

Guralnick, M. J. 1976. The value of integrating handicapped and nonhandicapped preschool children. Am. J. Orthopsychiatry 46:236–245.

Guralnick, M. J. 1978. Integrated preschools as educational and therapeutic environments. In M. J. Guralnick (ed.), Early Intervention and the Integration of Handicapped and Nonhandicapped Children, pp. 115–145. University Park Press, Baltimore.

Guralnick, M. J., and Paul-Brown, D. 1977. The nature of verbal interactions among handicapped and nonhandicapped preschool children. Child Dev. 48:254–260.

Hartup. W. W. 1977. Peer interaction and the processes of socialization. In M. J. Guralnick (ed.), Early Intervention and the Integration of Handicapped and Nonhandicapped Children, pp. 27–51. University Park Press, Baltimore.

Hartup, W. W., and Coates, B. 1967, Imitation of a peer as a function of reinforcement from the peer group and rewardingness of the model. Child Dev. 38:1003–1016.

Hartup, W. W., Glazer, J. S., and Charlesworth, R. 1967. Peer reinforcement and sociometric status. Child Dev. 3:1017–1024.

Haskett, G. J. 1974. The ecology and early organization of children's social relations. Paper presented at the American Psychological Association, New Orleans.

Hester, P., and Hendrickson, J. M. 1976. Establishing functional expressive language: The acquisition and generalization of five-element syntactic responses. Unpublished manuscript. George Peabody College, Nashville, Tenn.

Hill, A., and Strain, P. S. 1978. Increasing the overhand ball throwing of a severely retarded male. Research in progress.

Johnston, J. M., and Johnston, G. T. 1972. Modification of consonant speech-sound articulation in young children. J. Appl. Behav. Anal. 5:233–246.

Karen, R. L. 1965. Operant conditioning and social preference. Unpublished doctoral dissertation. Arizona State University, Tempe.

Kazdin, A. E. 1973. The effect of vicarious reinforcement on attention behavior in the classroom. J. Appl. Behav. Anal. 6:71–78.

Kazdin, A. E., Silverman, N. A., and Sittler, J. L. 1975. The use of prompts to enhance vicarious effects of nonverbal approval. J. Appl. Behav. Anal. 8:279–286.

Keller, M. F., and Carlson, P. M. 1974. The use of symbolic modeling to promote social skills in preschool children with low levels of social responsiveness. Child Dev. 45:912–919.

King, M. 1966. Interpersonal relations in preschool children and average approach distance. J. Genet. Psychol. 109:109–116.

Kirby, F. D., and Toler, H. C. 1970. Modification of preschool isolate behavior: A case study. J. Appl. Behav. Anal. 3:309–314.

Koegel, R. L., and Rincover, A. 1977. Research on the difference between generalization and maintenance in extra-therapy responding. J. Appl. Behav. Anal. 10:1–12.

Kohn, M. 1966. The child as a determinant of his peers' approach to him. J. Genet. Psychol. 109:91–100.

Kopstein, D. 1972. Effects of accelerating and decelerating consequences on the social behavior of trainable retarded children. Child Dev. 43:800–809.

Lee, L. C. 1973. Social encounters of infants: The beginnings of popularity. Paper presented at the biennial meeting of the International Society for the Study of Behavioral Development, Ann Arbor, Mich.

Lott, A. J., and Lott, B. E. 1974. The role of reward in the formation of positive interpersonal attitudes. In R. L. Huston (ed.) Foundations of Interpersonal Attraction, pp. 171–192. Academic Press, New York.

Mahoney, G. J., and Seely, P. B. 1976. The role of the social agent in language acquisition: Implications for language intervention. In N. R. Ellis (ed.), International Review of Research in Mental Retardation, Vol. 8. Academic Press, New York.

Marshall, H. R., and McCandless, B. R. 1957. A study in prediction of social behavior of preschool children. Child Dev. 28:149–159.

Moerk, E. L. 1976. Processes of language teaching and training in the interactions of mother-child dyads. Child Dev. 47:1064–1078.

Morris, W. N., Marshall, H. M., and Miller, R. S. 1973. The effect of vicarious punishment on prosocial behavior in children. J. Exp. Child Psychol. 15:222–236.

Mueller, E. 1972. The maintenance of verbal exchanges between young children. Child Dev. 43:930–938.

Nordquist, V. M. 1977. A behavioral approach to the analysis of peer interactions. In M. J. Guralnick (ed.), Early Intervention and the Integration of Handicapped Children, pp. 53–84. University Park Press, Baltimore.

O'Connor, R. D. 1969. Modification of social withdrawal through symbolic modeling. J. Appl. Behav. Anal. 2:15–22.

O'Connor, R. D. 1972. The relative efficacy of modeling, shaping, and the combined procedures for the modification of social withdrawal. J. Abnorm. Psychol. 79:327–334.

Parton, D. A. 1976. Learning to imitate in infancy. Child Dev. 47:14–31.

Patterson, G. R., Littman, R. A., and Bricker, W. 1967. Assertive behavior in children: A step toward a theory of aggression. Monogr. Soc. Res. Child Dev. 32:113.

Peck, C. A., Apolloni, T., Cooke, T. P., and Cooke, S. A. 1976. Teaching developmentally delayed toddlers and preschoolers to imitate the free-play behavior of nonretarded classmates: Trained and generalized effects. Unpublished manuscript. Sonoma State College, Sonoma, Ariz.

Ragland, E. U., Kerr, M. M., and Strain, P. S. Effects of peer social initiations on the behavior of withdrawn autistic children. Behav. Mod. In press.

Rheingold, H., Gewirtz, J. L., and Ross, H. W. 1959. Social conditioning of vocalizations in the infant. J. Comp. Physiol. Psychol. 52:68–73.

Rincover, A., and Koegel, R. L. 1975. Setting generality and stimulus control in autistic children. J. Appl. Behav. Anal. 3:235–246.

Rosenkrans, M. A. 1967. Imitation in children as a function of perceived similarity to a social model and vicarious reinforcement. J. Personal. Soc. Psychol. 1:307–315.

Shatz, M., and Gelman, R. 1973. The development of communication skills: Modifications in the speech of young children as a function of listener. Monogr. Soc. Res. Child Dev. 38 (5).

Shores, R. E., Hester, P., and Strain, P. S. 1976. The effects of amount and type of teacher-child interaction on child-child interaction during free-play. Psychol. Schools 13:171–175.

Skinner, B. F. 1953. Science and Human Behavior. Free Press, New York.

Snow, C. E. 1972. Mothers' speech to children learning language. Child Dev. 43:549–565.

Stone, L. J., Smith, H. T., and Murphy, L. B. (eds.). 1973. The Competent Infant. Basic Books, New York.

Strain, B. A. 1975. Early dialogues: Reciprocity in vocal interaction between mothers and their three month old infants. Unpublished doctoral dissertation. George Peabody College, Nashville, Tenn.

Strain, P. S. 1977. Effects of peer social initiations on withdrawn preschool children: Some training and generalization effects. J. Abnorm. Child Psychol. 5:445–455.

Strain, P. S. 1978. Modification of social isolation between handicapped and nonhandicapped children. Except. Child. In press.

Strain, P. S., and Carr, T. H. 1975. The observation study of social reciprocity: Implications for the mentally retarded. Ment. Retard. 13:18–19.

Strain, P. S., and Cooke, T. P. 1976. An observational investigation of two elementary-age autistic children during free-play. Psychol. Schools 13:82–91.

Strain, P. S., Cooke, T. P., and Apolloni, T. 1976. Teaching Exceptional Children: Assessing and Modifying Social Behavior. Academic Press, New York.

Strain, P. S., and Pierce, J. E. 1977. Direct and vicarious effects of social praise on mentally retarded preschool children's attentive behavior. Psychol. Schools 14:348–353.

Strain, P. S., and Shores, R. E. 1977. Social interaction development among behaviorally handicapped preschool children: Research and educational implications. Psychol. Schools 14:493–502.

Strain, P. S., Shores, R. E., and Timm, M. A. 1977. Effects of peer social initiations on the behavioral of withdrawn preschool children. J. Appl. Behav. Anal. 10:289–298.

Strichart, S. S. 1974. Effects of competence and nurturance on imitation of nonretarded peers by retarded adolescents. Am. J. Ment. Defic. 78:665–674.

Wahler, R. G. 1967. Child-child interactions in free-field settings: Some experimental analyses. J. Exp. Child Psychol. 5:278–293.

Walker, H. B., and Hops, H. 1973. The use of group and individual reinforcement contingencies in the modification of social withdrawal. In L. A. Hamerlynck, L. C. Handy, and E. J. Marsh (eds.), Behavior Change: Methodology, Concepts, and Practice, pp. 269–307. Research Press, Champaign, Ill.

Walters, R. H., Parke, R. D., and Cone, V. A. 1965. Timing of punishment and the observation of consequences to others as determinants of response inhibition. J. Exp. Child Psychol. 2:10–30.

Wehman, P. 1977. Helping the Mentally Retarded Acquire Play Skills: A Behavioral Approach. Charles C Thomas, Springfield, Ill.

5 TEACHING GAMES AND HOBBIES

Jo Ann Marchant

The leisure time of developmentally disabled persons has become an area of increasing concern to special educators. Many educators recognize that developmentally disabled individuals must learn how to engage in appropriate leisure activities to fill in time unoccupied by employment, activities, or community-based recreation programs geared to meet their needs. Because skills for participation in leisure time activities often do not evolve in developmentally disabled persons without instruction, educational programs must be designed.

This chapter is concerned with teaching games and hobbies to the developmentally disabled. Games are defined as activities that have rules or set procedures and usually involve two or more participants. Hobbies include pastimes or amusements that may or may not have rules, and that may be done alone or with others. In this chapter games are classified in two broad categories: (1) quiet or table games, and (2) active games involving gross motor skills. The purpose of this chapter is to provide direction in selecting and teaching appropriate games to individuals working with developmentally disabled persons. A hierarchy of game skills is proposed with suggestions as to where commercially available games should be placed in this hierarchy and how they can be taught using a task analysis approach. Special emphasis is placed on selecting and teaching games to severely developmentally disabled persons. Methods for involving parents in teaching games are discussed, as are games for developmentally disabled adults.

RATIONALE FOR TEACHING GAMES

Acquisition of Leisure Time Skills

Handicapped individuals often spend long periods of time engaged in passive activities like watching television because they have not acquired skills for engaging in a greater diversity of leisure time activities (Katz and Yekutiel, 1974). Once a repertoire of games and hobbies has been acquired, decisions can then be made regarding better use of free time. Carlson and Ginglend (1961) state that acquisition of skills for participation in leisure time activities should foster growth in the mental health of exceptional individuals, resulting in greater happiness and better self-control.

Wehman (1977) points out that developmentally disabled persons often have a stronger need for play and diversion activities than non-disabled persons because their living or working conditions may provide little joy in their lives. Severely developmentally disabled persons often live in drab institutional settings with little guidance in the use of leisure time, while mildly disabled individuals may live alone and work at repetitious jobs where there is little opportunity for cooperative interaction with co-workers. Frequently there is little opportunity to learn how to use leisure time appropriately. The development and maintenance of game and hobby skills will provide handicapped individuals with guidance and direction in the use of their leisure time.

Games and Socialization

In addition to providing entertainment for leisure time, games provide an excellent way for developmentally disabled persons to learn lessons in a group. Examples of this include taking turns, following rules, and winning or losing a competitive activity. Developmentally disabled individuals often do not interact with their peers spontaneously (Whitman, Mercurio, and Caponigri, 1970; Burney, Russell, and Shores, 1977). Frequently games present excellent opportunities for acquisition of skills that may enhance the development of cooperative behavior. Social interaction skills assist in the normalization process by allowing the disabled individual to function successfully with nonhandicapped individuals (Peterson and Haralick, 1977). Development of socialization activities has proved to be especially beneficial to the disabled individual's personal development and adjustment in the community and in vocational settings. This is particularly true when the activities learned are similar to activities of nonhandicapped persons (e.g., Bernhardt and Mackler, 1975; Day and Day, 1977; Wehman et al, 1978).

Games with rules are particularly useful in educational settings to promote cooperative play skills as well as to facilitate competitive social behavior. Mithaug and Wolfe (1976) indicate that task or curricular activities can be arranged for task interdependence among two or more children, thereby increasing the likelihood of social responding. Table games and many active games include cooperation procedures in which the reinforcers of all participants are at least in part dependent upon the responses of the other individuals involved (Hake and Vukelich, 1972).

Carlson and Ginglend (1961) expanded social development to include progress in self-help skills, improved health and safety habits, increased interest span, increased ability to cope with stimulation, and the development of new interests. Learning game skills may foster progress in some of those aspects of social development as well as in the development of cooperative and competitive social behavior.

Appropriate social behavior skills, such as those established in successful game experiences, will likely be helpful in providing opportunities for more positive social experiences in other areas of life.

Learning New Skills Through Games

Fun is an essential ingredient for leisure time program success, but a game program should seldom be developed for fun alone. In addition to facilitating socialization, games should be used to foster acquisition and retention of other target behaviors. A well designed individualized education program (IEP) for a developmentally disabled student will have well defined objectives in the areas of motor, language, conceptual, and social development, as well as objectives for prevocational and vocational skill development. Such objectives are formulated after the student has been assessed by the teacher and a team of auxiliary personnel who will be working with that student. Instructional programs and materials used in the classroom with each student should be developed or chosen to foster acquisition or retention of a specified skill or objective on the IEP for that student.

Games are valuable tools for teachers of exceptional children who realize that students need repeated exposure to material in order to learn and retain it. Carefully chosen games can provide practice that fosters acquisition and retention of the skill (Blake, 1974). An example of this would be the use of a "Lotto" game to practice matching or visual perceptual skills instead of repeated seat work. Another example would be playing "A Tisket a Tasket" to practice skipping. In a later section of this chapter, the relationship between games and different curriculum areas is carefully detailed.

A creative teacher can easily involve game activities in all aspects of daily planning, but care must be taken to ensure that the games used are on the correct developmental level of the student, and that the student possesses the necessary game skills, such as the ability to use dice or to read the game cards. A hierarchy of such skills is presented later in this chapter in an attempt to assist teachers in selecting appropriate game materials.

Game materials serve many purposes in educational settings ranging from simply providing fun and entertainment for students to reinforcing complex reasoning ability such as that required in problem-solving activities. An outstanding teacher will select game materials to provide practice in skills being developed according to specified objectives for each student, while keeping in mind the many other benefits of such materials, including the development of social skills. Whenever possible, such materials should be selected to meet more than one specified objective. An example of this would be the use of "Bingo" to foster development of fine motor eye-hand coordination skills and listening skills, and to reinforce recognition of numerals.

SELECTING GAMES FOR DEVELOPMENTALLY DISABLED INDIVIDUALS

The selection process for choosing games to use with developmentally disabled persons is a twofold process. First, the developmental or academic level at which the student is functioning must be considered; and second, the level of game skills at which the student is functioning must be assessed. The developmental or academic functioning level of the student will be assessed by the interdisciplinary team that formulates the individualized education program for that student. Examples of useful assessment devices include the *Denver Developmental Screening Test*, the *Learning Accomplishment Profile*, the *TMR Profile*, the *Metropolitan Readiness Test*, and the *Wide Range Achievement Test* (WRAT), as well as a wide variety of behavioral checklists and rating scales. These are employed in addition to the standard intelligence tests normally used to evaluate handicapped students. Once the general assessment of the student is completed, the teacher must then determine the specific skills to be taught or reinforced by the use of games in the classroom.

Skill Areas Where Games Can Be Utilized

Valett (1968) has proposed six skill areas of basic learning abilities. Included areas are gross motor development, sensorimotor development, perceptual motor skills, language skills, conceptual skills, and social skills. Each ability area is defined and broken down into component skills, which are also defined.

The skill areas and definitions as formulated by Valett are presented in Tables 5.1 through 5.6. Representative samples of commercial and group games that might facilitate acquisition of each skill area are included.

No attempt is made in these tables to define which developmental or academic level the games represent. Rather, an attempt is made to point out the many skill areas in which games can play a role in an educational setting. A teacher who has assessed a class can determine relevant games to introduce, based on the objectives that have been set for individual children. Care must be taken, however, that the skills being reinforced are neither too simple nor too difficult for the individual child involved. For example, once a student has mastered the number concepts being practiced in a "Bingo" game, playing the game is no longer educational in nature, and the teacher may wish to introduce a flashcard game involving simple addition facts or a board game involving addition of the two sets of numbers rolled on dice if addition is the next skill to be developed. "Bingo" can still be used for recreational and leisure time purposes

Table 5.1.   Games for gross motor development

Rolling—the ability to roll one's body in a controlled manner
  Games: Line games, obstacle courses
Sitting—the ability to sit erect in normal position without support or constant reminding
  Games: "Simon Says," circle sitting games
Crawling—the ability to crawl on hands and knees in a smooth and coordinated way.
  Games: Line and circle games, obstacle courses
Walking—the ability to walk erect in a coordinated fashion without support
  Games: Line and circle games
  Hobbies: Nature walks, hikes
Running—the ability to run without a change of pace
  Games: Line and circle games, relays, "Squirrels in Trees"
  Hobbies: Jogging
Throwing—the ability to throw a ball with a reasonable degree of accuracy
  Games: Line and circle games, relays
  Hobbies: Dribbling and throwing baskets
Jumping—the ability to jump simple obstacles without falling
  Games: Line games, imitative games, "Jack Be Nimble"
  Hobbies: Jumping rope
Skipping—the ability to skip in normal play
  Games: "A Tisket a Tasket," "Follow the Leader"
Dancing—the ability to move one's body in coordinated response to music
  Games: Statues
  Hobbies: Dancing
Self-identification—the ability to identify one's self
  Games: "Who Knows Where ____ Is?", simple rhythms
Body localization—the ability to locate parts of one's body
  Games: "Simon Says Touch," "Put Your Finger"
Body abstraction—the ability to transfer and generalize self-concepts and body parts
  Games: "Funny Face," "Mr. Potato Head," "Cootie"
  Hobbies: Drawing pictures of people
Muscular strength—the ability to use one's muscles to perform physical tasks
  Games: All active games, Indian wrestling
  Hobbies: Gymnastics
General physical health—the ability to understand and apply principles of health and hygiene and to evidence good general health
  Games: "Go and Grow Game," "Circulation Game"

by that child, but the arithmetic lesson should include new game activities.

The teacher of severely developmentally disabled individuals can also make use of the ability areas presented by Valett but may have to plan

Table 5.2. Games for sensorimotor integration

Balance and rhythm—the ability to maintain gross and fine motor balance and to move rhythmically
Games: Hopscotch, "A Tisket a Tasket," "Pat-a-Cake"
Hobbies: Dancing, swimming

Body-spatial organization—the ability to move one's body in an integrated way around and through objects in the spatial environment
Games: "Follow the Leader," obstacle courses, relays
Hobbies: Walking, biking

Reaction-speed dexterity—the ability to respond efficiently to general directions or assignments
Games: "Simon Says," "Boggle"
Hobbies: Candle or sculpture making

Tactile discrimination—the ability to identify and match objects by touching and feeling
Games: "Feeley Meely"
Hobbies: Making collages

Directionality—the ability to know right from left, up from down, forward from backward, and directional orientation
Games: "Simon Says," "Tic-Tac-Toe," Hopscotch
Hobbies: Square dancing, biking

Laterality—the ability to integrate one's sensorimotor contact with the environment through establishment of homolateral hand, eye, and foot dominance
Games: "Simon Says," line and circle games, "Twister"
Hobbies: Ballet, gymnastics

Time orientation—the ability to judge lapses in time and to be aware of time concepts
Games: "Tell Time," "Quizmo," "Hide and Seek"
Hobbies: Cooking, TV watching, pet care

Table 5.3. Games for perceptual-motor skills

Auditory acuity—the ability to receive and differentiate auditory stimuli
Games: "Turn to the Noise," "Touch What You Hear"
Hobbies: Listening to records

Auditory decoding—the ability to understand sounds or spoken words
Games: "Simon Says," "Bingo"
Hobbies: Exercise records

Auditory-vocal association—the ability to respond verbally in a meaningful way to auditory stimuli
Games: Spelling bee, "Go to the Head of the Class"
Hobbies: Poetry or story reciting

Auditory sequencing—the ability to recall in correct sequence and detail prior auditory information
Games: "I'm Going On a Trip," "Instructo" storytelling games
Hobbies: Acting, puppet shows, singing

Visual acuity—the ability to see and differentiate meaningfully and accurately objects in one's visual field
Games: "Spin and Say," car traveling games
Hobbies: Collecting groups of items

Visual coordination and pursuit—the ability to follow and track objects and symbols with coordinated eye movement
Games: "Busy Bee," ball games, electric screen games
Hobbies: Cutting, bowling

Visual-form discrimination—the ability to visually differentiate the forms and symbols in one's environment
Games: "Lotto," matching card games, "Tic-Tac-Toe," "Checkers"
Hobbies: Reading, coloring, collections

Visual figure ground differentiation—the ability to perceive objects in foreground and background and to separate them meaningfully
Games: "GNIP GNOP," "Hide and Seek," "Dominoes," electric screen games
Hobbies: Star watching, use of word game books

Visual memory—the ability to recall accurately prior visual experiences
Games: "Memory," "Jack in the Beanstalk Memory Game"
Hobbies: Coloring and painting about experiences

Visuo-motor–Fine-Motor Coordination—the ability to coordinate fine muscles such as those required in eye-hand tasks
Games: "Lotto," "Jumbo Tiddledy Winks," "Qubic," all board games
Hobbies: Painting, pasting, cutting, needlework, shop projects

Visuo-motor spatial form manipulation—the ability to move in space and to manipulate three-dimensional materials
Games: "Blockhead," relays, jacks
Hobbies: Craft and shop projects

Visuo-motor speed of learning—the ability to learn visuo-motor skills from repetitive experience
Games: "Pick Pairs," obstacle courses
Hobbies: Knitting, weaving

Visuo-motor integration—the ability to integrate total visuo-motor skills in complex problem solving
Games: "Checkers," "Connect Four," foosball, pinball machines, poker, charades
Hobbies: Taking trips, playing musical instruments, letter writing

---

games on a lower ability level. An example of this would involve the games suggested for use in training body-spatial organization. If the profoundly retarded child does not have game skills necessary to move through an obstacle course, the teacher may want to plan the game to involve only moving through one item, such as a tunnel, initially. Another example of this would include games to develop auditory acuity. "Touch What You Hear" is a game in which each child is blindfolded and moves about the room looking for the spot where the drum or cymbals are being played, with the winner being the one who finds the noise the quickest. A teacher of profoundly retarded students may adapt this game by hiding behind the students and having them turn to the noise. The winner would be the person who turned first.

While it should be evident that games can be used for a multitude of purposes in most special education settings, it is extremely important that teachers have an understanding of what abilities

Table 5.4. Games for language skills

Vocabulary—the ability to understand words
    Games: "Language Category Games," "Hung Up"
    Hobbies: Crossword puzzles
Fluency and encoding—the ability to express oneself verbally
    Games: "Spin and Say" games, storytelling games
    Hobbies: Telling stories, acting
Articulation—the ability to articulate words clearly without notable pronunciation or articulatory problems
    Games: Picture card games
    Hobbies: Using phone
Word attack skills—the ability to analyze words phonetically
    Games: "Uno"
    Hobbies: Crossword puzzles and word games
Reading comprehension—the ability to understand what one has read
    Games: "Go to the Head of the Class," "Mother's Helper"
    Hobbies: Reading
Writing—the ability to express oneself through written language
    Games: "Read Around"
    Hobbies: Keeping a diary, letter writing
Spelling—the ability to spell in both oral and written form
    Games: "Scrabble for Juniors," "Got a Minute Game," "Hangman," Spelling bee
    Hobbies: Use of word game books

Table 5.5. Games for conceptual skills

Number concepts—the ability to count and use simple numbers to represent quantity
    Games: "Stepping Stones Numerals and Number Patterns," "Ride in the Country," "Parchessi"
    Hobbies: Counting collections of items
Arithmetic processes—the ability to add, subtract, multiply, and divide
    Games: "Count Your Change," "Arithmetic Quizmo," "Math Flashcards," "Addo"
Arithmetic reasoning—the ability to apply basic arithmetic processes in personal and social usage of problem solving
    Games: "Count Your Change," "Monopoly," "Easy Money"
    Hobbies: Traveling
General information—the ability to acquire and utilize general information from education and experience
    Games: "Energy in the Community," "Mother's Helper"
    Hobbies: Pet care, craft projects, life science activities
Classification—the ability to recognize class identities and to use them in establishing logical relationships
    Games: "Sort-a-Card," "Clue," "Checkers," "Twenty Questions"
    Hobbies: Collecting sets of items
Comprehension—the ability to use judgment and reasoning in common sense situations
    Games: "Baretta," "Easy Money," "Clue"
    Hobbies: Crafts, pet and child care, traveling

the games reinforce so that no student acquires isolated skills that have no functional application. Games should not serve only as time-filling devices. An example of teaching a child an isolated skill with no functional role would be having a profoundly retarded child play letter-matching "Lotto" games when no reading is included in his long range educational program. It would be more beneficial for the child to learn games utilizing concepts being taught in language or other curriculum areas. To assist teachers in sequencing game activities, a hierarchy of active games and one of table games are proposed in the next sections of this chapter.

Sequencing Active Games

Active games should be used in classrooms for a variety of reasons. They provide a change in routine from quiet seat work and facilitate gross motor development, language, sensorimotor integration, perceptual-motor skills, and conceptual skills. In addition, they provide the first organized group experiences for many young children, and assist in developing needed game skills for organized sports in intermediate-age children.

Although active games serve valuable purposes, many teachers encounter difficulty in teaching or implementing the games in special education settings. As games are attempted, chaos often ensues because of the large space required for instruction.

Table 5.6. Games for social skills

Social acceptance—the ability to get along with one's peers
    Games: All group games and table games involving more than one person
    Hobbies: Moving about neighborhood
Anticipatory response—the ability to anticipate the probable outcome of a social situation by logical inference
    Games: Open ended storytelling
    Hobbies: Dating, attending dances
Value judgments—the ability to recognize and respond to moral and ethical issues
    Games: "Energy in the Community"
Social maturity—the ability to assume personal and social responsibility
    Games: All group activities
    Hobbies: Pet and child care

Cratty (1968) suggests structuring games activities in such a way that a developmentally disabled individual can progress from simple to complex activities. For example, line games are less complex and easier to manage than circle games, while base games are more complicated than either line or circle games.

Careful selection of appropriate active games should minimize difficulties encountered in their use. For this reason, a hierarchy of active games, based on Cratty's suggested sequencing, is presented in Table 5.7. Representative samples of game activities have been included.

Utilizing this type of skill hierarchy will assist teachers working with all levels of disabled students in selecting and structuring active games successfully. A teacher of severely and profoundly retarded students may wish to adapt a circle game to be done in a line if the class involved does not possess the needed skills for playing in a circle. For example, the "Farmer in the Dell" game can initially be played with the children seated in chairs in a line. The "farmer" can stand on another line facing the chairs as he chooses his

Table 5.7. Hierarchy of active group game skills

1. *Imitative group games*
    "Peek-a-Boo," "Pat-a-Cake," "Where Is Thumbkin," "Jack Be Nimble," "I'm a Little Teapot"
2. *Line games*
    "Simon Says"
       a. "Do this!"
       b. "Hop to the other line," etc.
    "Follow the Leader"
    Ball games—passing, rolling, throwing the ball
3. *Circle games*
    Ball games—passing, rolling, throwing the ball
    "A Tisket-a-Tasket," "London Bridge," "Farmer in the Dell"
    Rhythm games
4. *Base games*
    Simple one- or two-base ball games
    Tag, "Snake in the Gutter"
    "Squirrels and Trees"
5. *Serial memory tasks*
    Obstacle courses
    Memory games
6. *Grid games*
    Hopscotch
    Letter or number grid games
7. *Reasoning games*
    "Hide and Seek"
    Charades

Table 5.8. Hierarchy of table game skills for mildly and moderately developmentally disabled students

1. *Matching games*
    "Lotto" games, "Old Maid," Simple card games
2. *Simple track games*—using cards to match. Playing piece is introduced. Card is drawn to effect a move. "Candyland," "Chutes and Ladders"
3. *Track games using a spinner and colors* "Happy Little Train," "Three Little Pigs"
4. *Track games using dice* "Gingerbread Man," "Silly Sandwich"
5. *Track games using a spinner and numbers* "Hi-Ho Cherry-O"
6. *Games using dice and three-dimensional playing pieces instead of a board* "Cootie"
7. *Simple games requiring beginning reading skills* "Mother's Helper," "Scrabble for Juniors"
8. *Complex games requiring reasoning ability, reading, and/or math skills* "Pay Day," "Go to the Head of the Class," "Easy Money," TV game show games, complex card games
9. *Table game sports* Foosball, table hockey, pinball machines

wife, and so on. As the class acquires the ability to follow the game procedure, the chairs can be faded gradually, and finally the children can be taught to form a circle around the farmer. Structured procedures facilitate acquisition of active game skills by developmentally disabled students, and should enable the teacher to maintain control of the group while providing assistance where it is needed.

Sequencing Table Games

Table games involve the use of numerous skills to which developmentally disabled students may not have been exposed previously, and which may be frustrating to students if they are not taught sequentially as the students develop intellectually or physically. Such skills include use of spinners, dice, and game cards that require reading or matching skills. These skills will probably not be acquired unless specific instruction is provided. To simplify table game selection and instruction, a hierarchy of table game skills for mildly and moderately handicapped students is proposed in Table 5.8. Representative commercial games are suggested.

Large toy stores and mail order stores have hundreds of games available. Using the proposed game skill hierarchy, teachers should be able to easily select table games that involve appropriate game parts while incorporating academic or readiness concepts which are being taught in the classroom. For example, "Hi-Ho Cherry-O" is a spinner game that involves counting skills, while "Funny Face" is a spinner game involving matching skills. Thus, if one objective of the game period is to have the student practice counting, "Hi-Ho Cherry-O" would be the appropriate game to select.

Table Games for Severely and Profoundly Handicapped Individuals

Severely and profoundly handicapped individuals may not acquire table game skills as easily as mildly or moderately disabled persons, and perhaps will never acquire the skills necessary for playing complex table games as presented in Table 5.8. However, a review of the limited literature involving training of table games to severely handicapped persons suggests that the necessary behaviors can be learned and generalized (Bates, 1976; Wehman, 1978). Acquisition of the skills necessary for playing simple table games enables severely handicapped students to interact socially with their peers, siblings, and parents in activities similar to those enjoyed by the nonhandicapped persons. Parents are often delighted to have game materials to use at home with the students.

Table 5.9 indicates a hierarchy of table game skills for use with severely and profoundly handicapped individuals. Some commercial games are suggested; however, teacher-made materials will

Table 5.9. Hierarchy of table game skills for severely and profoundly handicapped persons

1. *Picture-matching game using separated game pieces*
   Color-matching games
   Shape-matching games
      "Lotto" games, simple card games
2. *Simple track game*—left to right straight across page. Use big blocks with pictures to match, but introduce the concept of a playing piece. Draw cards to effect a move.
3. *Track game with a curve*
4. *Simple games using spinners and colors*
      "Happy Little Train," "Funny Face"
5. *Simple commercial games using cards and/or spinners*
      "Candyland"
6. *Simple commercial board games using dice*
      "Gingerbread Man," "Silly Sandwich"

probably be most appropriate for areas in which commercial materials are too advanced or too complicated because of the use of too many words, designs, or curves.

The hierarchy for this population involves an easy-to-complex sequencing of skills and includes instruction in using a game piece on a straight track and then on a curved one. Breaking down table game skills into such components should facilitate development of these skills. It is especially important that all persons playing the games with severely and profoundly handicapped students understand which skill is being taught and use the same teaching techiniques. Since severely and profoundly handicapped individuals do not make generalizations easily from one learning situation to another, programming must include careful selection of verbal cues, settings, and other variables that might inhibit the student's meeting success with the game materials.

ADAPTING AND DESIGNING GAMES

Developmentally disabled individuals often have physical or perceptual problems that inhibit them from using commercially made game materials successfully. Teachers of these individuals have the option of either securing the commercial materials and adapting them to meet the needs of the students or of designing and making table games for the students. As with eating and other self-help devices, the teacher must remember that adapted game materials should be used only when it is absolutely necessary because of the tendency for persons to become dependent upon such adaptations. It is also important to remember that one goal of game instruction is normalization, so whenever possible game materials should be identical to those used by nonhandicapped persons.

When adaptations are necessary, they should be done to meet the individual needs of the student, and whenever possible auxiliary staff persons, such as physical, occupational, or speech therapists, should participate in the planning of such adaptations.

Students with poor fine motor skills may need to have game cards or playing pieces built up by being placed on heavy cardboard to make them easier to grasp. For these same students it may be necessary to tape the game board down or use a piece of dyacem to hold it in place on the table. If pictures on the game board are too close together, it may be necessary to cut the pictures and separate them on a larger board so the pieces are easier to place. Positioning a student in a prone position over a roll or wedge instead of at a table may facilitate manipulation of playing pieces if the student needs better extension of the upper extremities.

For a student with perceptual problems many game boards are too cluttered with fancy designs so that the student cannot determine where the track begins or goes. Such figure-ground difficulties can be reduced by covering all unnecessary designs on the board with solid colored contact paper and by using prompts such as big stars to indicate where to begin and arrows to point to the correct pathway. The prompts can be faded as game skills are acquired.

The above examples represent ways the materials themselves might be adapted. In addition to adapting materials, it may also be necessary to adapt the rules of commercial games to meet the needs of disabled persons. This may be done to reduce the length or complexity of a commercial game, and should be done to meet the individual needs of students with whom the games will be used. Rules may be adapted also to permit nonverbal students to use manual language or to point out their reply on an answer sheet.

Endless adaptations of games are possible for the determined teacher, but in some instances commercial games are not available or cannot be adapted to be used for a particular objective. Teacher-made games can fill this void if care is taken in planning and making them.

Such games should be made with large, clear pictures that are uncluttered and should usually contain only one item. Items in the game should be spaced appropriately for the students with whom the game will be used. Game materials should be realistic and colorful when possible and should be made of durable materials. Lamination, clear contact paper, or dry mounting should be used on the games, particularly if the students exhibit drooling problems. Colorful tape borders should be put around boards to discourage students from pulling off the coverings, and rubber cement rather than glue is suggested as an adhesive for paper pictures to ensure proper placement and sticking. When carefully made, the laminated or covered games can be wiped clean and used for several years.

Playing pieces should be large enough to be grasped and released easily by the students. Blocks or other small toys can be used as can poker chips if the students can handle these easily.

The rules for teacher-made games should be written down sequentially and should include the objectives and materials for the games. They must be clear and easily understood so that the game can be played the same way by all players. Initially the game should be implemented with another adult so that necessary changes can be made before instructing students to use the game. All materials and the rules should be kept together in a box, and lost or destroyed pieces should be replaced immediately.

TEACHING GAMES TO DEVELOPMENTALLY DISABLED PERSONS

Systematic instruction of games should follow the same sequence used for instructional programs in other curriculum areas. The first step in this sequence involves assessing the current level of functioning of the student. When this assessment is completed, annual goals in the area of leisure skills will be identified. Selection of game skills should depend on the skills that will assist the student in functioning in complex heterogeneous community settings as an adult. It is also necessary to consider why the skills should be taught, and whether or not there are other important skills that might be trained more quickly and efficiently.

From the annual goals in the leisure skills area, instructional objectives must be set. These are precise statements of what the learner will be able to do following instruction (Mager, 1962). The instructional objective should contain three components: the criterion level of performance required, description of observable behavior, and condition. These objectives reflect what specific games the student will play, and instructional procedures or methods reflect how the games will be taught. Evaluation reflects the effectiveness of instruction and progress made by the child.

Knapczyk and Dever (1977) portray instructional problem solving in a paradigm that includes teacher and learner behaviors as well as teaching tools to effect the desired outcomes. This model is presented in Figure 5.1. Several examples of how

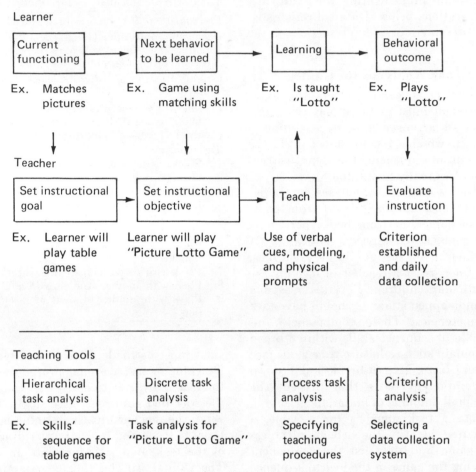

Learner

| Current functioning | → | Next behavior to be learned | → | Learning | → | Behavioral outcome |

Ex. Matches
pictures

Ex. Game using
matching skills

Ex. Is taught
"Lotto"

Ex. Plays
"Lotto"

Teacher

| Set instructional goal | → | Set instructional objective | → | Teach | → | Evaluate instruction |

Ex. Learner will
play table
games

Learner will play
"Picture Lotto Game"

Use of verbal
cues, modeling,
and physical
prompts

Criterion
established
and daily
data collection

Teaching Tools

| Hierarchical task analysis | | Discrete task analysis | | Process task analysis | | Criterion analysis |

Ex. Skills'
sequence for
table games

Task analysis for
"Picture Lotto Game"

Specifying
teaching
procedures

Selecting a
data collection
system

Figure 5.1.   Instructional problem-solving paradigm with examples of programming for table game skills. (Reprinted with kind permission of Knapczyk and Dever, 1977.)

instruction in game skills fits into the model are also provided.

With this instructional model, task analyses are characterized as teaching tools. In a task analysis, behavior is divided into smaller steps that are taught sequentially to a student. A task analytic method of presenting instructional material is useful in several ways (Wehman, 1977):

1. It makes the learning task easier for the student because the material is taught in small steps.
2. It is good for assessing the exact skill level of the student and assists in placement of the student at a certain program level to begin instruction. It also aids the teacher in grouping students at similar skill levels homogeneously.
3. It assists the teacher in following a specific order and sequence.

4. It simplifies program evaluation and assessment of student progress.
5. It facilitates replicability of instruction because different adults working with the student can adhere to the same order and sequence.

A hierarchical task analysis involves a simple-to-complex sequencing of the skills involved in a broad curriculum area. Such hierarchies for active games and table games are included in Tables 5.7, 5.8, and 5.9 of this chapter. A discrete task analysis in game training focuses upon the exact steps a student goes through to play a specific game. Process task analysis involves a sequencing of what the teacher does to teach a certain game skill, and criterion analysis involves selecting a data collection system and establishing the level of acceptable performance for specific game skills. Formulation of task analyses for games and teach-

ing procedures for implementing them are discussed in the sections below. Data collection suggestions are presented in a later section of the
chapter.

Formulating Task Analyses for Games

A task analysis of a game reflects the exact
responses a student must make to play the game.
The responses are arranged in steps according to
the sequence in which they must occur. If the
teacher is careful in sequencing the steps, instruction in the game is greatly facilitated.

Teachers may secure task analyses for games
from available curriculum guides, from commercial kits of games, or from books pertaining
to games or elementary physical education. A
perfunctory search of the available resources,
however, may not assist a teacher in meeting the
needs of particular children. For this reason a
teacher of handicapped students should have task
analysis competencies. These competencies include being able to sequence skills within a broad
curriculum domain such as leisure time skills (see
Chapter 1), and being able to break a skill down
into small component parts that present the
student with small amounts of material.

To formulate a task anaylsis for a game, a
teacher must first identify the behavioral objective for the game and then list the component
skills for playing the game in the logical sequence
in which they occur in the game. Prerequisite
skills for playing the game must also be established. Below are listed several different types
of games and the instructional objectives, as well
as prerequisite skills for these games: 1) a "Lotto"
or matching game, and 2) a simple board game using a spinner.

Teachers must practice breaking skills down
into their component parts, and should actually
act · out a game task analysis with input from
another adult before using it in the classroom.
Doing this should alleviate some instructional difficulties, but it is possible that further changes
like breaking steps down even further might be
necessary once instruction is begun with a student.

An example of a task analysis for a simple table
game, "Picture Lotto," is included in Table 5.10,
and Table 5.11 includes a task analysis for "Hi-
Ho Cherry-O," a board game with a spinner.

Teaching Procedures for Game Instruction

Once a teacher has a task analysis comprised of
the steps a student must do to play a game, deci-

Table 5.10. Task analysis for "Picture Lotto" game

Prerequisite skill: Picture-matching ability.
Behavioral objective: Given the table game "Picture
 Lotto," the student will play the game independently
 with no errors four out of five times.
Games consists of: Picture cards, boards for each
 player.
Playing procedures: Players take turns drawing cards,
 looking to see if there is a match. The winner is the
 person who has all pictures on his board covered first.
Task analysis:
1. Stacks cards in a pile between teacher and himself.
2. Draws one card.
3. Matches card to his board if it matches or puts it
 face down in a reject pile.
4. Waits for teacher to draw and match card.
5. Draws a second card.
6. Plays until one person has all three picture cards
 matched.
7. Plays with six cards instead of three.
8. Plays with another student with adult assistance.
9. Plays with another student with no adult intervention.

sions must be made as to *how* to teach the game.
Teaching or instructional procedures reflect what
the teacher will do to assist the student to acquire
the specified skills set forth in the task analysis.
First, the teacher must determine how much material to teach and in what order. Each of the steps
of the task analysis represents an isolated skill.
The skill(s) can be taught separately and then
combined with another step, or several of the steps
can be taught at one time. Chaining is the term
used to refer to connecting the steps together.

In forward chaining, Step 1 of the task analysis
would be taught, then Step 2 would be taught, and
then Steps 1 and 2 would be chained together.
Step 3 would be taught next and chained to Steps
1 and 2.

In backward chaining, the last step of the task
analysis would be taught first and then chained to
the next to the last step and so on. Teacher ingenuity must be put into action to determine
whether a game skill is taught more easily through
the use of forward or backward chaining or
whether or not several steps of the task analysis
should be grouped together for instruction.

For example, Marchant and Wehman (1978)
determined that teaching Steps 1 through 6 of the
"Picture Lotto" task analysis (see Table 5.10)
together provided more excitement and quicker
success for four severely handicapped children
than if Step 1 had been taught in isolation and
then chained to Step 2 and so forth. If backward

Table 5.11. Task analysis for "Hi-Ho Cherry-O"

Prerequisite skills: Simple counting skills.

Behavioral objective: Given the table game "Hi-Ho Cherry-O," the student will play the game independently with no errors four out of five times.

Game consists of: Spinning dial, 40 cherries (10 to each tree), and a cherry bucket.

Playing procedures: Student spins arrow, picks indicated number of cherries off of his tree or puts the indicated number of cherries back on his tree. The first player to pick all 10 cherries off of his cherry tree wins.

Task analysis:
1. Gives teacher one cherry. Requires student to give teacher one cherry. (Use whatever system for value counting that works for you.)
2. Gives teacher two cherries.
3. Gives teacher three cherries.
4. Gives teacher four cherries.
5. Puts indicated number of cherries in bucket. (Give the student verbal instruction on how many cherries you want him to pick off the tree. Require student to then place cherries in bucket. Encourage student to count each cherry out loud as he puts them in the bucket. Picking, counting, and placing cherries in bucket one at a time helps to alleviate mass confusion.)
6. Spins the arrow.
7. Identifies what the arrow lands on. (The spinning dial also has pictures of a dog, a bird, and a spilled cherry bucket on it. Cover these three pictures for now. Student is required to count how many cherries the arrow is pointing to.)
8. Puts indicated number of cherries in bucket. Student is now required to put all previous steps together. Spins arrow, indentifies what arrow lands on, puts indicated number of cherries in bucket.
9. Plays game with teacher.
10. Lands on bird. (Uncover the dog, bird, and cherry bucket. You can uncover them one at a time or all at once.) Student is required to put one cherry on his tree.
11. Lands on dog. Student is required to put one cherry back on his tree.
12. Lands on spilled bucket. Student is required to return all cherries in bucket to tree.
13. Plays game with teacher and another student.
14. Plays game with others.

Adaptations:
1. Original game rules indicate that two cherries should be returned to tree when landing on bird or dog. If only one cherry is in the bucket it must be returned. To alleviate unnecessary confusion, the student is only required to put one cherry back.
2. Glue a piece of felt on the arrow end of the spinner for easier identification.

chaining had been implemented, the students would have played until six pictures were covered, and they might have lost interest. Once the idea of winning by covering all the pictures was established, it was easier to increase the number of pictures on the game board.

In addition to determining the amount of material to teach and in what order, it is also necessary to determine what teaching techniques will be used to assist the student to make correct responses on the steps of the task analysis. The way in which a teacher presents materials, along with the level of assistance provided, influences how quickly the student learns.

Successful instruction of game skills requires that only as much teacher assistance and reinforcement as is absolutely necessary be used. Ideally, active involvement in game activity will become sufficiently motivating so that little or no adult reinforcement is necessary.

An instructional model that offers minimal adult assistance is one in which verbal cues alone are offered first to the student. If the student does not respond to verbal directions or cues, then the teacher models or demonstrates the desired response. If the student still does not respond, then the teacher physically prompts or guides the student through the desired response. Verbal or tangible reinforcement will be given for any correct student response initially and will be phased out gradually as the skill is acquired. An example of using these techniques to teach a skill in a game task analysis can be seen in Step 1 of the "Picture Lotto" Task Analysis included in Table 5.10. The student is told to "Stack the cards in a pile." If he does, he is rewarded verbally or with an edible. If the student does not respond, the teacher says, "Stack the cards in a pile," as she stacks the cards in a pile. The student is then given a chance to respond and is rewarded for a correct response. If the student still does not respond, the teacher physically guides the student through the act of stacking the cards and rewards the student for assisting in the task.

Stimulus-fading or color-coding techniques can be incorporated into this instructional model to enhance instruction in game skills. An illustration of a stimulus prompt is using a large star made of brightly colored felt to indicate where the playing piece is placed at the beginning of a track game like "Candyland." As the student acquires the skill of positioning his playing piece, the star is made smaller and eventually faded or removed altogether. Another example of stimulus fading would be using broad red lines to designate the game path initially, gradually reducing the lines, and finally using the narrow lines just as they exist on a commercially made board game.

Color coding can be used in teaching card games like "Old Maid." Matching cards can be glued on tagboard of the same color, or colored tape can be put at the edges of matching cards, so that the color as well as the pictures will serve as clues to the student as to which cards go together. As the student learns to play the game, the color cues should be removed gradually.

Instructional strategies utilizing such concepts are endless, and their implementation only requires teacher ingenuity. It should be noted that whenever possible a multisensory approach should be used in introducing games and other instructional programs. Prompts are most valuable if the student can both see and feel them. The felt star used in the above illustration is a good example of a multisensory stimulus.

Verbal cues, modeling, physical prompts, and stimulus prompts should be used only as long as they are needed to evoke a correct response from the student. This is also true with verbal or edible reinforcement used in game instruction. Expressive clapping, hugging, or edible reinforcement have proved to be effective in instilling the concept of "winning" a game and also assist in teaching handicapped persons other game skills (Bates and Rankin, 1977). Students may become dependent upon adult prompts or reinforcers like these, however, and thus some care should be taken to phase them out as the game skills are acquired. All student-initiated game endeavors should be rewarded as students begin to play games with peers or siblings without adult intervention since this type of socialization represents the terminal goal of all game programming.

Physical adaptations of the game materials also serve as necessary modifications when teaching desired game skills. These adaptations were discussed in an earlier section of this chapter, but are mentioned here as instructional procedures because the use of them should be included in written instructional procedures. This will be helpful to all persons implementing the program.

All of these suggestions reflect *how* teachers can teach handicapped students game skills. Arranging the classroom for game instruction is discussed in the section below.

Structuring Game Instruction

In addition to systematic instructional strategies, structured classroom arrangements also facilitate game training. Such arrangements include strategies for physically engineering the classroom and personnel strategies such as moving from simple one-to-one instruction in games to group instruction.

For table game instruction the physical environment should include a child-sized table and chair from which the student's feet can reach the floor. Initially all training should be done at the same location and by the same trainer. The spot chosen should be isolated from any distractions that inhibit the student from attending to the game. The trainer should be on the level of the student and should establish eye contact and give clear, direct instructions to the student.

When each of two students has met criterion on the game when playing with the trainer, the two children can then be taught to play together with the trainer providing prompts as needed. Throughout all training the trainer should be seated next to or closely behind the students so that physical prompts can be offered if necessary. This proximity should be faded as the students acquire the game skills. Attention should be given to placing children with hand-dominance problems or physical limitations so that these difficulties are minimized.

After the needed skills for a game have been acquired at the original training site, instruction can be carried out by other adults and in other settings. This will facilitate transfer of the skills to other environments and persons. The game materials can also be sent into the home or ward at this stage. The same instructional procedures should be used by all persons using the game materials.

The suggested techniques for structuring table game instruction are recommended particularly for teaching table games to severely developmentally disabled persons, but the simple-to-more-complicated structure should facilitate game playing abilities in all handicapped individuals.

Carefully organizing instruction for active games is even more crucial for success in teaching these games. A clearly designated area of the room should be used initially, and each student should be given a physical prompt, such as a chair or mat, to indicate the spot to sit or stand at the be-

Code: + = step was carried out independently
                      − = step was not carried out independently

Name of student _____

I.   Steps in "Picture Lotto" task analysis

1. Child stacks card in a deck between himself and partner.					
2. Child draws and matches one card. If he does not have a match, he places card in a new pile next to the first pile.					
3. Second player draws a card and follows same procedure.					
4. Play continues until one player has all three pictures matched and is declared the winner.					
5. Child plays with six cards instead of three.					
6. Child plays six-picture game with an adult.					
7. Child plays game with another child under adult supervision.					
8. Child plays "Lotto" with another child with no adult help.					
Criterion: Completion of a step independently for three consecutive days.					

II. Steps in "Color Lotto" task analysis

1. Child stacks cards in a deck between himself and the other player.					
2. Child draws and matches one card. If he does not have a match that is not covered, he puts card in second pile.					
3. Second player does same.					
4. Play continues until one player has six pictures covered and is declared the winner.					
5. Child plays game with an adult.					
6. Child plays game with an adult and another child.					
7. Child plays game with another child with no help.					
Criterion: Completion of a step independently for three consecutive days.					

III. Steps in "Shape Lotto" task analysis

1. Child stacks cards in a deck between himself and partner.					
2. Child draws and matches one card. If he does not have a match that is not covered, he puts card in second pile.					
3. Second player does the same.					
4. Player continues until one player has six pictures covered and is declared the winner.					
5. Child plays game with an adult.					
6. Child plays game with an adult and another child.					
7. Child plays game with another child with no help.					
Criterion: Completion of a step independently for three consecutive days.					

Figure 5.2.   Sample data sheet for "Lotto" games.

ginning of the game. A large rug might be designated as the game area for an active game. Masking tape is especially useful in designating the circle for a game like "A Tisket a Tasket" if the student has eye-foot coordination to skip on the circle. Rug remnants are excellent prompts to show a student where to stand or sit for a circle game. Several adults should be placed around the circle to offer physical guidance as skills are being taught. If adequate staff is not available, the teacher should work with only several children at a time before trying to carry out any large group instruction.

Kohl (1971) points out the necessity of keeping all explanations simple and brief. In addition, the teacher should be close to the student to whom directions are being given. In active group games teachers of handicapped individuals should not lecture or give directions from a distance because several students are likely to respond if it is not clear to whom the direction is being given.

Other points of emphasis in organizing the class for both active and table game instruction include the importance of the teacher's knowing the games well and participating as a model and motivator when the games are being taught. Developmentally disabled persons enjoy repetition and will enjoy the same games for long periods of time. Adults who work with these persons must strive to maintain a high level of enthusiasm. A final point in classroom organization for game instruction includes the importance of insisting that students help put away equipment and materials used in the games. Doing so facilitates knowledge of where the materials are located if the student wishes to use them with his peers and also serves as a prevocational skill of keeping the classroom neat.

Keeping Records of Game Skill Acquisition

The final component of an instructional program for game training includes selection of a data collection system in order that progress made by the students can be measured and so that the instructional techniques can be evaluated. With a task analysis approach to instruction data collection is simplified because small components of a task are identified and a student's ability to perform the steps can be indicated. Figure 5.2 includes a data sheet used for three "Lotto"-type games.

When using this data sheet, the student is told at the end of a 20-minute training session in the game to "Play 'Lotto'." A plus is given on the data sheet for each step completed independently by the student, and a minus is given for any step not completed (Marchant and Wehman, 1978). Use of this data sheet permits the teacher to readily identify the step of the task analysis at which the student's ability to play the game breaks down and allows this step to be pinpointed as the place where training needs to be carried out.

Such information can be presented graphically by placing the percentage of steps of the task analysis completed independently on the vertical axis of a graph and the session number or date on the horizontal axis of the graph. This data collection system is given only as an example. Individual teachers will likely choose one of many available systems of data collection to keep records regarding student progress.

In addition to collecting information regarding the specific game skills being trained, teachers should also keep records to indicate how long, i.e., the duration of time, a student engages in a game activity. This information will reflect a student's increase or decrease in interest as well as an increased attention span if the student enjoys a game for an extended period of time. Information regarding the number of times, i.e., the frequency, a student initiates playing a game with a peer or an adult should also be recorded because this, too, indicates an increased interest in game activities as well as growth in socialization skills.

DEVELOPING HOBBY SKILLS

Hobbies are leisure time activities that may or may not have rules, and that may be carried out by an individual or by a group of persons. These activities could include gardening, baking, pet care, acting, art and craft activities, compiling collections of various items such as coins or stamps, or engaging in outdoor exercises like going for a walk, hiking, or bicycle riding. Activities like these require a large amount of self-directed behavior and are thus somewhat more complex than the game activities discussed in this chapter.

Many hobbies provide for creative expression. Because it is very difficult to assess the diversity of interests in any group of persons, an effort should be made to expose handicapped persons to a wide range of hobby experiences so that a choice of hobbies is provided. Community recreation programs, school programs, and family activities in the home should all be involved in exposing these individuals to a full range of such leisure activities.

However, simple exposure to available activities is not likely to lead to successful participation by the handicapped persons. Therefore some systematic instruction in hobbies, as in game skills, is necessary. Corbin and Tait (1973) point out that the greatest motivation to participate in leisure activities is skill and that a person's skill in any activity must be developed.

Instructional programs to develop hobby skills in the school setting can utilize the same instructional strategies suggested above for teaching games. After a student has been taught the varying skills associated with several hobbies, opportunities should be provided for the person to independently choose and engage in, on a regular basis, the activity that is most reinforcing for him. Hobby centers could be established in the classroom, and perhaps one hour on Friday afternoons could be set aside for students to choose and work on the hobby of their choice.

The teacher must plan for transfer of the hobbies learned in school to other environments, such as the home and recreation center. Parents and other persons working with the student should be taught the teaching procedures used in the classroom, and must also be given information as to where needed materials can be purchased. They should be encouraged to understand that hobby items made by the student allow for creative expression, and, if possible, the items should be displayed in the home, even if they do not resemble adult artwork.

In addition, teachers must play an active role in helping parents learn how other leisure time skills like bicycle riding in the community or pet care can be taught in the home. Parents should be instructed to teach such activities in small steps, proceeding from simple to complex behaviors, which the student must demonstrate.

An example of this would be a father teaching his son to ride a bicycle around the neighborhood. The father should first ride around one block on his bike with his son until the son knows exactly where he is allowed to go on the bicycle. Then the son could be allowed to go from the last corner to his house alone, then half way home alone, then around the whole block while the father waits in the yard, and finally around that one block alone.

The child could be taught gradually to ride in other areas of the neighborhood, using the same technique of fading adult assistance through backward chaining.

Pet care also could be taught to a severely handicapped child at home. Initially the student could be taught to carry the filled bowl of food each day to the correct feeding spot, which should be color coded by a large circle of red contact paper the size of the diameter of the bowl. After the student has learned the daily routine of carrying the bowl at the same time to the same place, he can be taught to fill the bowl and put the dog food away. The parents should be instructed as to how to remove their physical prompts gradually as the child learns to feed the dog. Skills of providing water and brushing the dog could be introduced and taught through use of the same systematic procedures.

Teachers should make frequent contacts with parents and other persons working with their students in the community so that suggestions can be made for developing appropriate leisure skills in the students and so that transfer of training is carried out from the classroom to the home and community environments of the students. Additional suggestions for involving parents in the teaching of games and hobbies are discussed in the following section of the chapter.

INVOLVING PARENTS IN GAME AND HOBBY TRAINING

Games and hobbies provide valuable opportunities for handicapped students to interact with their family members in pleasurable activities. Parents are often pleased to have materials that allow them to carry out leisure time activities with their handicapped children similar to those engaged in by the nonhandicapped siblings (Bates, 1977; Marchant and Wehman, 1978). For this reason parents should have an active role in determining what types of leisure skills will be included in the long range individual educational plans of their children. When skills are introduced, parents should be made aware of what the game rules are, and of what specific instructional procedures are being used to teach the games or hobbies.

During the summer, leisure time activities should be considered as a part of total educational planning, which should assist parents in understanding the global or overall nature of the program for their child. This is essential because follow-up of school objectives in the home is crucial in all curriculum areas if transfer of training is to occur. The importance of this type of planning is mentioned here also because teachers would be unwise to encourage parents to play games or carry out hobbies with their children while ignoring the necessity of home follow-up of self-help training being carried out at school.

Once instructional procedures for games or hobbies are determined, parents can be taught to use the materials in several different ways. The parent can come to the school to learn the instructional procedures, can observe the student being taught the activity, and can then participate in the activity with the student so that the teacher can make suggestions. This type of parent involvement also allows parents to observe the student in a group situation at school. Another approach to parent involvement is to have the teacher go into the home, teach the parent to play the game by actually playing it with the parent, and then observe and make suggestions as the parent plays the game with the student. It would be ideal if a combination of these approaches could be used whereby the parent would visit the school and the teacher would visit the home.

Video-tape equipment offers another approach to parent involvement if the parent cannot come to the school to see the student doing the activity. The training situation could be taped and taken to the parent. This equipment also allows the parent to be taped while working with the child so that the parent can view the tape and determine needed areas of improvement.

Regardless of how parent training is effected, certain guidelines should be adhered to in planning for transfer of game or hobby skills into the home environment. For example, it is important that the same verbal cues and same teaching procedures be used at home and at school. Playing pieces must be called by the same labels, and parents must be certain of the exact rules of the game or procedures for teaching a specific hobby. In addition, parents should be encouraged to play enthusiastically and to offer social and/or edible reinforcement as is done at school. Specific training techniques that have proved effective in the school setting also should be used in the home. To illustrate, if having a child place her hands in her lap between turns assists in helping her attend to the game, parents should be instructed to use this type of game structure when playing at home.

Parents should be taught how to involve other siblings in game or hobby activities with the handicapped child, and should be helped to understand the importance of fading adult help as it is no longer needed.

In addition to these guidelines, it is necessary to consider at which point instruction should be carried out at home as well as at school. Students should have acquired the necessary skills well enough so that no confusion will result when other persons or settings are involved.

In teaching table games to severely handicapped students, it may be advisable to require the child to play the game with the teacher and a classmate for a number of days before initiating game play in the home. It is very important that the same materials be used in both settings; thus teachers may need to make a set of identical materials to send home, or at least will have to tell parents where to acquire materials and exactly how to make the game. Marchant and Wehman (1978) found that four severely handicapped students generalized game skills for three matching games with no difficulties when these guidelines were followed.

If parents are willing to do so, they should be taught to keep records of student progress by using the same data collection techniques the teacher uses. The task analytic approach to instruction suggested in this chapter provides a sequential list of steps the student is to go through in playing a game and provides an easy instrument for a parent to use in recording what the student was able to do independently each time the activity was carried out. Teachers must determine how often they would like parents to keep records of activities being done at home. It is necessary to maintain close contact with parents to ensure that activities are being done regularly and that no difficulties are being encountered in home instruction. Teachers can also use these regular contacts to reinforce or praise parents who are working consistently with their children, and to encourage all parents to follow up school activities at home.

Planned involvement of parents in leisure time programming should ensure that games and hobbies taught at school do not become isolated skills, but rather that they assist the students in functioning more normally in their home environments.

GAMES AND HOBBIES FOR DEVELOPMENTALLY DISABLED ADULTS

Developmentally disabled adults should be provided opportunities for social interaction with their normal peers in the community. Ginglend (1968) stated that broad personality changes in adults have been noted when they gain a sense of identity through a social situation. Unfortunately these persons may have had few previous experiences in the recreational area and may not have acquired needed skills.

Teachers and recreation specialists working with disabled adults must introduce activities that will provide opportunities for learning the basic social and physical skills required to play simple games or engage in hobbies. In choosing appropriate activities for this purpose, care must be taken that activities are not infantile. Activities should not be used that teach an isolated concept which will never be used in a functional way. An illustration of a nonfunctional concept would be having adults play games to learn the alphabet when they will never be involved in a reading program.

The limitations of individual adults must also be considered in choosing games or hobbies to teach so that materials can be adapted to alleviate difficulties. Leisure programs for severely and profoundly handicapped adults may have to include very simple activities, but creative measures must be taken to prevent them from resembling primary classroom activities. For example, if there are retarded adults who can do little artwork other than finger painting, such work should be laminated for use as placemats in the eating program. Another illustration of adapting materials to be more appropriate for adult handicapped persons involves the "Picture Lotto" game discussed earlier in this chapter. The adults should not be asked to match pictures of tricycles or other toys, but they could be taught to play the same game using household or workshop items, or seasonal concepts that might be included in their daily activites.

After activities for this age population are chosen carefully so that they are motivating and simple, but not demeaning, the same instructional strategies suggested for use in teaching games should be implemented. Numerous opportunities for acquiring and practicing the skills may be needed and must be provided for in daily programming to ensure that success is met.

SUMMARY

In this chapter game and hobby activities were described as being helpful in facilitating socialization and appropriate use of leisure time in developmentally disabled persons. Games were portrayed in a hierarchy, ranging from simple to complex in nature, and instructional strategies were discussed. Suggestions for teaching hobbies in the school setting and for planning for transfer of the activity to the home and community were made. Parent involvement in games and hobbies was discussed, as were considerations for planning game activities for adult-handicapped persons. The use of the systematic teaching procedures described in the chapter should facilitate developmentally disabled persons' engagement in games and hobbies that are similar to those enjoyed by nonhandicapped persons.

REFERENCES

Bates, P. 1977. Community transition: A behavioral approach with the severely profoundly retarded and their families. AAESPH Rev. 4:217–224.

Bates, P. 1976. Language instruction with a profoundly retarded adolescent: The use of a table game in the acquisition, generalization, and maintenance of verbal learning skills. Unpublished master's thesis. University of Wisconsin, Madison.

Bates, P., and Rankin, C. 1977. Teaching the severely retarded to play Candyland. In P. Wehman (ed.), Helping the Mentally Retarded Acquire Play Skills. Charles C Thomas, Springfield, Ill.

Bernhardt, M. A., and Mackler, B. 1975. The use of play therapy with the mentally retarded. J. Spec. Educ. 9(4):409–414.

Blake, K. A. 1974. Teaching the Retarded. Prentice-Hall, Englewood Cliffs, N.J.

Burney, J., Russell, B., and Shores, R. 1977. Developing social responses in two profoundly retarded children. AAESPH Rev. 2(2):53–64.

Carlson, B., and Ginglend, D. 1961. Play Activities for the Retarded Child. Abington Press, New York.

Corbin, H., and Tait, W. 1973. Education for Leisure. Prentice-Hall, Englewood Cliffs, N.J.

Cratty, B. 1968. Learning and Playing—Fifty Vigorous Activities for the Atypical Child. Educational Activities, Freeport, N.Y.

Day, R., and Day, M. 1977. Leisure skills instruction for the moderately and severely retarded: A demonstration program. Educ. Train. Ment. Retard. 12:128–131.

Ginglend, D. 1968. Recreation programming for the adult retardate. In Programming for the Mentally Retarded. American Association for Health, Physical Education, and Recreation, Washington D.C.

Hake, D., and Vukelich, R. 1972. A classification and review of cooperation procedures. J. Exp. Anal. Behav. 18:333–343.

Katz, S., and Yekutiel, E. 1974. Leisure time problems of mentally retarded graduates of training programs. Ment. Retard. 12(3):54–57.

Knapczyk, D., and Dever, R. 1977. Instructional problem-solving in programming for the severely handicapped. AAESPH Rev. 4:224–232.

Kohl. M. Games for Children. Cornerstone Library, New York.

Mager, R. 1962. Preparing Instructional Objectives. Fearon Press, Palo Alto, Cal.

Marchant, J., and Wehman, P. 1978. Teaching table games to severely handicapped students. Ment. Retard. In press.

Mithaug, D., and Wolfe, M. 1976. Employing task arrangements and verbal contingencies to promote verbalizations between retarded children. J. Appl. Behav. Anal. 9:301–314.

Peterson, N., and Haralick, J. G. 1977. Integration of handicapped and nonhandicapped preschoolers: An analysis of play behavior and social interaction. Educ. Train. Ment. Retard. 12(3):235–246.

Valett, R. 1968. A Psychoeducational Inventory of Basic Learning Abilities. Fearon Press, Palo Alto, Cal.

Wehman, P. 1977. Helping the Mentally Retarded Acquire Play Skills: A Behavioral Approach. Charles C Thomas, Springfield, Ill.

Wehman, P. 1978. Leisure skill programming in severely and profoundly handicapped persons: State of the art. Br. J. Soc. Clin. Psychol. 17(4).

Wehman, P., Renzaglia, A., Berry, G., Schutz, R., and Karan, O. 1978. Developing a leisure skill repertoire in severely and profoundly handicapped persons. AAESPH Rev. 3(3).

Whitman, T., Mercurio, J. R., and Caponigri, V. 1970. Development of social responses in two severely retarded children. J. Appl. Behav. Anal. 3:133–138.

6 COMMUNITY-BASED RECREATION PROGRAMS

Paul Bates and Adelle Renzaglia

Before World War II recreation programs for the developmentally disabled were virtually nonexistent. To a great extent this situation was a consequence of the eugenics movement and the seclusion of the vast numbers of developmentally disabled individuals in large residential institutions that were concerned solely with custodial care. When provided, recreation programs consisted merely of activities that were developed to consume time, prevent boredom, provide relief for custodial staff, and prevent the occurrence of behavior problems (CEC and AAHPER, 1966; Witt, 1971). It was not until after World War II, with the organization of parent groups (e.g., National Association for Retarded Citizens), that recreation became recognized as an integral part of education for disabled persons.

Although the parent movement served as a catalyst for increased services for mentally retarded children, provisions for recreation programs were slow to develop. Consequently recreation did not emerge as a distinct discipline until the 1960s (Witt, 1971), at which time the value of recreation for all people was recognized. Constructive use of leisure time has since been identified as an integral part of community living. Recreation programming has generally become accepted as an essential part of any educational or rehabilitative program for developmentally disabled persons (Luckey and Shapiro, 1974).

VALUE OF PLANNNED COMMUNITY RECREATION

Educators increasingly have recognized the importance of play and recreation in the development and socialization of all people. The developmentally disabled are no exception. It has been suggested that active participation in planned recreational activities within the community will result in positive gains in the following areas: 1)

health and physical fitness, 2) mobility, 3) language, 4) social skills, and 5) self-fulfillment or self-image (CEC and AAHPER, 1966; Wilson, 1974). Although little empirical research is available to support these contentions, it would seem that they are not unreasonable considering the nature of recreational activities.

Substantial amounts of time, as much as one-half of our adult waking hours, are available for leisure activities (CEC and AAHPER, 1966). Constructive use of this time may provide educational experiences that maximize chances for adjustment within community settings. Although participation in recreational activities should be voluntary, few developmentally disabled persons are self-directed or even aware of their options in this area. Therefore, community recreational activities must be planned carefully with specific goals in mind in order to facilitate the acquisition of leisure skills.

The constructive use of leisure time depends to a great extent upon the skills and interests an individual has acquired, and these skills and interests develop as a result of planned, systematic experiences with specific activities. Planned recreation and leisure time programs are designed to equip participants with the skills necessary for successful participation in recreational activities.

Community recreation provides developmentally disabled individuals (regardless of degree of disability) with opportunities for success, which they rarely experience in other facets of learning. Hitzhusen (1975) suggested that through fun, games, and competition mentally retarded individuals have an opportunity to establish social interaction skills and gain social acceptance from peers.

COMMUNITY INTEGRATION

Recent federal and state legislation (e.g., Education for All Handicapped Children Act, P.L. 94-

---

The contribution of both authors is considered equal.

97

142; Rehabilitation Act of 1973) has mandated the right of handicapped persons to placement within the least restrictive environment. As a result, large numbers of developmentally disabled persons have been placed in community living and employment situations. The deinstitutionalization and normalization movement has shifted the responsibility for programming from self-contained residential institutions to community agencies.

Several researchers have surveyed the activities of postschool developmentally disabled individuals residing in the community (e.g., Gozali and Charney, 1972; Stanfield, 1973; Katz and Yekutiel, 1974). The number of individuals surveyed ranged from 26–520, and the results were surprisingly similar. These studies suggested that as many as 80% of developmentally disabled adolescents and adults never leave their immediate neighborhood to travel or participate in community functions. The most commonly cited forms of leisure time activities for these people were watching TV, listening to the radio, and occasionally attending movies with family members. None of these activities required any social interaction behaviors with handicapped and/or nonhandicapped peers (e.g., Katz and Yekutiel, 1974).

Gozali and Charney (1972) surveyed 26 educable mentally retarded individuals one year after the termination of their involvement with a work adjustment training program. Their results indicated that most of these individuals were doing well in their job placements. However, not a single person participated in any of the organized sports or social activities offered in their home communities. Gozali and Charney concluded that educable mentally retarded persons have demonstrated the ability to adapt in a community situation. However, as professionals we have not yet developed programs that provide opportunities for the acquisition of necessary social skills for improving the quality of the educable mentally retarded's afterwork life.

Corcoran and French (1977) suggested that developmentally disabled individuals have not had experiences in living and coping with the demands of a "normal" community life and this decreases their chances for successful placement within community settings. Consequently, a number of educators have strongly emphasized the continuing need for recreation programs

designed to assist handicapped individuals in acquiring the social skills and competencies necessary for using community leisure time and recreational facilities (Luckey and Shapiro, 1974; Pomeroy, 1974; Corcoran and French, 1977).

Recreation specialists have attempted to meet the needs of the developmentally disabled through a variety of programs. This has resulted in a controversy within community agencies: some educators advocate total integration of handicapped persons with their normal peers, while others contend that segregated activities within a community structure best fulfill their needs. Stein (1977) suggested that there is a need for both sheltered and integrated community programs. Furthermore, the type of program should be determined by the past experiences, physical fitness, social adjustment, and degree of retardation of the individuals to be served.

Although the need for a variety of programs has been recognized, Wolfensberger (1972) maintains that the ultimate goal of any program should be that of preparing a person for independent and normative functioning. This is the major thrust of the normalization principle (Nirje, 1969). Normalization involves providing opportunities for handicapped individuals to experience the conditions of everyday life as close to the norms and patterns of society as possible. Wolfensberger (1972) contends that many failures of the developmentally disabled to adjust to community living are a result of insufficient and unrealistic preparation. He suggests that too often training has been conducted through sheltered, segregated programs, the goals of which are unrealistic in terms of the expectations of a normative community setting. As a result, placement from sheltered programs into the community has failed.

Leisure time and recreational activities play a major role in the lives of most community residents. Therefore, these activities should also be made available to developmentally disabled individuals residing in the community. Disabled persons should be encouraged to participate in regular programs when possible, and, when necessary, special, sheltered programs should be available.

Regardless of the nature of the program. Wolfensberger (1972) strongly emphasizes the importance of some form of integration. He maintains that integration is one of the major means of achieving and recognizing societal acceptance as well as achieving adaptive behavior change. Recreation programs that are designed exclusively for developmentally disabled individuals should, at least, be physically integrated into the community so as to maximize the opportunities for social integration. In other words, Wolfensberger would suggest conducting activities in a facility where other people are present in order to expose developmentally disabled persons to their normal peers and, conversely, to expose normal peers to developmentally disabled persons.

For example, instead of organizing large groups of developmentally disabled individuals to participate in activities like swimming or bowling, it is more desirable to attend these activities in small numbers so that it is not necessary to reserve an entire facility for developmentally disabled participants alone. This will enable a physical, if not social, integration of normal and handicapped peers. Furthermore, such an approach will maximize the opportunities for social interaction and learning through imitation of normal peer models.

Although the controversy over segregated versus integrated programs has not been resolved, the program suggestions provided by Wolfensberger (1972) seem to be based upon valid assumptions. The advantages for both the developmentally disabled individuals and the community at large are potentially great. However, there is a definite need for more research in this area to assess the comparative effects of integrated and segregated programs on both developmentally disabled individuals and normal community residents.

Whether or not a program is integrated, segregated, or represents a combination of these two modes, the general concensus is that recreational activities should be determined by the needs and desires of the individuals involved (CEC and AAPHER, 1966; Carlson and Gingland, 1968; Pomeroy, 1974). Each individual should receive and participate in a program tailored for his needs. Therefore, the development of a program that incorporates both sheltered and integrated activities will facilitate individualization by providing educators with a number of options for any one person's participation in community recreation.

To develop an effective model for community recreation, we must first be aware of the data regarding past program effectiveness. The remainder of this chapter first provides the reader with an overview of the data-based community recreation programs and the component activities that can and have been included. After this review, the authors provide the reader with a model for community recreation followed by a delineation of the areas that require further research.

COMMUNITY RECREATION PROGRAM REVIEW

The rationale for the development of community recreation opportunities for the developmentally disabled seems to be well established from both a theoretical and practical perspective. The influences of normalization and deinstitutionalization (Nirje, 1969; Wolfensberger, 1972) have contributed toward a positive atmosphere for the development of community-based recreation services. In addition, several reports (e.g., Stanfield, 1973) have identified that the developmentally disabled adult has ample leisure time available, but rarely participates in community recreation during this free time. By not participating in community recreation the social isolation of the developmentally disabled individual is accentuated. Furthermore, the potential benefit in overall social adjustment accruing from such participation has been suggested by several community recreation advocates (e.g., Hitzhusen, 1975).

In this section, survey and program evaluation data regarding component areas of community recreation are presented. For purposes of analysis, community recreation is divided into the following subcategories: physical activities, cultural activities, social activities, outdoor education activities, and mental activities. Before presenting a summary of research in each of these component areas, the results of several needs assessment surveys in the area of community recreation are presented. This section concludes with a brief discussion of two comprehensive recreation programs and an overall data summary of the area.

Community Parks and Recreation Services

Several surveys have been conducted in various parts of the country to assess the availability of community recreation to special populations (e.g., Andres, 1967; Hayes, 1969; Thompson, 1969; Edginton et al., Compton and Goldstein, 1976). Each of these studies relied extensively on distributing questionnaires to various professionals within the community who might be involved in recreation and/or programming with the developmentally disabled.

In two statewide surveys (Hayes, 1969; Edginton et al., 1975) and one national survey (Lancaster, 1976), the needs assessment results have generally been supportive of one another. The reasons that community recreation services were not offered for the developmentally disabled in the Edginton et al. (1975) survey closely paralleled the program development priorities listed earlier by Hayes (1969). These included lack of funds, inadequately trained professional personnel, and unawareness of need.

Most communities surveyed in the statewide surveys and the national survey indicated that they accepted the responsibility for developing recreation services for the developmentally disabled. Since the need to develop services is accepted by most communities, it seems that funding, expertise, and awareness are the major factors detracting from expansion of community recreation opportunities.

Physical Activities

Physical activities including exercise, individual sports, and team sports are community recreation outlets for millions of individuals. Participation of the developmentally disabled in these activities may be hindered by the unavailability of opportunity and the lack of physical skills.

In a review of research on physical fitness and mental retardation, Campbell (1973) concluded that mentally retarded persons were generally inferior to normal children on most measures of physical fitness. This inferiority in physical fitness must be evaluated with reference to these individuals' lack of opportunity to develop physical skills. For instance, regarding a mildly disabled population, Brace (1968) reported that public school physical education services were inadequate. When a more severely disabled population is considered, these deficiencies are even more appalling. As late as 1976, Spradlin and Spradlin stated: ". . . To the critics' knowledge, no systematic work has been reported on teaching children with severe behavioral limitations such physical fitness and motor performance activities as pull ups, sit ups, standing jump, running, and throwing."

Recently task analysis and contingent reinforcement have been used successfully to teach developmentally disabled persons a variety of physical activities. By breaking physical skills into their component parts, i.e., by using task analysis, and by reinforcing improvements on each of these components, the severely disabled have acquired such basic skills as rolling a ball, riding a sliding board, riding a tricycle, and jumping on a trampoline (Wehman and Marchant, 1977). Successful use of playground equipment also has been acquired via similar teaching procedures (Keeran, Grove, and Zachofsky, 1969).

Other physical skills that have been included in data-based instructional sequences are swimming (Bundschuh et al., 1972), bowling (Seaman, 1973), and exercises (Wehman et al., 1978).

The effect of participation in extracurricular physical activity, e.g., basketball and square dancing, on social acceptance of a mildly disabled group of inner city youth was investigated by McDaniel (1971). Based on a pre/post comparison of social acceptance scores, McDaniel (1971) found that the group involved in the extracurricular activities improved in social acceptance while the control group did not.

In conclusion, few data-based instructional sequences are available to the practitioner to assist him in developing the physical activity skills of the developmentally disabled. However, an instructional strategy based on task analysis and contingent reinforcement has proved useful and could be expanded to a wider variety of physical skills. With increased availability of opportunity and with improved instructional sequences, the involvement of the developmentally disabled in community-based physical recreation should be increased.

Cultural Activities

Cultural activities, such as arts and crafts, dancing, theater, music, and spectator events, have not been studied systematically with regard to the individual's ability to participate and/or benefit from involvement in such activities. Several authors have suggested the importance of creative arts for the developmentally disabled (e.g., Maynard, 1970; Burmeister, 1976), but only a few have engaged in any program evaluation.

Two studies that attempted to determine the effect of dancing activities on overall social adjustment were undertaken by Eichenbaum and Bednark (1964) and Chaney (1969). Eichenbaum and Bednark (1964) used teacher subjective reports to evaluate the effect of participation in square dancing. Positive changes attributed to the square dancing program included an improvement in overall attitude and a reduction in violent outbursts.

Chaney (1969) conducted a similar study regarding the effect of involvement in dance and rhythmical activities. In this study the experimental group evidenced significant improvement on both IQ and coordination measures, but made no improvements in social acceptance.

Equivocal results such as the Eichenbaum and Bednark (1964) and the Chaney (1969) studies preclude definitive conclusions about the value of participation in dance activities on social adjustment. On the whole, more research of a better quality is required in this area to investigate both skill acquisition and involvement benefit.

Social Activities

Few research efforts have been directed toward the social activities available through community recreation. The skills necessary for an individual to participate successfully in dances, social clubs, parties, field trips, etc., have not been evaluated critically. Research neglect in this area is alarming when one considers the importance attached to the development of more appropriate social behaviors in the adult developmentally disabled population (e.g., Stanfield, 1973).

Recently an increased sophistication in analyzing the skills necessary for the developmentally disabled to participate in community activities has been witnessed. Social activities must be available, individuals must possess the prerequisite behaviors necessary for participation, and these individuals must be able to travel to and from the activities.

Recognizing the complexity of issues surrounding the successful integration of developmentally disabled persons into community activities, Certo headed a task force to determine the minimum objectives necessary for individuals to use selected stores and services in the community (Certo and Swetlik, 1975). Table 6.1 presents a sample task analysis developed by Certo to teach the skills required for formal dining in a restaurant.

Similar task analyses were also developed by Certo to teach use of clothing stores, grocery stores, and other restaurants. Independent travel was a component skill in each of the community activities analyzed by Certo. Along this line Certo,

Table 6.1. Task analysis for use of a formal restaurant

Steps:
1. Teach function of formal restaurant.
2. Choose a formal restaurant.
3. Independently travel to the restaurant.
4. Wait for hostess/host and then wait for waiter/waitress.
5. Read menu.
6. Order food.
7. Eat food properly with appropriate manners.
8. Pay for food.
9. Independently travel home.

Adapted from Certo et al., 1975, unpublished manuscripts.

Schwartz, and Brown (1975) reported a successful program for teaching severely handicapped individuals to use city transportation. Because transportation is often a logistical constraint to the expansion of social recreation opportunities, teaching independent travel is an important concern.

In a recent presentation Marholin and his associates (1977) reported an empirical verification, via a multiple baseline analysis, of a community skills treatment package for severely developmentally disabled adults. This package consisted of prompting, modeling, corrective feedback, social reinforcement, and occasional, brief timeouts. The target behaviors in this successful study were bus riding, purchasing, and restaurant skills. The program involved teaching appropriate restaurant skills in a McDonald's hamburger stand.

Sex education is also a skill development area that has received limited attention with the developmentally disabled. If these individuals are to become involved socially with members of the opposite sex in community recreation activities, they will need to learn appropriate heterosexual behaviors. Recently Hamre-Nietupski and Williams (1977) reported the results of a 3-year sex education program involving severely developmentally disabled adolescents. The sex education and social skills acquired as a result of this data-based program should facilitate appropriate adult functioning of these individuals in heterosexual social activities.

There has also been an increased interest in teaching developmentally disabled individuals more effective interpersonal communication behaviors (e.g., Bates, 1976; Hynes and Young, 1976; Perry and Cerreto, 1977). Improvements in social conversational skills should facilitate successful participation of these persons in social activities in their home communities. In one such study severely handicapped individuals were instructed in how to initiate social activity requests over the telephone (Nietupski and Williams, 1974). Further study of how best to improve the interpersonal communication skills of the developmentally disabled is warranted.

As more social activity opportunities are made available to developmentally disabled individuals, more extensive social skill repertoires will be called for. A few studies have been reported that have addressed the need to develop social skill acquisition programs (e.g., Nietupski and Williams, 1974). Additional program research is required, as well as empirical investigation of the benefits of involvement in social activity programs.

Outdoor Activities

Numerous studies have been reported regarding camping programs for the developmentally disabled. Some of these programs have involved only developmentally disabled persons, while others have included both handicapped and normal individuals.

In one study the effect of a normal counselor companion assigned to each developmentally disabled camper was investigated experimentally (Burnes and Hassol, 1966). As a result of this "companion model" of camping, the disabled campers improved significantly in social competence over the duration of a summer program. Two studies that have investigated integrated camping arrangements have generally concluded that both the handicapped and normal campers benefitted from such involvement (Fiax and Peters, 1969; Hayes, 1969). However, Hayes (1969) suggested that active programming may need to be conducted to facilitate interactive behaviors between normal and disabled campers when such interaction fails to occur spontaneously.

Research on outdoor activities has been plagued with methodological problems. Future studies should concentrate more specifically on the component behaviors involved, should use acceptable research designs, and should utilize behavioral measurements rather than subjective evaluations.

Passive Leisure Activities

The involvement of the developmentally disabled in passive leisure activities, such as table games, card games, adult education, public library activities, etc., has received limited experimental investigation. Research in each of these areas would be beneficial in investigating skill acquisition programs as well as the potential influence of such activity on other variables (e.g., self-concept, social interaction, etc.).

Comprehensive Integrated Programs

Comprehensive community recreation programs have been investigated to determine the effect of involvement on self-esteem (Seaman, 1975) and to determine the type of individual that will succeed in a community program (Pumphrey et al., 1970). Based on subjective ratings by recreation directors, all developmentally disabled persons involved in Seaman's (1975) study evidenced gains in self-esteem after participation in the municipal recreation program. In the Pumphrey et al. (1970) investigation, 31 of the 41 developmentally disabled individuals who participated in the integrated recreation program were judged as doing satisfactorily to very well. The individuals who were judged as obstructive to the program were the overactive adolescents in the lowest educable range of mental retardation. In this study withdrawn individuals were accommodated more easily in the integrated program than were active persons.

Data Review Summary

Research involving community recreation and the developmentally disabled can be generously described as inadequate. The need for better research has been described as critical by recreation professionals; yet the need for better research has not been matched by the development of trained personnel in community recreation. Linford and Kennedy (1971) reported that the therapeutic recreation professional's background in quantitative methods was sufficient to guide only the most simple of doctoral dissertations. With the increasing emphasis on accountability, there is an urgent need to develop applied research methodology in community research. From such research viable recreation training programs can develop and sensitive program effectiveness measures can evolve.

COMMUNITY RECREATION ACTIVITIES

To help stimulate progam development in the area of community recreation for the developmentally disabled, diversified listings of potential activities might prove useful. Based on the variety of recreational activities enjoyed by normal individuals in the community, several lists of activities are presented below. These activities are presented in the areas of physical, cultural, social, outdoor education, and mental recreation.

By encouraging the development of a multitude of recreation opportunities for the developmentally disabled, we hope to emphasize the unique role that recreation participation can play in enriching the life of each individual. As normal individuals choose to participate in community recreation events that satisfy personal interests (e.g., camping to get away from it all), so should the developmentally disabled have that same opportunity. For these individuals to have this opportunity, recreational activities must be available to them. They must have the technical and social skills to participate, and they must receive some benefit from their participation. If all of these conditions are ensured, the developmentally disabled population would then have the opportunity to select or omit recreational outlets that best suit their needs. In a subsequent section of this chapter, suggested steps for meeting each condition are outlined.

Many of the activities that are listed as community recreation actually could be enjoyed at home or in the community. Because the emphasis of this chapter is on community recreation resources, it is our intention that each activity be considered as occurring away from one's residence. Furthermore, most activities are listed in a single recreation category but easily could be listed multicategorically. For instance, participation in a team sport could be listed as physical recreation as well as social recreation.

Physical Activities

Exercise is a very important activity from both a health and a recreational perspective. Physical activities are some of the most common ways in which community members interact together. For both a healthy and an enjoyable combination it is hard to beat participation in physical recreation activities. These activities may consist of individual, dual, or team events.

Physical fitness activities are enjoyed by millions, both individually and in the company of others. Table 6.2 presents a listing of potential physical fitness activites. With the increasing

Table 6.2. Physical fitness activities

Body mechanics	Roadwork
Calisthenics	Royal Canadian Air Force
Circuit training	Program (RCAF 5BX
Climbing training	and 10BX)
Isometric exercises	Rope skipping
Jogging	Swimming
Medicine ball	Walking
activities	Weight training
Obstacle course	Yoga

popularity of jogging clubs and exercise groups, physical fitness may become more of a social recreation event in the future. Group participation may also provide additional incentives for individuals to maintain physical fitness routines. Community settings in which physical fitness activities may be conducted include local parks, health spas, YMCAs, and YWCAs.

There are a variety of other individual events that involve vigorous physical activity. Some of these might be competitive, while others are simply participated in for fun. In Table 6.3 several of these individual sport activities are presented. Many communities have teams or clubs made up of individuals interested in a particular sport activity, e.g., archery club. These teams or clubs might provide an excellent integrated setting for developmentally disabled participants.

As communities have expanded the variety of sporting events that are available for all residents, the possibilities for including the developmentally disabled have been increased. Both dual and team sport activities should be made available. Tables 6.4 and 6.5 provide the reader with a detailed listing of dual and team sports. For each dual event, team competition could result by combining several individual participants and totaling a team score, e.g., tennis team.

Table 6.3. Individual sports activities

Archery	Punching bag activities
Baton twirling	Roller skating
Bicycling	Skiing
Diving	Swimming
Frizbee tossing	Track and field events
Hiking	Trampoline jumping
Horseback riding	Walking
Ice skating	Water skiing
Judo	Weight training
Karate	Wheelchair racing
Kite flying	

Table 6.4. Dual sporting events (individual or team activity)

Badminton	Jarts
Billiards	Loop tennis
Bocci	Marbles
Bowling	Miniature golf
Boxing	Paddle ball
Clock golf	Paddle handball
Croquet	Paddle tennis
Curling	Pool
Darts	Ring toss
Deck tennis	Roquet
Fencing	Shuffleboard
Golf	Squash racquets
Gymnastics	Table tennis
Handball	Tennis
Hopscotch	Tetherball
Horseshoes	

The composition of the teams could be segregated by disability or integrated. In a similar fashion the competition between teams could vary from being between only developmentally disabled teams to competition with all normal teams.

D'Alonzo (1976) reviewed the status of the rights of exceptional children to participate in interscholastic athletics and concluded that many are legally excluded from participation on the regular high school teams. Recommendations from D'Alonzo's (1976) review were to remove exclusionary barriers that prevent integrated team participation and also to develop a range of alternatives for those individuals unable to make the regular high school teams.

Normal individuals have long enjoyed the benefits of active participation in sporting events, while the developmentally disabled have been excluded. By providing appropriate instruction in physical activities, removing exclusionary clauses preventing integration, and developing a range of participation alternatives, the chances that a developmentally disabled person will become involved in a personally satisfying physical recreation experience are maximized.

Table 6.5. Team sport activities

Baseball	Lacrosse
Basketball	Rugby
Dodgeball	Soccer
Floor hockey	Softball
Football (tackle, touch, flag)	Stickball
	T-ball
Hockey	Volleyball
Kickball	Water polo

Cultural Activities

Arts and crafts, dancing, music, and theater are all activities that people enjoy during their free time as both participants and observers. From such involvement individuals can experience a sense of accomplishment and enhanced feelings of self-worth. Furthermore, many cultural activities provide one with the opportunity for creative expression through active participation.

Table 6.6 lists several arts and crafts activities that developmentally disabled persons might find interesting. Adult education classes, church clubs, and local craft guilds are but a few of the community settings in which arts and crafts can be enjoyed.

According to CEC and AAHPER publication (1966), the potential benefits from participation in arts and crafts programs include the following:

1. Development of new skills and hobbies
2. Construction of objects of usefulness and beauty
3. Discovery of outlets for the inherent desire to create
4. Relief of nervous tensions and promotion of emotional adjustment
5. Provision of an acceptable outlet for self-expression
6. Gain of personal satisfaction and feelings of achievement and success

Table 6.6. Arts and crafts activities

Basketry	Photography
Batik work	Pottery
Bead craft	Printing
Candle making	Quilting
Carving	Refinishing furniture
Ceramics	Rug making
Clay modeling	Sand craft
Copper enameling and tooling	Sculpturing
	Sewing
Costume jewelry making	Silk screening
Crocheting	Sketching
Drawing	Soap carving
Dressmaking	Stone craft
Embroidery	Tempera painting
Etching	Tie dying
Finger painting	Toy making
Flower arranging	Upholstering
Knitting	Water color painting
Leather craft	Weaving
Metal work	Whittling
Model building	Wood craft
Needlepoint	Woodworking
Oil painting	Yarn craft

Table 6.7. Dramatic activities

Amateur nights	Masquerades
Carnivals	Mimetics
Charades	Minstrel shows
Circuses	Operettas
Dramatic plays	Pantomimes
Fairs	Parades
Festivals	Puppetry
Follies	Variety shows
Impersonations	Vaudeville shows
Marionettes	

Table 6.9. Music activities

Vocal:	Instrumental music:
Barbershop groups	Bands
Caroling	Bugle corps
Choirs	Drum and Fife corps
Choruses	Instrumental playing:
Folk music	Autoharp, drums,
Glee clubs	guitars, harmonica,
Operettas	kazoo, mandolin,
Song contests	percussion instruments,
Whistling groups	ukulele, etc.
	Rhythm bands

If in fact any of these benefits are realized, expansion of arts and crafts experiences for the developmentally disabled is warranted.

Another area in which the developmentally disabled might attain satisfaction is dramatics. A variety of clubs and organizations in most communities regularly sponsor dramatic activities. Table 6.7 presents a listing of suggested dramatic activites that all individuals, including the developmentally disabled, might enjoy. By actively participating in dramatic productions yet another avenue for creative expression would be opened for the developmentally disabled.

Table 6.8 includes a variety of different dances that are major free-time activities for many people. Dancing has always been a popular leisure time activity in our culture, ranging from traditional polkas to today's disco dancing. The atmosphere that surrounds most dance activities is an excellent setting for people to enjoy music and being with each other. Adult education classes, dance clubs, and social clubs are all community organizations through which dance activity might be engaged.

In addition to dance activities, many persons participate in vocal and instrumental music activities (refer to Table 6.9). Several community organizations regularly sponsor vocal and instrumental musical performances. The developmentally disabled might choose to participate in these integrated musical activities or form their own musical groups (see Chapter 8).

As people benefit from active participation in cultural activities, they also can attain a great deal of pleasure from watching others participate. Table 6.10 presents a list of cultural activities that have always been the source of spectator interest. Attendance at community-sponsored cultural presentations would be an excellent way for developmentally disabled persons to both socialize in an integrated setting and benefit from viewing a cultural event.

Social Activities

Virtually all community recreation events can be considered social if involvement requires interaction with other persons. However, certain activities are participated in mainly for the fun of being with other people. Table 6.11 includes several such activities. In each of these the fun of socializing together is a major reason for the activity being enjoyable.

Most communities have several clubs and organizations in which social activities are emphasized. Table 6.12 lists several of these organizations in which developmentally disabled individuals might participate. Although these clubs have a variety of purposes other than social interaction, they do provide a setting in which positive interactions are facilitated. Because the social isolation of the developmentally disabled individual is often a topic of concern, expansions on the development of social interaction opportunities are critically needed.

Table 6.8. Dancing activities

Ballet	Grand marches
Ballroom dancing	Modern dancing
Creative dancing	Polkas
Disco dancing	Square dancing
Eurhythmics	Tap dancing
Folk dancing	

Table 6.10. Spectator cultural activities

Art fairs	Musicals
Art museums	Operas and operettas
Ballet	Parades
Concerts	Plays
Dance recitals	Theater—drama and
Movies	comedy

Table 6.11. Community social activities

Amateur nights	Holiday celebrations
Barbecues	Informal conversations
Bingo	Informal socials
Church activities	Marshmallow roasts
Clubs and organizations (see Table 6.12)	Parties
	Picnics
Dances	Potlucks
Dating	Record Parties
Eating in a restaurant	Scavenger hunts
Field trips	Spectator events
Games (e.g., pinball, bumper pool, pool, billiards, etc.)	Teen centers
	Wiener roasts

Outdoor Education Activities

The natural environment surrounding us has always been a major source of recreational activity and a focal point of study. Outdoor sporting events (e.g., fishing), nature study, and camping are but a few of the many reasons why people have always enjoyed participating in outdoor activities.

The developmentally disabled have been included frequently in supervised camping programs, but little has been done to explore the endless possibilities of their involvement in the variety of other outdoor activities. Table 6.13 provides a list of numerous activities that developmentally disabled persons have only infrequently had the opportunity to enjoy. An expansion of outdoor education opportunities for these individuals should be quite beneficial in providing enjoyment and productive use of leisure time.

Mental Activities

As people enjoy the more physical community recreation activities, e.g., bowling, they may also attain great satisfaction and pleasure out of

Table 6.12. Organized clubs and organizations

Boy's Clubs	Hi Y and Junior Hi Y
Boy Scouts	Junior Red Cross
Brownies	Junior Achievement
Campfire Girls	Neighborhood Houses
Church youth groups	Red Cross
Cub Scouts	Tri Hi Y
Catholic Youth Organizations	Salvation Army
	Settlement houses
Diners Club	Y Teens
Explorer Scouts	YMCA
4-H Clubs	YMHA
Girl's Clubs	YWCA
Girl Scouts	YWHA
Gra-Y	

Table 6.13. Outdoor education and recreation

Animal lore	Hiking
Aquatics (see Table 6.17)	Horseback riding
Backpacking	Hunting
Bait casting	Indian lore
Beach activities	Insect collection and study
Bicycle caravans	
Birdwatching	Landscaping
Boating	Mountain climbing
Campfire cookery	Nature study
Canoeing	Picnics
Day camping	Pioneering
Explorations	Reptile study
Field trips	Residential camping
Fire building	Sledding
Fishing	Tenting
Flower growing	Tobogganing
Fossil hunts and mounting	Trail tours
	Tree study
Gardening	Water skiing

mental activities, e.g., playing chess. Adult education, games, and library events are all mental activities that may be enjoyed in community settings (refer to Table 6.14). Because each person is unique, the range of community recreation activities should be broad enough to include activities of interest to everyone. An expansive lists of "mental" recreation activities should provide something of interest to everyone.

PROGRAM DEVELOPMENT

Although the need for expanded services has been established and a variety of activities has been suggested, community recreation programs for handicapped persons are far from adequate. This seems to be attributable to the fact that community agencies and associations are unsure of how to develop and implement a recreation program designed to meet the needs of developmentally disabled persons. The following section is designed to address a number of areas pertinent to the development and successful implementation of community recreation programs. Specifically, we attempt to provide a systematic approach for

Table 6.14. Mental activities

Adult education classes

Games (e.g., bingo, checkers, chess, monopoly, lotto, old maid, poker, bridge, war, scrabble, etc.)

Hobbies (e.g., collections, photography, plant care, magic tricks, stamp collecting, etc.)

Library activities (e.g., reading, listening to stories, watching movies, poetry reading, etc.)

identifying needs and providing services for developmentally disabled persons within a community structure. The areas to be evaluated and discussed include: 1) program planning, 2) assessment, 3) training and skill development, 4) maintenance and generalization of recreational skills, and 5) future research needs.

Community Recreation
Program Planning—Logistics

Wilson (1974) delineated several steps that communities should follow in developing comprehensive recreation services for the developmentally disabled. These steps are as follows:

1. Determine what the community has done, is doing, and plans to do in recreation for the developmentally disabled. This step should also include identification of the community's developmentally disabled population.
2. Analyze data obtained in Step 1 by continually asking: Who? Why? What? When? Where? and How much?
3. Determine what can be done effectively within the community's recreation structure.
4. Establish goals.
5. Determine priorities.
6. Plan recreational activities, involving consumers and their families in the planning.
7. Develop budgets.
8. Staff development (recruitment, training, assignment, and continuing in-service training).
9. Review existing services again to determine how facilities, equipment, and supplies can be adapted to best meet the needs of the developmentally disabled population.
10. Implement program.
11. Program evaluation to assess effectiveness, and revise program accordingly. After program evaluation, begin again at Step 4 and proceed through the sequence again.

Community Needs Assessment

The first three steps listed above involve a community needs assessment. A needs assessment should include: 1) investigation of the recreation services presently in existence for both normal and developmentally disabled persons, 2) determination of the community's willingness to include developmentally disabled individuals in recreation programs, 3) survey of the professional back-

grounds and attitudes of the personnel working in community recreation, 4) identification of the community recreation activities presently engaged in by the developmentally disabled and those activities in which they would like to participate, and 5) evaluation of the community recreation competencies of the developmentally disabled population.

There are many recreation services in the community that are potentially available to the developmentally disabled. According to Berryman and her associates (1971), these services may be offered by public recreation departments, community centers, commercial organizations, religious organizations, libraries, museums, zoos, youth agencies, camping facilities, hospitals, service clubs, school systems, and military organizations. A thorough analysis of each of these potential recreation resources could provide a catalog of community activities.

At the same time that existing resources are investigated, the willingness of community members to integrate the developmentally disabled into existing programs also should be assessed. This assessment should include the degree of handicap accepted and also the amount of integration tolerable. For instance, some programs might encourage full integration of the mildly handicapped while at the same time rejecting any integration of the severely disabled.

The professional background of the recreation personnel in a given community might provide information regarding the extent of the in-service training that will be necessary. Although a background in therapeutic recreation would be an asset, an individual's desire to learn and willingness to work with the developmentally disabled may be even more important staff characteristics.

With the identification of activities in which developmentally disabled are engaged presently and the activities with which they would like to become involved, the program developer may have useful information from which decisions regarding program expansion and future development can be made. The interests and needs of the population to be served in the community programs should be considered foremost in making programmatic decisions. For the severely developmentally disabled, who are unable to express their recreation interests in a productive fashion, care should be exercised to ensure that they are involved in a recreation program designed appropriately for their needs.

Assessment of the individual's skills necessary to participate in community recreation is very important for program development. If the individual does not have the skills required to bowl, the existence of integrated bowling leagues will do him little good. An expansion of the issues surrounding individual skill assessment follows in a subsequent section.

Goals and Priorities

A thorough analysis of the assessment information obtained in the areas previously discussed should enable the recreation developer to realistically appraise the possibilities for community recreation in a given community. By critically scrutinizing questions such as Who?, Why?, What?, When?, Where?, and How much? initial goals (Step 4) and program priorities (Step 5) can be established. In setting these program priorities the consumers should be integrally involved (Stein, 1977).

Activity Planning

Consumer involvement need not stop at setting program priorities but should continue into the actual planning of recreational activities. The direct consumers (developmentally disabled persons) and their families should be encouraged to take an active role in the planning of the program (Wilson, 1974). By encouraging active participation during the planning stage from those individuals directly affected by the program's success, the chances that the program will best meet the community recreation needs of its developmentally disabled population should be maximized.

If professionals fail to initiate program expansion in community recreation, Berryman, Logan, and Lander (1971) have outlined specific steps that parents can take to assess, plan, and implement activities for the developmentally disabled. When community program development is at issue, no one can deny the powerful force that parent groups have exercised in the development of much needed services. Often the parents have moved well ahead of the professional community in securing programs for their disabled children.

Budget Development

In addition to involving significant community members in program planning, e.g., consumers, parents, recreation directors, detailed attention must be given to the many components involved.

Budgets must be developed to account for the many variables included in community recreation services, e.g., transportation, staff, supplies, facilities, etc.

Table 6.15 is a suggested budgetary procedure for community recreation services which was taken from Wilson (1974). For particular high cost items in a budget, e.g., staff and transportation, communities might choose to take advantage of the variety of volunteer organizations that could provide these services free of charge (Pomeroy, 1974). With an expanded public relations network (Cappel, 1974), the possibilities for recruiting volunteer staff are enhanced. Such public relations activity may also secure material donations that would assist in program development and implementation.

Staff Development

Personnel development has been a long standing concern of those working in community recreation (Lancaster, 1976). Such development must include recruitment, training, assignment, and continuing in-service. Wilson (1974) suggested that students from special education, physical education, recreation, therapeutic recreation, social work, and general education could be excellent resources for staff recruitment. Although a technical background in the area of recreation and/or special education is desirable, the necessity of an empathetic positive attitude cannot be underestimated.

Along with recruitment the training of staff persons in pre-service and in-service programs is an essential aspect of staff development. The content of these training programs has been a source of much controversy. In 1975 Stein surveyed professional physical education and community recreation personnel in an attempt to determine critical professional competencies, academic degree level, and practical experiences that are essential for community recreation program implementation. Based on Stein's (1977) survey the following conclusions were offered: 1) the ability to work with individuals and groups of both handicapped and nonhandicapped is essential; 2) since cooperative efforts between disciplines are essential for integrating recreational experiences, interpersonnel skill training for professionals should be included; 3) personnel need to appreciate the learning potential of the mentally retarded; 4) a minimum of a B.A. should be required with background in regular physical

Table 6.15. Budgetary procedures

Budgets

Knowing the size of the community, the scope of the program, the demands for service, the quantity and quality of program objectives, the number of handicapped individuals to be served, and the staff already interested and capable of working will help in determining funding requests.

The budgetary (funding) request should indicate:

1. The name of the sponsoring agency or department having responsibility for the program
2. The period of time the budget encompasses
3. A brief statement of the general aims
4. A statement of specific program objectives
5. A statement about staffing and in-service education
6. A statement regarding the seasonal (or year-round) aspects
7. What provision will be made for staff training and for volunteer service and training
8. What specific facilities, supplies, and equipment will be used
9. What responsibilities other members of the "team" will have
10. The dates, days, and hours when the activities will be conducted
11. How the children are to be transported
12. What handicaps will be accepted
13. What age groups and sexes will be accepted
14. How many handicapped will be served on the basis of the funding request
15. Possibilities of supplementary funds from parents of participants, grants, gifts, and other sources
16. How the program will be evaluated and who is to evaluate it
17. The grand total of the dollar request

The summary of the items listed ought not to take more than two typed pages, single spaced

A third page should indicate the program category, breakdown, amount, and total. An example follows:

Category	Breakdown	Amount	Total
Activity	Administration		
	Supervision		
	Leadership		
	In-service education		
	Clerical service (this item should include the number of persons, expected hours of service, and the proposed hourly rate)		
	Also include the number of volunteers and estimated value of their service		
Transportation	Number of bus trips at cost per trip		
Plant operation	Costs of engineer/fireman or janitorial/custodial service on a per hour basis		
	Costs of heat, light, and other plant operation costs, building supplies		
Fixed charges	Costs of insurance, employees' fringe benefits, unemployment compensation, etc.		
Subtotal			

A fourth page should indicate:

Category	Breakdown	Amount	Total
Equipment	Proposed items of nonexpendable equipment needed		
Supplies	Proposed needs for expendables in physical, cultural, social, and special activities item by item		
	Proposed costs of food- or drink-associated items		
	Costs of testing and evaluation forms, mimeographing, etc.		
Subtotal			

Adapted from Wilson (1974).

education to acquaint personnel with the variety of recreation activities available for all persons; and 5) personnel should be involved in practical experiences at an early time in their educational career in order to gain exposure to the handicapped in a recreation setting.

Specific professional skills that have proved valuable in teaching recreation skills to the severely developmentally disabled are task analysis and behavior-shaping techniques. These skills have been utilized to teach behaviors as basic as performing a sit up to those as complex as dining in a formal restaurant.

Another competency that should prove to be increasingly valuable is program evaluation. With the recent emphasis on accountability and the constant problem of tight budgets, the ability to document the effectiveness of a community recreation program through applied research would be quite helpful.

Training programs for community recreation personnel should be designed to meet each of the above mentioned skill areas. Many skills could be taught in pre-service academic programs, while others may be more appropriately taught during in-service training. With the constant changes that community programs must endure, a dynamic in-service component can best ensure that personnel are equipped to meet those changes.

In addition to professional preparation programs, each community must accommodate the training needs of the many volunteer and part-time staff that they utilize. As community recreation for the developmentally disabled expands, the development of innovative personnel preparation programs in this area would be quite helpful.

Review and Adaptation

Before implementing the recreation program, the community's resources should be reviewed again to determine how adaptation of these services can best meet the needs of the developmentally disabled. According to Wilson (1974) "adaptation" is the key word in recreation. Through adaptation of staff, facilities, program, activities, equipment, and budget, sensitive responses to the special needs of the handicapped can be made. For the more severely disabled, more adaptation will be required than for the mildly disabled.

Program Implementation and Evaluation

After community recreation programs have been implemented, steps should be taken to ensure periodic evaluation of program effectiveness. Recreation program research should be conducted to investigate specific recreation skill training sequences, the effect of recreation involvement on other behaviors, e.g., self-concept, and the effects of integrated recreation programs composed of different mixtures of developmentally disabled and normals.

Both single-subject research designs and group designs could be used in recreation research. One particular single-subject design that has been used effectively is the multiple baseline (e.g., Wehman and Marchant, 1977). With the multiple baseline the effect of a program contingency is demonstrated by introducing a contingency at different points in time. If behavior change is associated consistently with the introduction of the contingency, a multiple baseline demonstration of program effectiveness will have been evidenced (Kazdin, 1975). This design is applicable across recreation behaviors (e.g., jogging, calisthenics, weight lifting), individuals (e.g., Jack, Betty, Bill), and situations (e.g., community recreation center, public park, YMCA). An advantage of this particular design is that program contingencies do not have to be reversed; they only have to be administered sequentially to demonstrate program effectiveness. As a result, program gains do not have to be lost in order to provide support for program contingencies.

The multiple baseline can also be applied to groups of individuals by summing their scores and treating the group as a single entity. For example, a group's participation in several different community recreation activities could be recorded. After a period of time, positive contingencies could be applied to the group's participation in one of these activities. If participation in this activity increased when the contingencies were implemented and if subsequent activities were similarly influenced by the contingencies, a multiple baseline demonstration of the program's effectiveness will have been evidenced.

The changing criterion is another single-subject design which might be useful in programs designed to increase frequency, rate, or duration of particular recreation behaviors. This design demonstrates the effect of a contingency by showing that behavior matches a criterion set for reinforcement (Kazdin, 1975). For physical skills such as jogging and weight lifting this design might prove particularly appropriate because it allows for the gradual shaping of increased performance. Groups of individuals could also be included in changing criterion contingencies.

Group designs relying on parametric and non-parametric statistics have been used widely in applied educational areas but have been used only infrequently to verify recreation program success. Campbell and Stanley (1963) have provided an excellent reference that should assist the community recreation researcher in selecting designs appropriate for specific research questions.

For sophisticated program evaluation to be conducted, money must be allocated and personnel must be trained for research purposes. Based on program evaluation information a program could be revised accordingly so as to improve services. Program evaluation could also be used to document successful efforts, the findings of which could be disseminated to assist other communities in developing recreation programs. In the future, data-based documentation of program success may be necessary for funding on the federal, state, and local levels.

Each of the above program planning steps and the related discussion should contribute toward a well organized community recreation program for the developmentally disabled. By attending to the details and logistics of the overall program plan, the success of the program can be ensured. In addition to the development of an organizational plan, specific attention must be given to individual programming concerns. These concerns include assessment, training, and transfer of training.

CLIENT ASSESSMENT

It was stated previously that community recreation programs should be tailored to the individual needs of each participant (e.g., Pomeroy, 1974). This can only be accomplished through the use of assessment procedures designed to identify individual performance levels and interests. However, because of the availability of standardized measurement instruments, educators frequently emphasize norms and standard scores rather than the skills and gains of the individual (Stein, 1977). Unfortunately standard scores do not provide recreation personnel with information pertinent to instruction. Therefore, the use of these instruments is at best questionable.

Stein (1977) has suggested that the use of an evaluative device is justified primarily in the way it facilitates instruction. Because of the diversity of skills of developmentally disabled persons, a variety of criterion-referenced assessment procedures may facilitate effective programming.

Competency Checklists and Interest Inventories

Initial assessment procedures should provide program personnel with data regarding an individual's general skill level and interests. Competency checklists and informal interest inventories may serve these purposes adequately. Table 6.16 presents a representative sample of a general competency checklist in a number of areas specifically related to community recreation. A more detailed checklist can be utilized for specific recreational activities (see Table 6.17).

In addition to, or as a part of, initial assessment procedures, it is important to obtain information regarding the type of program (e.g., integrated with normal peers, maintenance, or skill development) best suited for the individual. This can be accomplished by requiring responses to checklists that indicate the specific skill level of each participant. For example, a choice of the following responses would provide this needed information: 1) *Can't do,* 2) *Can do, but doesn't do consistently,* and 3) *Does do consistently.* A *Can't do* response would indicate to recreation program staff that a skill development program would be most appropriate for the individual in this area. A response indicating that the individual can perform a skill but is not consistent may indicate a motivational problem, and therefore an incentive program may be most appropriate. Finally, a *Does do* response would suggest that the developmentally disabled individual has the skills and uses them when given the opportunity. Therefore, an ongoing, possibly integrated program in the area assessed would be an appropriate placement for this individual.

Informal interest inventories may be especially useful in identifying appropriate placements for mildly handicapped persons. It is important, however, that these idividuals have had an adequate sampling of a number of activities so that their responses reflect genuine interest in some activities over others. If the number of recreational experiences has been limited, their choices may only reflect a lack of knowledge of the opportunities available. For individuals who have

Table 6.16. General competency checklist for assessment of recreation skills

Name _____   Date: Pretest _____

Posttest _____

Can't do	Can do	Does do	
			Mobility
————	————	————	Controlled movement in group activity—stop, starting, jumping
————	————	————	Skilled runner—uses cross pattern
————	————	————	Alternately hops from one foot to the other one
————	————	————	Balances on one foot, eyes closed
————	————	————	Jumps from standing position, feet together, and lands on both feet
————	————	————	Hops forward on one foot
————	————	————	Balances on preferred foot, eyes open
————	————	————	Jumps over obstacle
————	————	————	Walks alone
————	————	————	Stands alone
————	————	————	Ambulatory
————	————	————	*Total*
			Manual Ball Skills (12-inch softball—soft)
————	————	————	Throwing: throws, stepping with foot opposite throwing arm, with proper weight shift
————	————	————	Catching: consistently catches ball using two hands
————	————	————	Hitting: able to hit pitched ball consistently with bat (using playground sport ball)
————	————	————	Throwing: throws, stepping with foot opposite throwing arm, with proper weight shift (15–20 feet)
————	————	————	Catching: consistently catches ball thrown directly (without bounce)
			Hitting
————	————	————	With bat
————	————	————	With hand
————	————	————	With feet
————	————	————	Catches a playground sport ball bounced to him
————	————	————	Throws a ball
————	————	————	Kicks or hits a ball
————	————	————	Catches and throws playground ball that is swinging from rope
————	————	————	Touches or hits ball that is swinging from rope
————	————	————	Stops rolling ball with feet or with hands
————	————	————	Rolls ball on floor
————	————	————	Grasps ball
————	————	————	Watches moving ball—rolled, tossed, kicked
————	————	————	*Total*
			Manual Dexterity
————	————	————	Models recognizable forms in clay
————	————	————	Prints name
————	————	————	Ability to draw
————	————	————	Coloring
————	————	————	Scribbling
————	————	————	Some form either within lines or free
————	————	————	Recognizable figures
————	————	————	Painting
————	————	————	Draws recognizable face
————	————	————	Cutting with scissors
————	————	————	Snipping
————	————	————	Cutting on a line
————	————	————	Cutting a shape
————	————	————	Free cutting
————	————	————	Pasting
————	————	————	Pasting object
————	————	————	Target paste or simple shapes

Table 6.16. (continued)

Can't do	Can do	Does do	
_____	_____	_____	Stringing large beads
_____	_____	_____	Puts circles, squares, triangles in form board
_____	_____	_____	Imitates vertical and then horizontal line
_____	_____	_____	Builds tower of three blocks
_____	_____	_____	Marks with pencil or crayon held in fist (might scribble)
_____	_____	_____	*Total*
			Language Competency
_____	_____	_____	Communicates ideas meaningfully
_____	_____	_____	Reads with understanding
_____	_____	_____	Listens and retains what he hears
_____	_____	_____	Enjoys dramatic plays
_____	_____	_____	Enjoys table games
_____	_____	_____	Can count to 100 by 1s and by 10s
_____	_____	_____	Able to recall a story or a song
_____	_____	_____	Knows basic colors
_____	_____	_____	Knows primary colors
_____	_____	_____	Enjoys listening to stories
_____	_____	_____	Ability to recognize written names and signs
_____	_____	_____	Knows own sex
_____	_____	_____	Can count from 1 to 10
_____	_____	_____	Recognizes his spoken name
_____	_____	_____	Knows meaning of "yes" and "no"
_____	_____	_____	Verbalizes his needs
_____	_____	_____	*Total*
			Social Interaction
_____	_____	_____	Exercises self-control
_____	_____	_____	Forms close personal friendships
_____	_____	_____	Plays organized group games
_____	_____	_____	Strives for social acceptance
_____	_____	_____	Associative group play
_____	_____	_____	Gets along well with other children
_____	_____	_____	Plays well with one playmate
_____	_____	_____	Shows cooperation
_____	_____	_____	Postpones gratification for later reward
_____	_____	_____	Some parallel play
_____	_____	_____	Plays by himself
_____	_____	_____	Socially responsible to adults and other children
_____	_____	_____	Onlooker or plays alone
_____	_____	_____	Plays with one child
_____	_____	_____	Plays with two children
_____	_____	_____	Plays with more than two children
_____	_____	_____	Unprovoked aggressiveness
			Friendly or affectionate
_____	_____	_____	Toward child
_____	_____	_____	Toward adult
_____	_____	_____	Cries, whines
_____	_____	_____	Smiles, laughs
			Seeks help, attention
_____	_____	_____	From child
_____	_____	_____	From adult
			Rejects help, attention
_____	_____	_____	From child
_____	_____	_____	From adult
_____	_____	_____	Hands at face
_____	_____	_____	Other self-conscious habits
			Talking with children
_____	_____	_____	Asks questions

Table 6.16. (continued)

Can't do	Can do	Does do	
————	————	————	Makes commands
————	————	————	General talk
————	————	————	Responds to commands
————	————	————	Responds to questions
————	————	————	Responds to general talk
			Talking with adults
————	————	————	Makes commands
————	————	————	Asks questions
————	————	————	General talk
————	————	————	Responds to commands/instructions
————	————	————	Responds to general talk
————	————	————	Responds to questions
————	————	————	*Total*
			Self-Image
————	————	————	Shows perseverance despite failure
————	————	————	Identifies right and left while facing other people
————	————	————	Shows self-confidence
————	————	————	Makes accurate judgments of self
————	————	————	Understands concepts in relation to self
————	————	————	Shows self-motivation
————	————	————	Understands body planes (front, back, side, etc.)
————	————	————	Shows appropriate emotional responses
			Identifies body parts
————	————	————	Head
————	————	————	Feet
————	————	————	Arms
————	————	————	Hands
————	————	————	Fingers
————	————	————	Toes
————	————	————	Face
————	————	————	Knees
————	————	————	*Total*
			Grand Total Score
————	————	————	Mobility
————	————	————	Manual Ball Skills
————	————	————	Manual Dexterity
————	————	————	Language Competency
————	————	————	Social Interaction
————	————	————	Self-Image
————	————	————	*Total Score*

Adapted from Wilson (1974).

not participated previously in community recreation, program staff may wish to encourage active participation in a number of different activities to cultivate interests and facilitate the ability to exercise a choice.

Task Analytic Assessment

Characteristic of many developmentally disabled individuals, especially the more severely handicapped, is their lack of recreational skills. The utilization of general assessment instruments, e.g., checklists and inventories may only identify areas of difficulty. It does not, however, provide educators with information regarding specific behavioral deficits. Severely handicapped persons may have a very limited leisure skill repertoire. Therefore, it is necessary to identify exactly where learning breaks down so that effective training programs can be developed. This will facilitate the acquisition of skills prerequisite to successful participation in community recreation.

Assessment procedures via task analysis provide this pertinent information. Task analysis consists of breaking down a specific recreational skill into

Table 6.17. Competency checklist for swimming activities

Name _____ Date _____

Can't do	Can do	Does do	
			Preswim Activities
			Undresses self
_____	_____	_____	Shirt or dress
_____	_____	_____	Pants
_____	_____	_____	Socks
_____	_____	_____	Shoes
_____	_____	_____	Puts on suit
_____	_____	_____	Showers
			Swim Activities
			Entrance into the water
_____	_____	_____	Down the steps
_____	_____	_____	Over the side
			Adjustment to the water
_____	_____	_____	Walks in water
_____	_____	_____	Washes face
_____	_____	_____	Places face in water
_____	_____	_____	Holds breath
_____	_____	_____	Blows bubbles
_____	_____	_____	Retrieves ring
_____	_____	_____	Sits on bottom
_____	_____	_____	Turtle floats
_____	_____	_____	Front floats
			Prone swimming
_____	_____	_____	Floats prone without aid
_____	_____	_____	Kicks at side of pool
_____	_____	_____	Kicks at side of pool, face in water
_____	_____	_____	Glides
_____	_____	_____	Glides with kick
_____	_____	_____	Flutter kick and front crawl arms
_____	_____	_____	Rhythmic breathing at side of pool
_____	_____	_____	Complete front crawl
			Supine swimming
_____	_____	_____	Walks backward
_____	_____	_____	Back floats
_____	_____	_____	Glides
_____	_____	_____	Kick glide
_____	_____	_____	Elementary back, arms
_____	_____	_____	Elementary back, legs
_____	_____	_____	Complete elementary back
			Deep water adjustment
_____	_____	_____	Hangs at side
_____	_____	_____	Bobbing
_____	_____	_____	Walks ladder to bottom and up
_____	_____	_____	Walks ladder to bottom and kick up
_____	_____	_____	Treading
_____	_____	_____	20-Yard swim front crawl
_____	_____	_____	20-Yard swim on back
_____	_____	_____	Jumps in
_____	_____	_____	Sitting dive
_____	_____	_____	Kneeling dive
_____	_____	_____	Standing dive
			Advanced skills (20-Yard stroke swim)
_____	_____	_____	Scissors kick
_____	_____	_____	Side stroke, arms
_____	_____	_____	Complete side stroke
_____	_____	_____	Prone frog kick
_____	_____	_____	Breast stroke, arms
_____	_____	_____	Complete breast stroke
_____	_____	_____	Back crawl, arms

Table 6.17.   (continued)

Can't do	Can do	Does do	
————	————	————	Complete back crawl
————	————	————	Surface dive
————	————	————	Underwater swim
			Survival swimming
————	————	————	Extension rescue
————	————	————	Disrobing
————	————	————	Clothing flotation
			Postswim Activities
			Leaves pool
————	————	————	Up the ladder
————	————	————	Over the side
————	————	————	Showers self
			Dresses self
————	————	————	Shirt
————	————	————	Pants
————	————	————	Socks
————	————	————	Shoes on
————	————	————	Shoes tied

Adapted from Wilson (1975).

its component behaviors. Task analytic assessment involves evaluating an individual's performance on each of these component behaviors. This should indicate exactly where the individual is competent and at what point his behavior is inadequate for successful performance. The recreational skills assessed via task analysis may be as simple as ball rolling (see Table 6.18) or as complex as community bus riding and ordering dinner at a McDonald's restaurant (see Tables 6.19 and 6.20). The assessment procedure itself consists merely of recording a plus (+) when a component step is completed successfully or a minus (−) when it is incorrectly performed.

Appropriate and adequate task analytic assessment involves the development of each task analysis before the assessment of an individual's skills. This should include natural verification of the component steps involved in successful task completion. It is also important to obtain data on each step in the task over trials. A one-trial assessment of an individual's skills may not be representative of what he is actually capable of doing. Therefore, assessment via task analysis should be conducted a number of times so as to enable an adequate evaluation of skill level. It is evident that evaluating skill level utilizing task analytic procedures provides recreation specialists with information directly related to instruction.

TRAINING AND SKILL DEVELOPMENT

The development of community-based recreation programs should be a direct result of a needs assessment and evaluation of the individual skill levels of the developmentally disabled persons to be served. Community recreation services designed to serve a wide range of disabilities will most likely involve a number of different training and skill development programs. As was stated previously, program participants should be encouraged to take part in integrated programs designed for "normal" community residents when possible and sheltered programs when necessary (e.g., Wilson, 1974).

A cohesive program designed to meet the needs of this wide range of skill levels should involve transitional movement from segregated, restrictive activities to integrated, nonrestrictive activites. Therefore, severely developmentally disabled persons who lack the basic skills prerequisite to involvement in organized or group activities may best be served in sheltered, individualized training programs, while mildly handicapped persons who have demonstrated high levels of skills may benefit most by involvement in integrated programs that maximize contact with normal peer models.

As a result of this wide range of recreational needs, community recreation programs must

Table 6.18. Task analysis: Assessment of ball throwing

Record plus (+) for correct completion of a step in the task analysis and minus (−) for incorrect step completion.

Date

Task components														
Name _____														
Month _____ Team _____														
Program _____														
1. Child sits on mat.														
2. Child holds ball in front of body with fingers.														
3. Child's body is facing direction of target person.														
4. Child brings arms back to side of body.														
5. Ball is released by extending fingers with palm of hand facing target person.														
6. Child rolls ball through extension of arms.														
7. Ball is rolled to target person 1 foot away.														
8. Ball is rolled to target person 2 feet away.														
9. Ball is rolled to target person 3 feet away.														
10. Ball is rolled to target person 4 feet away.														
11. Ball is rolled to target person 5 feet away.														
12. Ball is rolled to target person 6 feet away.														
13. Ball is rolled to target person 7 feet away.														
14. Ball is rolled to target person 8 feet away.														

Task analysis reprinted from Wehman and Marchant (1977), by permission.

develop specific services designed to facilitate recreational involvement at many different levels. These services may be as simple as information centers that are designed to inform mildly disabled persons of the existing recreation programs available within the community. Information centers may also employ staff to contact integrated recreation programs about the possibilities of referring mildly disabled individuals for participation.

More involved services may consist of providing sheltered programs that are designed specifically for developmentally disabled participants. These sheltered programs may employ volunteers to serve as normal peer models for the developmentally disabled participants. Thus, the developmentally disabled and their normal peer volunteers may venture into the community to engage in the activities available.

Developmentally disabled individuals who are severely/profoundly handicapped may require very structured specific training programs designed to teach skills considered prerequisite to placement within less restrictive community recreation programs. These individuals, although they usually are not equipped to handle existing community activities without instruction, should always be taught with transition in mind. The ultimate goal of any recreation program must be movement into a less restrictive, more normative setting (Wolfensberger, 1972).

The type of program (integrated or segregated) should be determined by the specific needs of the individual. Consequently any one person may be involved in a number of different types of programs at any one time. For example, a developmentally disabled adult may have the social skills and/or physical ability to participate in a city bowling league with his normal peers but may require more structure and training to participate in swimming activities. Therefore, an appropriate swimming program may be one that is segregated and highly structured with the pupose of teaching rudimentary water skills.

Task Analysis and Skill Development

Assessment of skills via task analysis is related directly to instructional sequencing and skill

Table 6.19. Task analysis: Assessment of bus-riding skills

Record plus ($+$) for correct completion of a step in the task analysis and minus ($-$) for incorrect step completion.

Date

Name_____																		
Month_____Team_____																		
Program_____																		

Task components

1. Verbally states public transportation fare (25 cents, quarter).																			
2. Verbally states where to meet bus (e.g., Waverly Hall).																			
3. Verbally states time bus arrives (e.g., 3:30–3:40).																			
4. Arrives at correct bus stop (on steps).																			
5. Arrives at correct bus stop by 3:40.																			
6. Stands in clear view of bus as it approaches (on any of first four steps of building).																			
7. Verbally states at least one characteristic of bus (e.g., yellow).																			
9. Has bus fare (25 cents or one dollar).																			
10. Waits turn (gets in line) when boarding bus.																			
11. Fails to engage in incompatible behavior when boarding bus (e.g., stopping to talk to rider blocking aisleway).																			
12. Has exact bus fare (25 cents or one dollar).																			
13. Deposits exact fare in bus driver's hand.																			
14. Asks driver for bus's destination.																			
15. Sits in first empty double or single seat available.																			
16. Sits facing front of bus with two feet on floor.																			
17. Gets up within 10 seconds of clear aisle to depart.																			
18. Gets off bus without engaging in incompatible behavior (e.g., talking with driver and blocking aisle).																			
19. Asks driver for time of return trip.																			
20. Produces and stashes 25 cents for return bus trip.																			

Task analysis reprinted from Marholin et al. (1977), by permission.

development. As was indicated previously, a specific task analytic assessment should identify the task behaviors that have been mastered as well as an individual's skill deficits.

The success of teaching procedures based upon the analysis of task components has been attributed to a number of factors. Besides facilitating functional assessment, task analysis permits and encourages individualized instruction. Furthermore, instructional sequences based upon

Table 6.20. Task analysis: Assessment of restaurant (McDonald's) skills

Record plus (+) for correct completion of a step in the task analysis and minus (−) for incorrect step completion.

Date

Task components																	
Name_____ Month_____Team_____ Program_____																	
1. Verbal response to "What do we do when we get through shopping?"																	
2. Verbal response to "Where do we eat?" (McDonald's)																	
3. Verbal response to "When should we be there?" (5:00 p.m.)																	
4. Verbal response to "What do you want to eat?" (at least one main course)																	
5. Verbal response to "How much money will it cost?" (to nearest dollow in excess of exact cost)																	
6. Locates McDonald's (stops within 5 feet for at least 5 seconds).																	
7. Enters McDonald's.																	
8. Gets in line at functional cash register.																	
9. Remains in line until pays.																	
10. States what he wants (at least one main course) to waitress.																	
11. Makes himself understood (defined by waitress's correct response).																	
12. Holds other things in hand or puts them at a table.																	
13. Holds money and wallet in hand while items are rung up.																	
14. Takes appropriate amount of money to nearest dollar in excess of exact cost out of wallet.																	
15. Waits (physically oriented toward cashier) until transaction is completed.																	
16. Holds out hand to receive change from cashier.																	
17. Picks up tray.																	
18. Picks up napkin.																	
19. Selects table (pointing or verbal response).																	
20. Sits at table.																	
21. Uses napkin at least once during meal.																	
22. Puts all items (garbage) on tray at end of meal.																	
23. Takes and empties tray into garbage receptacle.																	

Task analysis reprinted from Marholin et al. (1977), by permission.

task analysis promote replication and consistency. Finally, task analysis facilitates program evaluation through frequent (daily or weekly) probe checks that are conducted in the same manner as initial task analytic assessment procedures.

Instruction based upon task analysis consists of using shaping, prompting, and modeling procedures to facilitate correct performance of each component behavior involved in task completion. It is, however, very important to allow the learner to complete each step with as little assistance or interference as possible. This will encourage independent performance and, consequently, will facilitate success. In addition, reinforcement for correct performance is an integral part of any instructional sequence. Especially for recreational activities, an enjoyable and rewarding experience is essential and will result in the increased likelihood of an individual's future participation in that activity.

Recreational skill development programs have utilized task analytic instructional techniques to develop a variety of skills. Nietupski and Williams (1974) employed task analysis and skill sequencing in teaching developmentally disabled individuals to use the telephone to initiate recreational activities with peers (see Chapter 1). Community bowling skills can be taught via task analytic instruction (see Table 6.21), as can basic recreational activities that do not require interactional skills.

MAINTENANCE AND GENERALIZATION OF RECREATIONAL SKILLS

Once an individual has demonstrated the ability to engage successfully in recreational activities within one setting, it should not be assumed that he will engage in those activities in other settings or continue to participate in community recreation after successful completion of a training program. Frequently behavior of the developmentally disabled is situation specific and does not occur under different circumstances or in different settings unless systematic transitioning is planned (Wehman, 1977b). However, there are a number of steps community recreation staff can take that will increase the likelihood of developmentally disabled persons using skills in various settings as well as continuing to engage in community recreation after formal training has been terminated.

Family Involvement

Many developmentally disabled individuals maintain residence with their families. Therefore, including a family component in community recreation programs may be one method of maintaining and/or increasing generalization of community recreation skills. Recreation programs may incorporate a weekly family night or occasional family activities (e.g., Saturday afternoon swimming, a picnic, community outings, shopping trips) so as to involve family members in recreational activities with their developmentally disabled children. Information regarding the objec-

Table 6.21.   Sample task analysis and skill sequence for teaching bowling

1. Push basketball from left or right side, while standing stationary, toward three pins 10 feet away.
2. Same as number 1, pins 15 feet away.
3. Same as number 2, using soccer ball.
4. Same as number 3, using 12-inch softball and six pins.
5. Same as number 4, using 14-inch softball.
6. Hold ball at waist, step forward with left foot, roll ball.
7. Step forward with right, then left foot, roll ball.
8. Same as number 7, pins 20 feet away.
9. Same as number 8, pins 25 feet away.
10. Same as number 9, pins 30 feet away.
11. Same as number 10, pins 35 feet away.
12. Same as number 11, pins 40 feet away.
13. Use very light (5-pound), small bowling ball—six pins at 40 feet.
14. Same as number 13—paint or tape "gutter" lines 60 inches apart between which student must keep ball.
15. Same as number 14, gutter lines 50 inches aparts.
16. Same as number 15, gutter lines 40 inches apart.
17. Use bowling alley, light ball at 40 feet—10 pins.
18. Same as number 17, at 45 feet.
19. Same as number 18, at 50 feet.
20. Same as number 19, at 55 feet.
21. Same as number 20, at 62 feet plus (foul line).
22–25+. Increase ball size and weight, gradually, to at least 8 pounds.
26–30+. Add two steps to delivery to develop a 4-step delivery.

Task analysis reprinted from Sengstock and Jens (1974), by permission.

Numbers 1 through 16 can be taught in a gym, on a playground or lawn, or even in a hall if the noise will not interfere with other programs.

tives of the program should be made available to family members, as should invitations to visit, observe, and take part in training programs.

Recreation staff may have to seek out family members actively by making contacts by phone or visiting homes. Although this may be costly and time consuming, the result of family participation should be quite beneficial. Providing families with opportunities to engage in enjoyable and rewarding activities together should enhance family interaction and maintain the involvement of developmentally disabled individuals in community functions. Furthermore, through in-service and information-giving sessions, family members may become aware of the opportunities within the community and the importance of recreation in the lives of developmentally disabled individuals (Hitzhusen, 1975). Parents and siblings may provide the encouragement and reinforcement necessary for the continued participation of their developmentally disabled members in community activities.

Enhancing Generalization of Skills

Characteristic of developmentally disabled persons is the fact that behaviors that are acquired in one environment do not occur when the environmental conditions have been altered significantly (Wehman, 1977b). For example, an individual who has learned to order lunch at a particular restaurant may not know what to do in the same restaurant when the shape and color of the menu have been changed. Therefore, community recreation programs must provide experiences that maximize the generalization of skills to varied situations and in the presence of unfamiliar people.

This can be accomplished by varying the training conditions as well as the people in the training environment. It should not be assumed, for example, that an individual is able to use all telephones because he has demonstrated the ability to use the telephone in the community YMCA. Instead, if the objective of a training program is to teach an individual to use different types of telephones, training should occur in many different settings on many different phones. Similarly, if a training objective is to teach a developmentally disabled individual to use community bowling facilities, that individual should be given varied experiences with community bowling. He should be taught to bowl when the facility is crowded, when it is empty, in many different lanes, and with different people. This will increase the likelihood of adequate performance under a variety of naturally occurring stimulus conditions.

Involving many different people (e.g., normal peers, professional staff, and volunteers) in training programs will also enhance maintenance and generalization of recreational skills. This provides developmentally disabled persons with the opportunity for interacting with a variety of people under a variety of conditions. Furthermore, increasing the number of people increases the number of sources an individual has for encouragement and reinforcement of continued participation in community activities.

Independence and Self-Maintenance

Wehman (1977b) suggested that an ideal way to maintain recreational skills is to provide an individual with experiences that are so enjoyable that he is eager to engage in these activities without external prompting or encouragement. The emphasis in community recreation should not be on performing a task but rather on having fun. Even if a person's skills are limited, criticism should rarely be given, whereas reinforcement for participation should be given in abundance. Increased positive interactions with peers (handicapped and nonhandicapped) and family in a recreational setting help to reinforce active involvement in programs, as will extra staff attention and praise.

Another step that can be taken to ensure the maintenance of community involvement of developmentally disabled persons is the encouragement of independent behaviors. Providing training programs that lead to the development of a repertoire of independent or self-initiated behaviors can serve to enhance the durability of participation in community recreation activities. For example, the lack of transportation to and from recreational facilities has been a limiting factor for developmentally disabled participants. However, if a training program is provided for teaching independent use of public transportation, developmentally disabled individuals then would be able to travel independently to and from community functions. Similarly, Nietupski and Williams (1974) developed a program for teaching severely handicapped students to use the telephone to initiate recreational activities with peers. These independent or self-initiated behaviors should be encouraged and reinforced by recreation staff and family members. Enjoyment and independence may result in increased participation as well as maintenance of recreational skills.

FUTURE RESEARCH

The present status of community recreation research has been presented and suggestions for a program model delineated. A critical ingredient of a community recreation model is a research component. Future research priorities for community recreation have been suggested by Stein (1977). These include:

1. *Hawthorne effect investigation.* Community recreation research should separate the value of participation in any activity from the value of participation in recreational activites. By not utilizing Hawthorne control groups (groups given equal attention but not recreation pro-

gramming), the effects of participation in recreation would be confounded.

2. *Efficacy of mainstreaming versus separate programs.* Many people have advocated completely integrated recreation programs, while others have supported segregated programs. However, there is little data to support the value of either of these proposals. Research is needed to determine which developmentally disabled persons (e.g., mild, moderate, severe) do better in special programs versus those that do better in regular activities. Furthermore, research should be of assistance in deciding at which point in a person's development transfer to regular recreation programming should be made.

3. *Development of objective measures of success, feelings of accomplishment, fun, etc.* Many advocates of community recreation have suggested that a variety of positive effects result from recreation participation. These positive effects have not been measured objectively in the past and hence have detracted from the development of a strong basis for community recreation expansion. If future research can objectify these affective behavior changes, the value of recreation for the developmentally disabled can be further substantiated.

Additional recreation research suggestions have been offered by Wehman (1977b). One of these calls for a determination of the effect of specific recreational activities on behavior and cognitive development. Another needed research area is the investigation of which recreational activities are appropriate for particular ages, levels, etc., of developmentally disabled. Finally the development of self-initiated use of recreation and investigation of transfer of training are critical research issues in community programming.

Individual recreational skill training sequences need to be validated, the effect of recreation involvement needs to be assessed, and comprehensive program evaluation needs to be conducted. The research that should be done in each of the above areas should be integrated into a useful body of knowledge. A conceptualization of community recreation research is needed that can account for the following: 1) the diverse subject populations included in the category of developmentally disabled, 2) the multitude of recreational activities that are available, and 3) the variety of settings in which recreation programs are conducted.

A three-dimensional conceptual model for community recreation research involving the developmentally disabled is proposed. This model

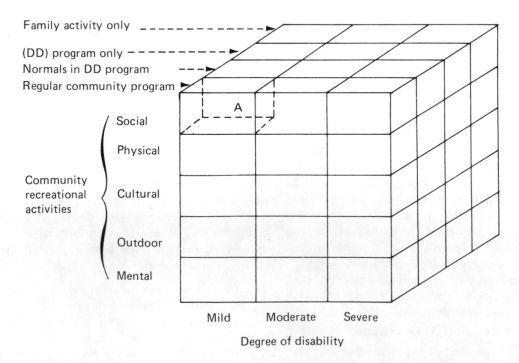

Figure 6.1. A conceptual model for community recreation research: Disability by recreational activity by program setting interaction.

represents a disability by recreational activity by program setting interaction (refer to Figure 6.1). This conceptualization could prove helpful for integrating existing research and for organizing and stimulating future empirical investigation.

Because community recreation programming for the developmentally disabled means different things to different people, a conceptual model must recognize these unique differences. For example, the nature of programming will vary as a function of degree of disability (e.g., mild, moderate, severe), the recreational activity considered (e.g., social, physical, etc.), and the nature of the program setting (e.g., regular community activity, segregated program, etc.).

Upon inspection of Figure 6.1, it becomes evident that specific research questions are more appropriate for particular cubic cells. For instance, the research questions that are of immediate concern when considering the social recreation behaviors of the mildly disabled in regular community programs (cell A of Figure 6.1) are different than these regarding a severely disabled population. With the mildly disabled the focus of research activity may need to be directed more toward their interpersonal social skills (Perry and Cerreto, 1977) than toward basic technical skills (e.g., mobility).

With increased research funding, improved personnel preparation, and the utilization of viable research models, an empirical body of knowledge may develop in the area of community recreation. From such a data base, program expansion could proceed.

SUMMARY

Although there has been a strong movement in the past few decades toward deinstitutionalization and normalization for developmentally disabled persons, provisions for participation in community recreation have been less than adequate. A review of the existing literature on community recreation for developmentally disabled community residents indicated that there are a number of recurring problems that frequently surface. These include: 1) a lack of funding sources, 2) a lack of trained personnel, and 3) a paucity of available programs or a lack of opportunity to engage in recreation programs. Furthermore, there are few methodologically sound studies that have investigated training techniques and service delivery systems. As was indicated, much research is needed in this

area so as to facilitate successful community involvement for developmentally disabled persons.

This chapter has attempted to evaluate existing literature, provide recreation personnel with a wide range of activities that may be appropriate for developmentally disabled community participants, and propose a systematic approach to program development. Realizing that the developmentally disabled population is far from homogeneous, future efforts in this area may be more beneficial if focused upon specific segments of developmental disabilities (e.g., mildly handicapped, severely handicapped, or physically handicapped, etc.) This may also provide answers to some of the many questions regarding program development and implementation.

The importance of recreational activities has been emphasized for all people, including the developmentally disabled. With an increase in research efforts as well as an expansion of community services, the recreational needs of all citizens should be met.

REFERENCES

Andres, C. 1967. The status of municipal recreation for the mentally retarded. Master's project. University of Minnesota, Minneapolis. Minn.

Bates, P. 1976. Language instruction with a profoundly retarded adolescent: Use of a table game in the acquisition, generalization, and maintenance of verbal labeling skills. Unpublished master's thesis, Department of Studies in Behavioral Disabilities, University of Wisconsin, Madison.

Berryman, D. L., Logan A., and Lander, D. 1971. Enhancement of recreation service to disabled children. (Final Report Grant No. C-202). Department of Health, Education, and Welfare, Washington, D.C.

Brace, D. K. 1968. Physical education and recreation for mentally retarded pupils in public schools. Ment. Retard. 6:18–20.

Bundschuh, E. L., Williams, W., Hollingworth, J., Gooch, S., and Shirer, C. 1972. Teaching the retarded to swim. Ment. Retard. 10(3):14–17.

Burmeister, J. G. 1976. Leisure services and the cultural arts as therapy for the mentally retarded individual. Ther. Recreat. J. 10(4):139–142.

Burnes, A. J., and Hassol, L. 1966. A pilot study in evaluating camping experiences for the mentally retarded. Ment. Retard. 4(4):15–17.

Campbell, D. T., and Stanley, J. C. 1963. Experimental and Quasiexperimental Designs for Research. Rand McNally, Chicago.

Campbell, J. 1973. Physical fitness and the MR: A review of research. Ment. Retard. 11(5):26–29.

Cappel, M. L. 1974. Providing community recreation services to special populations. Ther. Recreat. J. 8(2):72–77.

Carlson, B. W. and Ginglend, D. R. 1968. Recreation for Retarded Teenagers and Young Adults. Abingdon Press, New York.

Certo, N., Schwartz, R., and Brown, L. 1975. Community transportation: Teaching severely handicapped students to ride a public bus system. In L. Brown, T. Crowner, W. Williams, and R. York (eds.), Madison's Alternative for zero Exclusion: A Book of Readings, Vol. V. Madison Public Schools, Madison, Wis.

Certo, N., and Swetlik, B. 1975. Minimum objectives related to teaching severely handicapped students to use selected stores and services in the community. Unpublished manuscript. University of Wisconsin, Madison.

Chaney, R. 1969. The effects of a selected recreational activity on the IQ scores, social adjustment, and physical coordination of the educable mentally retarded child. Doctoral dissertation. Indiana University, Bloomington.

Compton, D. M., and Goldstein, J. E. 1976. Therapeutic recreation. Parks Recreat. 18:28–34, 95–98.

Corcoran, E. L., and French, R. W. 1977. Leisure activity for the retarded adult in the community. Ment. Retard. 15(2):21–23.

Cortazzo, A. D. 1968. An analysis of activity programs for mentally retarded adults. Ment. Retard. 6(6):7–9.

Council for Exceptional Children (CEC) and American Association for Health, Physical Education, and Recreation (AAHPER). 1966. Recreation and Physical Activity for the Mentally Retarded. AAHPER, Washington, D.C.

D'Alonzo, B. J. 1976. Rights of exceptional children to participate in interscholastic athletics. Except. Child. 43(2):86–92.

Edginton, C. R., Compton, D. M., Ritchie, A. J., and Vederman, R. K. 1975. The status of services for special populations in park and recreation departments in the state of Iowa. Ther. Recreat. J. 3:109–116.

Eichenbaum, B., and Bednark. 1964. Square dancing and social adjustment. Ment. Retard. 2(2):105–109.

Fiax, N., and Peters, E. N. 1969. Retarded children at camp with normal children. Children 16(6):232–237.

Gozali, J., and Charney, B. 1972. Agenda for the '70's: Full social integration of the retarded. Ment. Retard. 10:20–21.

Hamre-Nietupski, S., and Williams, W. W. 1977. Implementation of selected sex education and social skills to severely handicapped students. Educ. Train. Ment. Retard. 12(4):364–372.

Hayes, G. Z. 1969. Recreation services for the mentally retarded in the state of Kansas. Ther. Recreat. J. Third quarter, 13.

Hitzhusen, G. 1975. Therapeutic recreation services for the educable mentally retarded. Ther. Recreat. J. 9(4:)153–157.

Hynes, J., and Young, J. 1976. Adolescent group for mentally retarded persons. Educ. Train. Ment. Retard. 11(3):226–231.

Katz, S., and Yekutiel, E. 1974. Leisure time problems of mentally retarded graduates of training programs. Ment. Retard. 12(3):54–57.

Kazdin, A. E. 1975. Behavior Modification in Applied Settings. Dorsey Press, Homewood, Ill.

Keeran, C. V., Grove, F., and Zachofsky, T. 1969. Assessing the playground skills of the severely retarded. Ment. Retard. 7(3):29–32.

Lancaster, R. A. 1976. Municipal services. Parks Recreat. 18:18–27.

Linford, A. G., and Kennedy, D. W. 1971. Research— The state of the art in therapeutic recreation. Ther. Recreat. J. 5(4):168–169.

Luckey, R. E., and Shapiro, I. G. 1974. Recreation: An essential aspect of habilitative programming. Ment. Retard. 12(5):33–35.

McDaniel, C. O. 1971. Extra-curricular activities as a factor in social acceptance among EMR students. Ment. Retard. 10(2):26–28.

Marholin, D., O'Toole, M., Touchette, P. E., Berger, P. L., and Doyle, D. A. (October) 1977. "I'll have a Big Mac, large fries, medium coke, and apple pie . . . " or An experimental analysis of a training package to teach community skills. Paper presented at the 11th Annual American Association of Behavior Therapy Conference.

Maynard, M. 1976. The value of creative arts for the developmentally disabled child: Implications for recreation specialists in community day service programs. Ther. Recreat. J. 10(1):10–13.

Nietupski, J., and Williams, W. 1974. Teaching severely handicapped students to use the telephone to initiate selected recreational activities and to respond appropriately to telephone requests to engage in selected recreational activities. In L. Brown, T. Cowner, W. Williams, and R. York (eds.), A Collective of Papers and Programs Related to Public School Services for Severely Handicapped Students, Vol. 4. Madison Public School System, Madison, Wis.

Nirje, B. 1969. The normalization principle and its human management implications. In R. B. Kugel and W. Wolfensberger (eds.), Changing Patterns of Residential Care for the Mentally Retarded. President's Committee on Mental Retardation.

Perry, M. A., and Cerreto, M. C. 1977. Structured learning training of social skills. Ment. Retard. 15(6):31–34.

Pomeroy, J. 1974. The handicapped are out of hiding: Implications for community recreation. Ther. Recreat. J. 8(3):120–128.

Pumphrey, M. W., Goodman, M. B., Kidd, J. W., and Peters, E. N. 1970. Participation of retarded children in regular recreational activities at a community center. Except. Child. 36:453–458.

Seaman, J. A. 1972. The effects of a bowling program upon bowling skill number concepts and self-esteem of mentally retarded children. Doctoral dissertation. Indiana University, Bloomington.

Seaman, J. A. 1973. Right up their alley. Teach. Except. Child. 5(4):196–198.

Seaman, J. A. 1975. Effects of municipal recreation on social self-esteem of the mentally retarded. Ther. Recreat. J. 9(2):75–78.

Sengstock, W. L., and Jens, K. G. 1974. Recreation for the handicapped. Suggestions for program adaptations. Ther. Recreat. J. 8(4):172–177.

Spradlin, J., and Spradlin, R. Developing necessary skills for entry into classroom teaching arrangements. In N. Haring and R. Schiefelbusch (eds.), Teaching Special Children. McGraw-Hill Book Co., New York.

Stanfield, J. S. 1973. What happens to the retarded child when he grows up? Except. Child. 39:548, 550–552.

Stein, J. U. 1969. Professional preparation in physical education and recreation for the mentally retarded. Educ. Train. Ment. Retard. 4(3):101–108.

Stein, J. U. 1975. Annotated research bibliography in physical education, recreation, and psychomotor function of mentally retarded persons. Project No. OEG-0-72-5454-233563. American Alliance for Health, Physical Education, and Recreation, Washington, D.C.

Stein, J. U. 1977. Physical education, recreation, and sports for special populations. Educ. Train. Ment. Retard. 12(1):4–13.

Thompson, M. 1965. National survey of community recreation services to the mentally retarded and physically handicapped. Recreation 17:191–192.

Thompson, M. 1969. The status of recreation for the handicapped as related to community and voluntary agencies. Physical Education and Recreation for Handicapped Children. AAHPER and MRPA, Washington, D.C.

Wehman, P. 1977a. Applications of behavior modification techniques to play problems of the severely and profoundly retarded. Ther. Recreat. J. 11(1):17–23.

Wehman, P. 1977b. Helping the Mentally Retarded Acquire Play Skills: A Behavioral Approach. Charles C Thomas, Springfield, Ill.

Wehman, P., and Marchant, J. A. 1977. Developing gross motor recreational skills in children with severe behavioral handicaps. Ther. Recreat. J. 11(2):48–54.

Wehman, P., Renzaglia, A., Berry, G., Schutz, R., and Karan, O. 1978. Developing a leisure skill repertoire in severely and profoundly handicapped persons. AAESPH Rev. 3(2).

Wilson, G. T. 1974. Community Recreation Programming for Handicapped Children. National Recreation and Park Association, Arlington, Va.

Witt, P. A. 1971. A historical sketch of recreation for the mentally retarded (1920–1968). Ment. Retard. 9(1):50–53.

Witt, P. A. 1977. Therapeutic recreation: The outmoded label. Ther. Recreat. J. Second quarter, 39–41.

Wolfensberger, W. 1972. Normalization. National Institute on Mental Retardation, Toronto.

Wyatt, W. S., and Hunt, S. K. 1976. Using parents as evaluators of a therapeutic recreational camping program for the retarded. Ther. Recreat. J. (4):143–147.

7 SENSORY STIMULATION

Carol Granger and Paul Wehman

In recent years there has been a move to expand the amount and improve the quality of services available to severely developmentally disabled individuals. This has been evidenced in public schools, day care centers, and state facilities. One group within this population is nonambulatory individuals who are unaware of environmental stimuli and who also exhibit severe or profound mental retardation. Usually these individuals are grossly delayed in most areas of functioning, including language, sensory awareness, and all aspects of motor development.

A logical and necessary starting point of intervention for these individuals is to help them develop an awareness of the environment through developing orienting, attending, visual tracking, and reaching skills. These important developmental milestones are an integral part of all other functioning areas. Brazelton (1977) has indicated that the ways in which individuals respond are important in forming the first basis for learning about the world. Sensory stimulation is a significant aspect of environmental awareness and can be cultivated through exploratory play. This stimulation influences the central nervous system and subsequent motor responses toward the environment.

Sensory interaction is the ability to take in, sort out, and connect information from the world around us. It is controlled by the central nervous system. In normal development the sensory synthesizing of information takes place automatically. Its function is to provide an individual with differing systems for protection and survival, as well as allowing an individual to interact and learn from his environment.

Ayres (1972) reports that

> organizing and interpreting sensory information is the essence of perception. Perception usually is followed by a motor response to that which has been perceived. The development of this perceptual ability is dependent upon sensory feedback from the motor act which is elicited by the perceptual processes. The feedback mechanism enables the organism to check the accuracy of the perception as well as the effectiveness of the response.

Since severely disabled individuals frequently demonstrate deficits in motor performance, it is logical to suspect deficits in sensory processing which relate to delayed cognitive development and exploratory play.

It is important to note that sensory stimulation has neurological implications and derivatives (Kinnealy, 1973; Norton, 1975). When stimulation is provided, one is altering the neurological system, and for some persons the way in which alteration occurs is inadvisable.

Recent literature supports the positive effects that sensory stimulation has on extremely low functioning individuals (Neman et al., 1975; Safford et al., 1976). Sensory stimulation seems to be a potent means of improving sensorimotor awareness in the severely disabled; sensorimotor awareness, in turn, enables an individual to interact more effectively with his environment.

The purpose of this chapter is to discuss sensory stimulation as it relates to the development of low functioning individuals and to describe program guidelines for establishing a sensory stimulation program. The initial part of the chapter involves review of relevant literature in sensory stimulation, while the latter half is concerned with program development guidelines. The information contained in this chapter is devoted to those teachers and therapists who work with severely multiply handicapped and low functioning individuals.

SENSORY STIMULATION AND EXPLORATORY PLAY

Several theorists agree that the human infant's perceptual and manipulative explorations of objects constitute the most important learning experiences (e.g., Piaget, 1962). Exploratory behaviors are adaptive, that is, they involve visual tracking, scanning, and coordinated motor responses. On the other hand, play consists of behaviors and behavioral sequences that are organism dominated rather than stimulus dominated. For example, exploration is what can be done with the object, whereas play is what the individual can do (Weisler and McCall, 1976). For the purposes of this chapter exploratory play is considered to be actions on the toy or object. Sensory stimulation is the response of the individual as a result of the interaction of the organism. Because play involves the interaction of the individual with a toy, preferred toys (if identified) should be used in developing exploratory play. This will facilitate sensory awareness and coordinated motor responses.

Importance of Tactile Stimulation

In understanding sensory stimulation it is critical to discuss the interaction of various sensory systems, such as tactile, auditory, gustatory, visual, and olfactory, as they relate to the stimulation. Brazelton (1977) reports that the importance of touch can be observed in very premature babies. These babies, after receiving an extra 15 minutes daily of stroking while in the incubator, gained weight more quickly. They were also able to take more food, cope with problems of fragile circulatory adjustments, and adjust to temperature changes better when they came out of the incubator.

Another study, which was conducted with a group of premature infants, evaluated the effect of tactile stimulation using the *Neonatal Behavior Assessment Scale* (Solkoff and Matuszak, 1975). With tactile stimulation, the infants cried less and gained weight more rapidly. With kinesthetic, tactile, and visual stimuli greater alertness, better grasp reflex, and increased weight gain were noted. The study was conducted for only 10 days. The results showed change of two or more points on 26 scales, while the control groups and the premature infants gained two or more points on 11 scales.

There is also a close association with tactile perception and motor planning on the Gesell quotients in early life (Ayres, 1972). Reported are relationships between touch and visual stimulation. The results indicated that visual-only matching of stimuli was superior to tactile-only matching (Jones and Robinson, 1973; Raskin and Baker,

1975) for normal subjects but not for retarded subjects.

Raskin and Baker concluded in a study with normal and severely disabled individuals that tactual clues alone did not increase learning. It was indicated that effective classroom learning is better accomplished with multisensory stimuli.

The tactile functions are primitive; they serve as a protective or a discriminative source. The protective system responds to light or unexpected touch—often as a fight of flight response, warning of impending danger. The discriminative system responds to environmental stimuli, in which the response is related to the quality of the stimuli (Wilbarger, 1968; Weisberg, 1975). Many low functioning children who do not have a developed protective tactile system exhibit tactile defensiveness and related behavioral responses because the stimulation is interpreted as offensive or harmful, and thus the individual wants to withdraw, or "flight," from the situation. Because stimulation is offensive, the individual is unable to receive stimuli and is unable to develop exploratory play skills.

In severely developmentally disabled individuals tactile defensiveness is frequently evident. The tactile stimuli are interpreted as offensive. The individual may exhibit responses like scratching, wishing to get away, facial grimaces, somatic complaints, bodily movements, anxiety, and aggressive behaviors (Bauer, 1977). These avoidance responses make it extremely difficult for the teacher to use social and physical contact as reinforcement in developing play behavior. Furthermore, tactually defensive mentally retarded individuals often demonstrate hyperactive behavior, a short attention span, and distractibility (McCracken, 1975).

Tactile sensitivity is one of the primary modes of communication and is never wholly superseded by other systems. Many signals present symbolic significance. For example, individuals who are limited in early tactile experiences must wait until visual and auditory recognition and reception have developed sufficiently before beginning communication skills since touch for learning is not pleasant.

For the child with high rate hyperactive behaviors, remediation helps normalize neural pathways. These pathways elicit protective responses and develop more balance between the protective and discriminative systems. A touch pressure proprioceptive mode of treatment is optimal when the child receives tactile stimulation; this might involve rubbing with a dry washcloth or other type of cloth. Silk, velvet, or lotion are often the most acceptable media. The teacher must rely on the child's responses for information on the effect, as well as the type, duration, and frequency, of the tactile stimulation. It has been suggested that the back of the hands and the forearms provide the least defensive areas, whereas the stomach, chest, face, and feet are most responsive to stimulation. Should the individual demonstrate an avoidance response, the stimulation should not be discontinued altogether. This negative response can be interpreted as the individual's inability to organize this stimulus. Alternate modes of stimulation can be explored for a short intermediary time.

Cruickshank (1977) has noted that holding or touching the hyperactive child may reduce hyperactivity. It is also interesting to note that "touching oneself, whether directly or indirectly," and being touched by another are two different neurological processes and must be considered as such (Baker, 1973), especially in interpretation of responses to training. This is particularly evident when one is considering changes elicited by a severely disabled individual as a result of tactile stimulation. Another consideration, since tactual and visual integration are closely related, is that a child might show a negative response when someone casually touches him.

Auditory and Tactile Processes

The auditory system is usually related to communication and language functions. The neural processing of sound is considered one of the primal forms of sensory integration at the brain stem level (Ayres, 1972). The processing of auditory stimuli involves duration, frequency or tone, intensity, and sequence of sound. The auditory system has evolved from the vestibular system, thus suggesting a close relationship between hearing and balance (Baker, 1973). Recent literature supports a strong association between auditory learning and visual learning for mildly retarded persons (Bucham, 1974).

It has been suggested that "delays in mobility and locomotion were lessened when one was successful in providing early auditory-tactile experiences that sustained interest in the external world, encouraged physical activity and ultimately permitted sound to serve as a lure for forward progression" (Adelson, 1974). Most literature has supported the use of auditory-tactile experiences. Since earlier research encourages multisensory use of stimuli, and since auditory experiences are coupled with tactual and visual stimuli development, this is not surprising.

As noted earlier, with the close relationship between tactile and auditory stimulation and integration, it is understandable that tactile defensiveness and auditory defensiveness often go hand-in-hand in severely handicapped children. Therefore, an important goal is to diminish defensive behavior so the child is better able to receive and process auditory stimuli and, thus, demonstrate increased listening and attending skills. It is best to work with a trained audiologist in diminishing auditory defensiveness. This can be done by working with frequency and duration of sounds in a controlled manner initially, rather than only in the natural environmental setting of the individual. Of course, eventually training also must take place in the child's natural environment.

Auditory and Gustatory Stimulation

It is interesting to note that auditory and gustatory stimulation are also related in the newborn, and lack of response to these stimuli perhaps could be an indication of a hearing loss. In a noisy nursery a newborn sucking on a pacifier often does not respond to a loud noise designed to detect a hearing loss. However, when the infant is tested while sucking on a pacifier and hears a softer, more attractive noise, the infant will pause to listen and then resume sucking. This can also apply to oversatiation of a noise. An individual with no brain damage will respond to a sound, but will rapidly stop paying attention when it is repeated again and again. A brain-damaged child, however, will respond repeatedly because he cannot discriminate similarity. Furthermore, the normal infant will respond to the slightest changes in the sound, as detected in sucking responses (Brazelton, 1977). One might suggest that with low functioning individuals the sucking reflex could be used in an evaluation and as a subsequent indicator of change responses; this is based on multisensory stimulation for remediation. This could be demonstrated by changes in sucking duration and bursts.

Taste and Tactile Systems

The sense of taste is closely related to the tactile system because the cranial nerve for taste innervates the tongue. The structural concerns of taste are the tongue and the mouth, which in turn are associated with the oral reflexes. Engen, Lipsitt, and Peck (1974) demonstrated that taste preferences of infants could be determined by measuring the sucking response. The infants demonstrated a higher sucking rate with sucrose as compared to glucose or water. The study also suggested that taste patterns are innate, whereas odor patterns result from experience and training. Therefore, the sense of smell (olfactory) often changes one's responses to taste.

It has been demonstrated that there is a change in sucking bursts or groups of sucks with the introduction of different tastes. With increased sweetness the infant engages in more sucks per minute, more sucks in each burst, and deeper sucking at a slower rate. Furthermore, sensitivity to sweet and salty fluids is substantial, as demonstrated by the infant's sucking patterns (Brazelton, 1977). Along this same line, it has been found that babies use the suck-burst-pause pattern to demonstrate communication. When the baby is feeding on a bottle and pauses, the feeder often jiggles the bottle to encourage sucking. The baby often does not respond to the joggling with increased sucking and instead prolongs the pause as if to "savour the communications" with the feeder.

The demonstration that nonhandicapped infants do respond to fine discriminations in taste and that taste is related to tactile stimulation through neural innervation is indicative that gustatory and tactile stimulation may be important modalities in eliciting greater sensory awareness and movement in profoundly retarded, nonambulatory individuals. Further research with this population will be necessary to verify this generalization.

Importance of a Multisensory Approach

Many of the first-observed developmental milestones are visual in nature, such as visual pursuit and localization of object permanence. Visual responses are also consequences of cerebral nervous system development and can be affected by disorders of the system. The importance of a mild sensory deficit is greater in low functioning individuals because they are not able to compensate for sensory deficits as normal individuals can.

For example, learning is possible for the nonretarded blind individual through direct environmental experiences and use of other modalities. However, the severely retarded blind individual not only lacks use of the visual sense but also is often motorically handicapped and subsequently unable to perform exploratory actions necessary for learning and developing meaning from environmental experiences. Therefore, training efforts must be multisensory in nature. Low functioning individuals frequently exhibit seizure activity and abnormal motor patterns that interfere with central or peripheral visions. The oculomotor system problems are demonstrated through strong movement of the eyes, with dominance of abnormal reflex behavior and the Doll's Eyes Phenomenon (primitive compensatory eye movements in the opposite direction of head movement) (Fieber, 1977).

In reviewing the available literature there appears to be substantial research to support a theory that multisensory stimulation with structure for the severely developmentally disabled individual is the most effective medium for treatment of deficits and subsequent development of exploratory play actions (e.g., Safford et al., 1976). It is unlikely that many severely multihandicapped individuals can enter into meaningful play experiences without initially receiving substantial sensory stimulation under the supervision of an occupational therapist and teacher. The use of tactile, visual, auditory, and gustatory modes is important in improving the sensory awareness and alertness of the individual. The balance of this chapter is concerned with practical suggestions in assessment of, and stimulation (intervention) for, the low functioning multihandicapped child.

DEVELOPMENT OF A SENSORY STIMULATION PROGRAM

Assessment

Before selecting appropriate modes of stimulation, it is necessary to carefully assess the functioning level of the target population. Unfortunately there are few comprehensive tools for assessing the early developmental behavior of severely multihandicapped individuals. One tool, which has been found to be effective, and which was standardized on a profoundly retarded population, is the Awareness, Manipulation, and Posture Scale (AMP) (Webb, 1971). It assesses the child's response to tactile, kinesthetic, auditory, visual, gustatory, and olfactory sensory receptors. A portion of this scale is provided in Table 7.1.

Another assessment tool, which has been used in the Infant Development and Deaf/Blind Programs at the Meyer Children's Rehabilitative Institute, Omaha, Nebraska, is available mainly for targeting sensorimotor cognitive milestones that are associated with visual stimuli (see Fieber, 1977). Numerous developmental assessments, such as the Denver Developmental Screening Inventory (DDSI), Gesell Developmental Quotients, Portage Guide to Early Education, Comprehensive Developmental Evaluation Chart, Upper Extremity Motor Development Test (see Miller et al., 1955), and EMI Assessment Scale, have also been used by therapists in assessing developmental levels.

These types of checklist instruments provide valuable information initially on the child's level of behavior in the language, motor, and cognitive domains. To develop a program, however, it is necessary to complete these assessments over several days and collect more specific information through task analysis and skill sequencing formats. (See Chapter 3 for more detailed description.)

As sensorimotor deficits are identified through assessment, subsequent stimulation programs can be designed to ameliorate these problems. As is usually the case, multiple deficits, all extreme in nature, are verified and a multisensory approach is warranted. Regardless of the level or number of deficits, specific therapy objectives must be written into the child's individualized education program (IEP).

Intervention

After specific therapy objectives have been identified, a stimulation program must be designed to facilitate the child's optimum functioning and interaction ability. Each individual's program should be specific to meet his needs. There is no "one sensory stimulation program" that would be appropriate for all sensory deficit individuals. The mechanisms of a program must be structured to meet individual demands and responses. However, there are specific training techniques and activities for particular dysfunctions that can be discussed, as well as some general program guidelines.

Because sensory systems develop as tactile, auditory, and visual systems, it is appropriate to plan a sensory stimulation program that not only provides stimuli for these three sensory modalities but also provides gustatory and olfactory stimuli. Also, since the relationship between motor responses and sensory responses is critical in development, and stability comes before mobility, it is important that positioning be discussed in designing any sensory stimulation program for severely motorically involved individuals.

Positioning: An Important Prerequisite

The child's body must be maintained in the optimum position for the receipt of the stimuli. In order for the eyes or oculomotor muscles to be able to fixate and track a moving object, head stability should be secured. Whether it is voluntary or stabilized by another individual, the head should be slightly bent (flexed) and in the midline position. If the arms are generally hanging along the body or are extended (straight) away from the body, they should be brought into the midline position and stabilized, which will help stabilize the head. If the legs are usually straight (extended), they should be bent (flexed) slightly at the hips and knees to facilitate their straightening. Pictorially, the individual that looks like this:

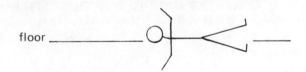

would look like this:

If necessary, a support at the base of the neck might be appropriate, and a beanbag chair could be considered to provide the desired position. If the child is seated in a personal chair which is appropriate for his needs, a lapboard could be used for the introduction of the sensory stimuli. All efforts should be made to present the appropriate

Table 7.1. AMP index #1 (7th revision) (Reprinted with kind permission of Ruth Webb, Ph.D.)

NAME _____ DATE RATED _____ _____ _____
CASE # _____ EVALUATOR _____ _____ _____
                                   OBSERVER _____ _____ _____

                    Total Awareness Score   _____ _____ _____
                    Total Manipulation Score   _____ _____ _____
                    Total Posture Score   _____ _____ _____
                        (Static and Dynamic)   _____ _____ _____

                    Awareness Index   _____ _____ _____
                    Manipulation Index   _____ _____ _____
                    Posture Index   _____ _____ _____
                    Total AMP Index   _____ _____ _____

Total AMP Index _____ 1 _____ / _____ 2 _____ / _____ 3 _____
                       0–75   76–150   151–225

(The number above the range interval into which the Total AMP Index score falls is the Total AMP Index.)

DIRECTIONS: Please rate the frequency of the action responses in capitals on the scale following each item. If the item contains two or more stimulus words (in parentheses), underline the appropriate stimulus words. Items should only be rated for responses during the testing period. For instructions in giving the individual items, please consult the manual.

RATING SYSTEM: Opposite each item are five columns (see below). They are headed "0", "1", "2", "3", and "Total". Present each item three (3) times. If the child responds to the item each time you present it, check "3." If he responds twice, check "2;" once, check "1." If he makes no response at all, check "0."

0	1	2	3	Total

The index for each section is found by summing the ratings for all items in the section and locating the total on the scale which follows each part of the AMP. The number on the scale above the total score is the Index for the individual AMP section. The score and Index for the complete AMP are found in a similar way: sum the scores for all parts of the AMP and locate the sum on the scale at the top of this page. The number above the score for the total AMP is the Index for the total AMP.

More than one column for the scores and indices is provided on the front page so that each form may be used at least three (3) times. It is suggested that ratings at different times be marked with different colored pens; green, red, and blue, respectively. BE SURE TO PUT THE DATE EACH TIME YOU USE THE FORM. A TEST IS USELESS WITHOUT THE DATE. Each time you use the form, be sure both the child's name and your name are on it.

BY: Ruth C. Webb, Ph.D., Director of Developmental Therapy, Glenwood State Hospital School, Glenwood, Iowa 51534

NAME _____ CASE # _____

*AWARENESS**

* Note: Sensory systems are designated by the abbreviations following each item: T—Tactility (Te—Temperature and P—Pain), K—Kinesthesia, V—Vision, A—Audition, G—Gustatory, O—Olfactory, Me—Memory, and At—Attention.

	0	1	2	3	Total

A. *Avoidance:*
1. STRUGGLES when held tightly (T, Pr) ....
2. DRAWS wrist or knee away from sharp tapping from rubber hammer (underline) (T, P) ....
3. DRAWS check away from sandpaper (T, P) ....
4. DRAWS right and left hands out of hot (120° F) water and cold (40° F) water (underline) (T, Te) ....
5. JUMPS or BLINKS eyes when metal basin is dropped 2 feet behind child (underline) (K, A) ....
6. TURNS away from strong light (V) ....
7. DRAWS away from unpleasant odors: A, potassium sulphate; B, turpentine (O) ....
8. DRAWS away from unpleasant tastes: A, lemon; B, salt; C, alum (G) ....
9. STRUGGLES to regain upright position (3–6 mos.) (K) .

B. *Approach:*
10. DRAWS closer or SMILES when cuddled (underline) (T) ....
11. MAINTAINS CONTACT with or PATS pliable materials for 10 seconds: A, sand; B, wet clay; C, water (underline) (T) ....
12. SMILES or TURNS toward bell (underline) (A) ....
13. SMILES, TURNS, or REACHES toward music (underline) (A) ....
14. SMILES when evaluator smiles (social response) (V) ...
15. TURNS toward hanging ball (V) ....
16. TURNS toward voice from behind (A) ....
17. REACHES toward pleasant odors: A, charisma perfume; B, oil of lemon; C, oil of cinnamon (underline) (O) .....
18. REACHES toward pleasant taste: sugar or sugar water (underline) (G) ....

C. *Integrating Memory with Present Stimuli:*
19. LOOKS at familiar person when named (A, V, Me) .....
20. OBEYS gesture command (raises arms in response to outstretched arms) (V, Me) ....
21. LOOKS in direction a block has been dropped (V, A, Me) ....
22. TURNS head or SMILES when name is called (underline) (A, Me) ....
23. SHIFTS attention from one toy to another (V, A, At) ...
24. TURNS toward objects as they are named (ball, spoon) (underline) (A, V, Me) ....
25. REACTS to re-appearance of evaluator (V, A, Me) .....

TOTAL *AWARENESS* SCORE _____

AWARENESS INDEX	1	/	2	/	3
	0–25		26–50		51–75

(The number above the range interval into which the Total AWARENESS Score falls is the AWARENESS Index. Please place the Total AWARENESS Score and the AWARENESS Index in the appropriate spaces on page one.)

NAME _____ CASE # _____

*MANIPULATION**

* Note: In addition to the sensory systems designated in the Awareness Scale, the MANIPULATION SCALE includes: GM—Gross Motor, FM—Fine Motor, I—Imitation, PP—Person Permanence, Int—Intentionality, Comm—Communications, and OP—Object Permanence.

	0	1	2	3	Total

A. *Responses to Objects:*
  26. REACHES for object with right, left or both hands (V, At, FM, Int) (underline) ....
  27. GRASPS object with right, left or both hands (V, FM, Int) (underline).....................................
  28. HOLDS object with right, left or both hands (V, A, FM, Int) (underline).....................................
  29. TRANSFERS toy from hand to hand (V, T, FM, Int) ...
  30. SQUEEZES ball (T, I, FM, Int) ....

B. *Responses to Commands: Gestures:*
  31. POUNDS table with block (V, T, A, I, FM, Int) ....
  32. PICKS up bead with finger and thumb (V, T, I, FM, Int) ....
  33. DROPS block in can (V, A, I, FM, Int) ....
  34. PUTS ring on stick (V, I, T, FM, Int) ....
  35. POURS sand or water from one can to another (V, T, I, FM, Int) (underline) ....
  36. IMITATES poking finger into hole (V, I,T, Int) ....
  37. PLAYS peek-a-boo (I, A, PP, Int) ....
  38. PAT-A-CAKES (V, I, A, Int) ....
Words
  39. In sitting position, PULLS toy across table toward self with string (V, FM, A, Int) ....
  40. REMOVES box covering candy (V, OP, A, Int).........
  41. THROWS ball purposely (A, V, Int) ....
  42. STACKS one block on another (A, Int) ....
  43. SCRIBBLES on paper (A, FM, Int) ....
  44. OBEYS verbal command (Give me your hand) (A, Int) .

C. *Expression of Intentionality:*
  45. EXPRESSES need by: 1) sounds; 2) eyes; 3) gestures; 4) words (underline) (V, A, Int, Comm) ....
  46. REMOVES towel from head (active avoidance) (V, FM, Int) ....
  47. PATS mirror image (V, T, Int) ....
  48. PULLS evaluator's arm to get balloon (V, FM, Int) .....
  49. PULLS evaluator's arm to indicate choice of toy (V, A, Int, Comm) ....
  50. RESISTS when treat is taken away (V, Int, Comm) ....

TOTAL *MANIPULATION* SCORE _____

MANIPULATION INDEX _____ 1 _____ / _____ 2 _____ / _____ 3 _____
                                0–25   26–50   51–75

(The number above the range interval into which the Total MANIPULATION Score falls is the MANIPULATION Index. Please place the Total MANIPULATION Score and the MANIPULATION Index in the appropriate spaces on page one.)

NAME _____   CASE # _____

POSTURE (Static and Dynamic)*

* Note: In this section, S for Static and D for Dynamic are shown in parentheses after each item. If the child walks with assistance, rate starred (*) items 51–55, 57–60, 62, 64–71 with "3".

	0	1	2	3	Total
51. *HOLDS up head for at least 1 minute (S)					
52. *ROLLS from stomach to back or from back to stomach (D)					
53. *ROLLS completely over (D)					
54. *MOVES on back purposely by pushing arms or legs (underline) (D)					
55. *MOVES on stomach purposely by pivoting arms and legs (D)					
56. GIVES ACTIVE ASSISTANCE when limbs are moved in reciprocal pattern (D)					
57. *SITS without support for 1 minute (S)					
58. *MOVES on seat (D)					
59. *MOVES forward on stomach by pushing with arms or legs or both (D)					
60. *CREEPS by moving arms and legs bilaterally (D)					
61. STAND on hands and knees (S)					
62. *CRAWLS bilaterally (D)					
63. CRAWLS translaterally (D)					
64. *PULLS to stand on knees (D)					
65. *PULLS to stand on feet (D)					
66. *STANDS supported in standing table for at least 1 minute (S)					
67. *STANDS holding chair at least 1 minute (S)					
68. *STANDS holding adult's hand at least 1 minute (S)					
69. *STANDS unsupported at least 1 minute (S)					
70. *WALKS with one hand held at least 10 feet (D)					
71. *WALKS with push cart at least 10 feet (D)					
72. WALKS alone at least 10 feet (D)					
73. ROCKS in a chair for at least 3 times (D)					
74. BOUNCES on bed or trampoline at least 3 times (D) ...					
75. MAINTAINS sitting position on balance board at least 3 rocks (S)					

TOTAL *POSTURE* SCORE _____

POSTURE INDEX	1	/	2	/	3
	0–25		26–50		51–75

(The number above the range interval into which the Total POSTURE Score falls is the POSTURE Index. Please place the Total POSTURE Score and the POSTURE Index in the appropriate spaces on page one.)

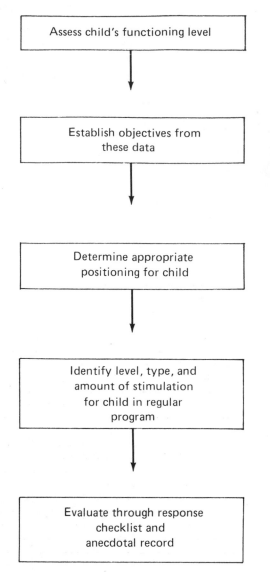

```
┌─────────────────────────────────┐
│  Assess child's functioning level │
└─────────────────────────────────┘
                 │
                 ▼
┌─────────────────────────────────┐
│     Establish objectives from     │
│            these data             │
└─────────────────────────────────┘
                 │
                 ▼
┌─────────────────────────────────┐
│     Determine appropriate         │
│     positioning for child         │
└─────────────────────────────────┘
                 │
                 ▼
┌─────────────────────────────────┐
│   Identify level, type, and       │
│   amount of stimulation           │
│   for child in regular            │
│   program                         │
└─────────────────────────────────┘
                 │
                 ▼
┌─────────────────────────────────┐
│   Evaluate through response       │
│   checklist and                   │
│   anecdotal record                │
└─────────────────────────────────┘
```

Figure 7.1. Sequence for starting a sensory stimulation program.

courage increased muscle tone. This will be important when the child begins to manipulate more graded and weighted toys in the environment.

Other positions, such as side-lying to the right or left, as well as a prone position (stomach-lying) over a wedge, are recommended, depending on the desired responses and reactions of the child. Proper positioning can prevent deformities and will allow the child to indicate a response to sensory stimuli. It will also increase opportunities for exploratory play. In addition to determining optimal positioning, medical reasons for the severely multihandicapped child's failure to respond to stimuli must be ruled out. These might include deficits in vision and hearing, and physiological-tactual deficits, such as those caused by peripheral nerve injuries and strokes (CVA).

After the desired position has been determined, and assessments have been conducted, a sensory stimulation program is implemented. Since most multihandicapped children do exhibit a wide range of severe deficits, the following sections are devoted to programming for a 10-year-old child who is functioning developmentally at a 1–3-month level. Varying positioning techniques are employed, and medical reasons for sensory deficits have been ruled out.

As previously mentioned, sensory stimuli develop through tactile, auditory, and visual muscles, but the multisensory approach has been considered the most effective media for remediation. Although the different sensory modes should be employed in conjunction, program guidelines are provided below for each one separately. Figure 7.1 depicts the sequence of events that should be followed in the program development process.

TACTILE STIMULATION

The touch pressure proprioceptive mode of treatment is often preferred. In some cases it may be less offensive for the individual to provide the tactile stimulation to himself than to have someone else apply the stimuli. Initially stimulation should be applied to the least offensive areas, such as the palms of the hands and forearms; the most offensive areas are usually the soles of the feet, the chest, and the stomach area. After the child receives stimulation via neutral warm lotion, velvet, silk, a washcloth, or other pleasant tactual experiences, exploratory play with items like a textured mobile or a cloth clutch ball or block

stimuli toward the midline and to diminish the possibility of abnormal reflexive behaviors.

Frequently, severely multihandicapped individuals are spastic or stiff. When this is the case, stimuli should be presented calmly and not quickly; this is because rapid presentation of stimuli could tend to set off the individual's arousal system and subsequently increase muscle tone. With the child who is floppy or "like a rag doll," a similar head position is also desirable (slightly bent or flexed), but the individual does not have to be completely bent up. If some head control is evident, the child can straddle the therapist's knee, which subsequently will en-

may be encouraged on a blanket or towel. If the child only shows adverse responses, i.e., withdrawal, increased muscle tightness, facial grimaces, excessive hitting or kicking, the stimulation should not be discontinued, but, rather, the duration and intensity of stimulation should be decreased. Anecdotal remarks or a checklist response sheet can be used to document these responses.

Tactual stimuli that have been used in preparing a child to receive multisensory exploratory play experiences and/or to diminish the tactile defensiveness include:

Cotton	Ice/Water
Sandpaper (all grades)	Leather, vinyl
Suede	Lotion
Terry cloth	Velvet
Silk	Flannel
Wool rug/blanket	Sand
Noodles/macaroni	Foam rubber
Vibrator	Feather

The stimuli included for each category of sensory stimuli are by no means all inclusive but represent stimuli that may be used to facilitate sensorimotor development. The 10 activities and suggestions below should be utilized under supervision of an occupational or physical therapist.

Tactile Stimulation Activities

The activities below include relevant suggestions for implementing a tactile stimulation program:

1. Place child's hand in macaroni, powder, sand, or water, and find familiar toy.
2. Wrap child in a blanket, and unroll him in the direction of a noise-making toy. (In general, when rolling or unrolling a child, provide stimulation at the hips and shoulder.)
3. Apply contrasting temperature lotion on the hands and arms, noting different responses of child. Use deep pressure, not light brushing.
4. Gently cuddle child, rubbing arms and legs. Have child actively participate during stimulation.
5. Have child roll from rug to clothed area to furry surface. At the end of one surface have a mirror, and at the other end have musical chimes that ring for child to roll toward.
6. Use washcloth or toy doll and play "Peek-a-Boo," putting toy on child's arm. After playing rub toy on child's arms and legs.
7. Tickle child's hand with a feather while he is not looking at it. Watch for head turning to the stimuli.
8. Tie scarf or necktie around trainer's neck. Lean over child so he can see your face and possibly touch the scarf. Shake the scarf so he can see it and reach for it. If he grabs it or touches it, smile to show him you are pleased. Initially move scarf toward child's hands so he does not need to reach for it as much (Shearer and Shearer, 1976).
9. Rub child with different textures (rough, smooth, soft, hard), and watch his reactions. Talk to him while applying the stimuli.
10. Put chalk or similar substance on child's arms and hands and encourage him to rub it off. If he does not do it, physically guide child through target response.

AUDITORY STIMULATION

Auditory responses, as startle responses at birth and later as localization responses, are normally evident in all individuals. Severely multihandicapped persons, however, often exhibit delayed or overexaggerated responses to auditory stimuli. When providing auditory stimuli to these individuals it is important that the auditory stimuli not be visible to the individual receiving the stimulation. Often a familiar voice is the best medium for eliciting initial appropriate responses to auditory stimuli. An inappropriate response does not necessarily indicate a hearing loss but may indicate inattentiveness or emotional withdrawal (Webb, 1971).

Once the child has been presented with the stimuli and has responded appropriately and/or has been prompted physically to respond, functional auditory stimuli may be presented to encourage exploratory play. Such stimuli include "Happy Apple," musical chimes, a record player, a radio, bells, and stimuli with auditory features that the individual can respond to, or be prompted physically to respond to, with a head turning (see Chapter 8 on Music Therapy). Auditory stimuli that have been used with severely developmentally disabled children include:

Bell	Horn
Rattle	Radio
Drum	Musical mobile
Commercial musical toys	Familiar voice/
("Happy Apple," chimes,	unfamiliar voice
piano, musical TV,	
talking toys)	

Auditory Stimulation Activities

Below are listed a number of program guidelines and suggestions for using auditory stimulation:

1. Hang a noise mobile in front, then to one side and the other of child. Encourage head turning and eye tracking to stimuli.
2. Sing and talk to child, varying the distance you are from the individual. Try not to let child see the trainer. Note the responses of child at the varying distances to changes in musical tone, as evidenced by head turning and eye blinking.
3. Position child correctly, and place musical toy, such as music chimes or "Happy Apple," in front of him. Encourage use of arms to hit at toy to make noise. Put a noise squeeze toy in front and to sides of child to encourage interaction. Physically prompt when necessary.
4. Tie bells to ankles and arms of child so that when he moves his extremities noise will be realized. Talk about the resulting noise when it occurs.
5. Crumble paper to make noise on either side of child's head, and note his responses.
6. Tie brightly colored ribbons with bells in various places near child. When they ring, encourage child's responses by head turning or eye tracking to noise.
7. Place rattle in child's hands. Encourage shaking of rattle. Respond to the shaking of the rattle by smiling at child.
8. Blow a whistle or horn at different distances and directions from child. Note varying responses from different places.
9. When child vocalizes noises, repeat noises and sounds.
10. Use radio at soft volume in the room. Be sure not to overstimulate so that child demonstrates no response or overexaggerated response to sound.

Note: If child seems to demonstrate no response to auditory stimulation, physically turn his head to the noise. Be sure child is in the optimum position for head turning.

GUSTATORY AND OLFACTORY STIMULATION

Gustatory and olfactory stimuli are discussed simultaneously because their relationships are difficult to differentiate in a testing situation. Gustatory stimuli experiences are administered to the tongue; olfactory stimuli experiences are administered to the nasal area usually through saturated cotton or by sniffing a container of the substance. Although these can be excellent modalities, there are several problems associated with administering the gustatory and olfactory stimuli. For example, some children dislike being touched around the oral (mouth) area; the presentation of stimuli is considered offensive, and withdrawal responses (turning head away and pushing trainer away) may occur. Therefore, the therapist must be able to differentiate avoidance responses to tactual and visual stimuli from avoidance responses to gustatory or olfactory stimuli.

Usually stimuli are divided into unpleasant items, such as vinegar, lemon, alum, salty, putrid odor, and resinous odor, and pleasant items, such as sugar or sugar water, perfume fragrance, spicy odors, and lemon odor and fragrance. Olfactory and gustatory stimuli frequently activate stimulatory receptors for the child and subsequently create an excitatory state. This may facilitate greater amounts of physical movement and responsiveness.

Gustatory and Olfactory Stimulation Activities

The following activities are suggested for use in developing a stimulation program through gustatory and olfactory modes.

1. Provide child with teether or teething toy (such as plastic bottle) and place different smells and tastes on the surface of the bottle. Note responses between pleasant and unpleasant odors. When changing odors on bottle be sure to wash thoroughly.
2. Hang mobile of different smells, such as cloves, cinnamon, garlic. Note if head turning is more to one type of odor or another. Change positions of odors.
3. Place child's hands into foods with different tastes, such as pudding, applesauce, salt, sugar; allow child to taste different foods.
4. Provide child with opportunities to go into shops with varying odors. Examples include soap shop, bakery, perfume department. Note if responses are to smell or to vision.
5. Identify pleasurable odor for child and place in area of toy. When child interacts with toy, allow him an opportunity to smell odor closely.

6. Have empty container saturated with varying smells with lids to take off and put on. Note varying responses to odors. If child is unable to actively take off lid, provide dowel handles on the lids. When necessary, provide physical prompts.
7. Provide itemizer with various smells and tastes, and allow child an opportunity to taste and smell each. Note any response of child to varying stimuli.

VISUAL STIMULATION

Responses to visual stimuli are present at 1 week of age in an avoidance response to a bright light and at 1 month in reaching toward stimuli. Visual responses are usually coupled with motor responses in visuo-motor, eye-hand coordination, and exploratory play skills. Fieber (1977) has divided sensorimotor-cognitive development for the first 2 years of life into seven stages (for assessment purposes):

1. Visual pursuit, localization, and object permanence
2. Development of means for obtaining desired environment events
3. Development of operational causality
4. Development of motor imitation
5. Development of vocal imitation
6. Construction of object relations in space
7. Development of schemes for relating to objects

Stimulation for cultivating visual awareness can best be coupled with appropriate motor responses and subsequent exploratory play activities.

Sensory stimuli to facilitate visual awareness includes the use of visual tracking or pursuit, using a pinpoint flashlight and brightly colored objects, which may help the child develop increased oculomotor control. Once objects can be localized, exploratory play actions (assuming motoric functioning is suitable), utilizing visual stimuli, may be encouraged.

Visual Stimulation Activities

Visual stimulation is a critical means of facilitating cognitive development. The activities listed below are inexpensive suggestions for implementing a visual stimulation program:

1. Hold an object (brightly colored) and/or a pinpoint flashlight in front of child's eyes to get his attention. After his attention has been gained, slowly move the object in an arc in front of child. Verbally say "Look." Each time attention is paid to the object, reinforce child. Initially perform with attention in the midline, then at 0°–45°–90°–135°–180°. Also move object varying distances from arc.
2. Place mobile in front of and to either side of child. Encourage him to look at moving object. Be sure to change position of the object.
3. Place a mirror in child's field of vision. Encourage looking at image in mirror, being sure to move mirror from side to side and up and down. Reinforce positive responses.
4. Place different brightly colored and interesting objects around the room, and encourage him to "Look at ____." Physically prompt when necessary.
5. Position child so his hand can be moved freely. Move hand into field of vision, and encourage him to look at his hand. Place brightly colored objects in child's hand and encourage his looking. Physically prompt when necessary.
6. Tie a helium balloon or balloon to child's wrist and have him follow the balloon. A face can be drawn on the balloon. Be sure to switch the balloon to each wrist.
7. After visual pursuit and localization are evident, encourage the child to reach. Place brightly colored necklace or scarf around your neck and prompt reaching behavior. Objects with noise are appropriate. Encourage both one- and two-handed reach.
8. Secure child's attention to an object on a towel out of his reach. Encourage him to grasp the towel to secure the object. Physically prompt if necessary. Use different sized toys to encourage varying grasp patterns.
9. Secure child's attention to an object. Let the object drop out of sight, and encourage him to look for object. Use brightly colored reinforcing objects.
10. Place a mobile or an object on a piece of elastic within the child's field of vision. Encourage him to pull the objects and create a pull/push type of effect. Place elastic object at different visual fields and distances.

MATERIALS DEVELOPMENT

Thus far, little has been said about design, construction, or adaptation of materials for use in a stimulation program. Many of the tenets and

Table 7.2. Materials development for sensory stimulation

1.	*Stimulus modes:*	Tactile, visual
	Material:	Soft doll
	Construction:	Use two clean washcloths sewn together, or a clean sock, and stuff and sew up. Faces can be made with crayon or bits of fabric or yarn. Use your imagination!

2.	*Stimulus modes:*	Tactile, auditory, visual
	Materials:	Rattles, noise makers
	Construction:	Take any plastic container washed well. Place something inside for noise, and taped tightly shut. It can be used as a mobile by tying it to a coat hanger. To make a soft toy sew material scraps together with yarn or stuff a clean sock and sew up. If something is put inside for noise, be sure it cannot be swallowed, thus causing problems.

3.	*Stimulus mode:*	Tactile
	Material:	Feeling bag
	Construction:	Put common household items (spoon, sponge, cup washcloth, etc.) in a paper bag. The child can feel the objects by sticking his hands into the bag. Use soft, hard, fuzzy, warm, cool, round, square objects. With each object the child picks up, tell him what it is.

4.	*Stimulus modes:*	Visual, auditory, olfactory
	Material:	Mobile
	Construction:	Take a coat hanger with knotted cording, material of different colors, and tin foil, and attach where the child cannot grasp. Bells or another noise maker sewn onto the material can be added. Also, dip the material into different smells, such as perfume, so the child can smell the material.

5.	*Stimulus mode:*	Gustatory
	Material:	Bottle
	Construction:	Take a small plastic bottle with no writing on it and wash it well. Let child use it as a mouthing toy for exploration. Put different tastes on it, being sure to wash off the tastes before applying another.

Table 7.2.   (continued)

6.	*Stimulus modes:*	Visual, tactile
	Materials:	Blocks, milk carton
	Construction:	Take a milk carton, open the top, and wash it thoroughly. Refold the top and tape it down. (A Carnation Milk box works well also.) The blocks can be covered with paper and colored, or you can cover them with colorful wrapping paper or with pages from magazines or material.

7.	*Stimulus mode:*	Visual
	Material:	Egg carton
	Construction:	Take an egg carton, use the top as the base and egg holders as hangers with yarn or string. The hangers can be painted, wrapped, or whatever to make them colorful. This will make a color mobile.

Table 7.3.   Response checklist for evaluation stimulation program

Name _____

Recorder _____

Date _____

(+) = indicates appropriate response
(−) = no response
If other than target response noted, record response in Comments.

		Positive/Approach response					Negative/Avoidance response				
	Sensory stimulation	Looks at person applying stimuli	Opens eyes wide	Smiles	Reaches toward stimuli	Laughs out loud or increases vocalization	Withdraws hand or extremity	Pushes stimuli away	Frowns	Increases muscle tone	Comments
Tactile	Lotion (Room temp.)										
	Sand paper										
	Cotton										
	Terry cloth										
Auditory	Bell										
	Horn										
	Drum										
	Rattle										
Gustatory	Sugar holt										
	Vinegar										
	Salt holt										
	Vanilla										
Olfactory	Lemon										
	Cinnamon										
	Rotten egg										
	Perfume										

guidelines advocated in Chapter 2 hold true here as well; as Williams, Briggs, and Williams note, it is wise to design materials for the lowest functioning handicapped child. Because the information in that chapter relevant to homemade construction is limited, Table 7.2 has been developed for those practitioners working directly with very low functioning children. It is hoped that the design guidelines in this table will be helpful.

EVALUATION OF STIMULATION ACTIVITIES

To determine the success or failure of a sensory stimulation program, anecdotal records and objective response checklists to specific stimuli are necessary. Table 7.3 indicates one possible checklist that might be employed. The frequency of response can be used to measure specific changes as a result of sensory stimulation. A time expectancy for changes, however, cannot be predicted specifically because each individual responds at a different rate. However, if no change has been observed for 6 months, assuming stimulation has been consistent, the therapist should reexamine presentation techniques and provide sensory stimulation in a different manner. This includes developing new stimuli, increasing lengths of presentation, and using multiple sensory modes.

SUMMARY

The present chapter has been concerned with sensory stimulation for low functioning handicapped individuals. The nonambulatory, profoundly retarded person receives very little attention from programmers and researchers and yet exhibits perhaps the most complex and frustrating physical and behavior problems of any handicapped population.

The review of literature and subsequent stimulation activities contained in this chapter will be helpful to those faced with many aspects of programming for severely multihandicapped children. Although these program activities are certainly not play and recreation as typically envisioned they are crucial prerequisites to any further behavioral development.

REFERENCES

Adelson, E., and Fraeberg, S. 1974. Gross motor development in infants blind from birth. Child Dev. 45:114–126.

Ayres, A. J. 1972. Sensory Integration and Learning Disorders. Western Psychological Services, California.

Baker, G. P. 1977. Tactile sensitive behavior in hyperactive and nonhyperactive children. Am. J. Occup. Ther. 31:447–453.

Bauer, B. A. 1977. Tactile sensitivity—Development of a behavioral response checklist. Am. J. Occup. Ther. 31(6):357–361.

Brazelton, T. B. 1977. The infant's world: How babies learn about taste, touch and smell. Redbook Mag. November:24–26.

Bucham, T., Butler, G., Eppes, F., Giles, J., Harris, T., Holzband, B., Lane, J., and Quisenberry, T. 1974. Effects of auditory reception on auditory and visual learning tasks. Educ. Train. Ment. Retard. 9:56–61.

Cruickshank, W. 1977. Referenced in: Sensory integration, an overview. Prepared by Occupational Therapy Division, Rehabilitation Medicine Department, Good Samaritan Hospital, Cincinnati. pp. 1–13.

Engen, T., Lipsitt, L. P., and Peck, M. B. 1974. Ability of newborn infants to discriminate rapid substances. Dev. Psychol. 10:741–744.

Fieber, N. M. 1977. Sensorimotor cognitive assessment and curriculum for the multi-handicapped child. The Severely and Profoundly Handicapped Child. Proceedings from the Second Annual Illinois Conference, Illinois on Severely/Profoundly Handicapped, Chicago.

Jones, B., and Robinson, T. 1973. Sensory integration in normal and retarded children. Dev. Psychol. 9:178–182.

Kinnealy, M. 1973. Aversive and nonaversive responses to sensory stimulation in mentally retarded children. Am. J. Occup. Ther. 27:464–471.

McCall, R. B. 1974. Exploratory manipulation and play in the human infant. Monogr. Soc. Res. Child Dev. 39.

McCracken, A. 1975. Tactile function of educable mentally retarded children. Am. J. Occup. Ther. 29:397–402.

Miller, A. S., Stewart, M. D., Murphy, M. A., and Jantzen, A. C. 1955. An evaluation method for cerebral palsy. Am. J. Occup. Ther. 9(3):105–111.

Neman, R., Roos, P., McCann, B. M., Menolascino, F. J., and Heal, L. W. 1975. Experimental evaluation of sensorimotor patterning used with mentally retarded children. Am. J. Ment. Defic. 79:372–384.

Norton, Y. 1975. Neurodevelopment and sensory integrating for the profoundly retarded multiply handicapped child. Am. J. Occup. Ther. 29:93–100.

Piaget, J. 1962. Play, Dreams, and Imitation. W. W. Norton, New York.

Raskin, L. M., Baker, G. P. 1975. Tactual and visual integration in the learning processes: Research and implications. J. Learn. Disabil. 8:108–112.

Safford, P. L., Gregg, L. A., Schneider, G., and Sewell, J.

M. 1976. A stimulation program for young sensory-impaired multihandicapped children. Educ. Train. Ment. Retard. 11:12–17.

Shearer, D., and Shearer, M. 1976. Portage Project Guide. Portage Public School District, Portage, Wisconsin.

Solkoff, N., and Matuszak, D. 1975. Tactile stimulation and behavioral development among low birthweight infants. Child Psychiatry Hum. Dev. 6(11):33–37.

Webb, R. C., and Staff of The Developmental Therapy Department. (January) 1971. Manual for AMP Index, #1, 7th Rev. Glenwood State School, Glenwood, Iowa.

Weisberg, P. 1975. Developmental differences in children's preferences for high and low arousing forms of contact stimulation. Child Dev. 46:975–979.

Weisler, A., and McCall, R. B. 1976. Exploration and play: Resume and redirection. Am. Psychologist 31:492–508.

Wilbarger, P. 1968. Activities for the remediation of sensorimotor dysfunction in primary school children. Unpublished manuscript. Goleta Union School District, Goleta, Cal.

8 MUSIC THERAPY Implications for Recreation Programming

George Giacobbe and Richard M. Graham

Practically every developmentally disabled individual will have had a considerable part of his life given to music or music-related experiences before ever coming to any setting for recreational experiences. One has only to take into account the amount of time during any given day when a person hears music while listening to the radio, viewing television, shopping in supermarkets, attending religious services, or sitting in waiting rooms of one kind or another. Add these moments to the time that the individual sings, whistles, plays musical instruments, dances, etc., and it becomes even more clear just how much our "normal environment" is, in fact, a musical environment. It becomes evident that to live in a "normal" environment music is essential. It is part of the very pursuit of humanness that all human service agencies attempt to implement in assisting those with developmental disabilities to adjust to life and living.

Music therapy is the use of carefully selected musical experiences to develop, restore, or maintain the good mental and physical health of developmentally disabled individuals. Such experiences are designed to assist in the efforts of agencies to humanize their services, i.e., to make the efforts toward habilitation, rehabilitation, recreation, or any form of assistance, more seated in enjoyment and happiness.

MUSIC AND THE DEVELOPMENTALLY DISABLED

Developmentally disabled individuals are very much like everyone else when it comes to music.

The contribution of both authors is considered equal.

A chapter of this nature has not been recorded previously. See Schwann, *Long-Playing Record Catalog,* April, 1978.

In any given population of people, one will find those who sing well and those who do not; those who play an instrument and those who do not; those who dance and those who do not dance; a few who create music and a great many who do not. This is the case in any grouping of developmentally disabled individuals. The one thing that all individuals have in common—to a greater or lesser degree—is enjoyment of music. The kind of music enjoyed varies from individual to individual, from social group to social group, and from nation to nation. It also varies as a function of age and is influenced by the type of developmental disability. The model presented in Figure 8.1 delineates one framework for analyzing the potential interaction among age level, disability type, and category of music activity.

In planning music experiences for the developmentally disabled, it is necessary for the recreation music leader to consider the cultural group from which clients come—their musical tastes and interests—as well as the type of developmental disability. With this in mind, it is valuable to look more closely at "music" and at the individuals who lead music activities for the developmentally disabled.

MUSIC: A SOCIALIZING AGENT

The anthropologist Meriam (1964, p. 27) writes that "music is a uniquely human phenomenon which exists only in terms of social interaction." The ability to interact socially is a basic goal of any recreation program with the developmentally disabled. In reference to this purpose, Gaston (1968, p. 21) has written, "It is precisely with such people (the handicapped) that music, because of its true nature, is beneficially influential in persuading toward better patterns of behavior."

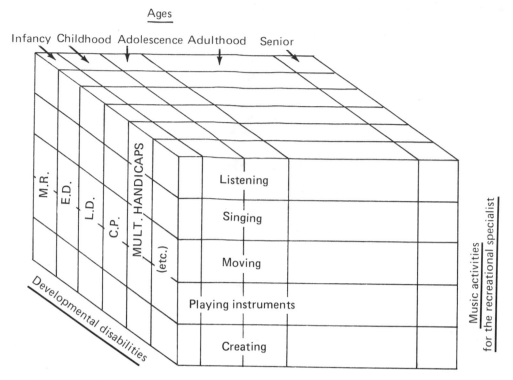

Figure 8.1. A framework for analyzing the potential interaction among age level, disability, and category of music activity.

The primary task of the recreation music leader in music therapy sessions is to organize group singing, listening, playing of instruments, dancing, creating of music, and production activities that will provide for the special sort of communications among participants and between participants and audiences that music provides. By properly coordinating these activities with the work of other professionals in the overall recreation program, the music program will qualify as music therapy.

MINIMUM SKILLS FOR CONDUCTING MUSIC THERAPY ACTIVITIES WITH DEVELOPMENTALLY DISABLED INDIVIDUALS

In the heterogeneity of the typical university class of recreation majors there are diverse skills, interests, and talents that can be utilized to emphasize several aspects of music. Many of these students have been high-school band, orchestra, or chorus members, or have sung for years in church or community choirs. These individuals bring with them certain skills that can be utilized effectively in an intelligently planned music therapy program for the developmentally disabled. As is the case in

every area of recreation, the recreation leaders must possess certain basic skills in order to function as leaders. The following list represents the minimum abilities and levels of interest the college student or in-service recreation leader must have in order to conduct music therapy activities on the lowest level of acceptability.

The pre-service or in-service recreation leader must be able to:

1. Sing a familiar song "on pitch"
2. Sing, clap, step, and dance to a simple musical beat (The leader must be able to do these separately and all together, i.e., walk in a circle to the beat of music in the background while singing the words and clapping the beat.)
3. Recognize off-pitch singing and playing by others
4. Recognize inaccurate clapping, stepping, and moving to a simple musical beat by others

Along with the above minimum skills there should be certain general knowledge that one interested in music should have accumulated in order to function successfully as a therapeutic recreation music leader. This includes the following:

1. The ability to identify personal music behaviors in relation to preferences, skills, and their interaction with daily, weekly, and yearly activities
2. Discovering and listing community resources that provide or promote music materials and activities, i.e community orchestras, choruses, bands, music and record stores, record libraries, concert halls, etc.
3. Interviewing clients (if possible) to indicate preferred and desired musical activities (The leader should observe them in various musical environments and identify times when they prefer music.)
4. Keeping in mind that music is to be used for a purpose
5. Knowing words and music to several songs and how to sing them effectively
6. Understanding that the various subcultures in the United States have different songs with which the members of these groups identify
7. Knowing how to sing songs from the various subcultures in, at least, a close approximation of the "proper" style, as dictated by the culture that produced the song
8. Understanding that no one "type" or "kind" of music is "better" or "worse" than any other kind of music, with respect to taste and inherent beauty or quality

Although the entering recreation student may possess the above skills and knowledge, it is also necessary to have an appropriate attitude. This should reflect:

1. An interest in music and a willingness to learn to sing or play a musical instrument
2. Some experiences in listening to music (not as background music, but for the simple pleasure of listening to music)
3. The fact that making or listening to music is one of the highest and most "human" endeavors available to human beings, disabled or nondisabled

MUSIC THERAPY ACTIVITIES

Music therapy can take place when one music leader and one developmentally disabled individual combine their efforts in a structured, goal-directed therapy session, using music to a greater extent than words. Such one-to-one sessions do occur from time to time and are desirable in some instances. This is but one aspect of music therapy, however. The leader can work in small groups or very large groups and in a variety of music settings. This chapter concentrates upon the skills, procedures, and information needed to conduct music therapy with small groups of developmentally disabled individuals. Table 8.1 outlines the types of music therapy experiences that are described throughout the balance of this chapter.

LISTENING IN MUSIC THERAPY

All that can be accomplished in music therapy depends upon the opportunities the client has to

Table 8.1.   Music therapy activities

Listening	Singing	Moving	Playing instruments	Creating
Background music	Informal singing	Eurhythmics	Rhythm instruments	Song making
Recorded music in listening groups	Community "sings"	Rhythms (e.g., Orff)	Simple melody instruments	Free improvisation on instruments
Music from radio (FM or AM) and television	Choruses	Action songs	Simple harmony instruments	Writing music
	Quartets and other ensembles	Singing games		Psychodrama with music (psycho-opera)
Live concerts	Glee clubs	Play games	Fretted instruments	
	Solos	Folk dances	Bands	Group improvisation ("jam sessions")
			Orchestras	
			Solos	
			Chamber groups and other combinations	

hear and listen to music. An essential and fundamental task of the recreation music leader is to provide opportunities for the client to listen to music of the client's choice.

Individual Listening

Listening to music is a very personal thing. No one, not even the leader, can listen for the client. If the listening session has prescribed specific (behavioral) goals (as should be the case), the leader must be prepared to deal with the individual motivations of each listener. It is fairly safe to say that few, if any, listeners in a music therapy session are interested in having their listening interrupted with musicological "analyses" or interpretations by the leader or other music "authority." This does not mean, however, that discussion should not be permitted.

Music for Group Interaction

The discussions that precede and follow any music listening session should be related directly to the therapeutic goals of the group. Group discussions may center around mood, programmatic ideas expressed in the music, past associations, feelings engendered, etc. The group may also discuss the more formalistic aspects of the music performed, e.g., harmonies, form, compositional devices, etc. Much of what is discussed will depend to a great extent upon the makeup of the actual listening group itself.

Organizing Compatible Music-Listening Groups When clients form a music therapy group (or become grouped) according to music tastes (likes as well as dislikes), the recreation leader can plan in terms of such natural groupings. This should not be interpreted to mean that only one type of music will be listened to by any particular group. It does mean that any departure from the accepted music norms will be worked out collectively among the group members. The means and reasons for selection of music for listening can be of great significance.

Benefits of Music Groups People normally listen to music in groups for varied reasons. One of the most common reasons seems to be a desire for group or "collective" responses and enjoyment of music. The great numbers of listeners who make up audiences of various sorts attest to this preference of people to share musical experiences with others. Gaston (1968) believes, in addition, that "the potency of music is greatest in the

group" and "music draws people together for the purpose of intimate, yet ordered, function." Most music listening will take place in groups. "Compatible" groups may extend the listening session to include attending live performances together and to the organization of recording tape (cassette, cartridge, reel-to-reel) clubs.

Group Attendance at Live Performances Clients may develop rapport to a considerable extent by attending live musical performances in "music interest" groups. There have been many reports of clients from large residential settings attending musical events. These groups are usually not kept together for other activities to build a cohesiveness, however. In cases where group attendance is but another aspect of an overall music therapy effort, live music experiences provide for additional opportunities for discrimination, exploration of feelings, and a sharing of aesthetic experiences. Although most of the discussion centering on music will emanate from the interest brought to the sessions by the listeners, there will be times, particularly during the first sessions, when the client will have to be motivated to listen.

Encouraging Listening When motivational techniques are necessary, the following approaches to listening have proved successful:

1. Comparative listening: The client will compare renditions being heard with others with which he might be familiar; he may also compare artists, accompaniments, interpretations, etc.
2. Supplementary information: Interest may be created by having clients read about music, e.g., information from record covers, biographies, anecdotes, etc.
3. Movement to music: Dance, action, or mime suggested by the music.
4. Visualizing stories or programmatic ideas: Thinking about story ideas, titles, or other subjects suggested by the music.
5. Familiarization with music and instruments: Recognition of instruments, voice qualities (soprano or alto?), dance steps, forms, etc.

Again it should be noted that there has been no suggestion that a client be led to "appreciate" music. Rather the emphasis has been upon using music that appeals in various ways to individuals, depending upon their previous background, experience, and exposure to music. If, however, as a result of the structure and music selection processes a client evidences greater desire to listen, and becomes more discriminating in his choices and responses to all kinds of music, one can state that the client is evidencing a greater appreciation of music.

Background Music

Frequently background music is provided in a variety of treatment settings for developmentally disabled individuals. Examples are music from recorded sources during mealtimes, during "intakes" in reception rooms, during visiting hours, and at other active occasions. Music may also be "piped into" individual rooms or wards. When the former is the case, provisions should be made for clients or attendants to turn the music off or on and to regulate the volume. Pillow speakers and small transistorized receivers make background music an even more individual experience.

When music is to be transmitted from some central area, important factors such as selection of materials, volume level, and length of transmitting times must be considered. The sound should never be so loud that people are required to shout above it to be heard. As a general rule, background music should probably not exceed five decibels above the threshold of sound for any given treatment room. (This will vary depending upon the nature and size of clientele served.)

It is usually a good idea to work closely with clients and staff in selecting music to be programmed from any central source. It is also important that music not be played continually throughout the day. Carefully selected music at critical periods during the treatment day is much more effective than any program of music that is played without interruption throughout the day. It is also worth mentioning that mealtimes may not always be the best time for effective background music. Frequently the period just after (or before) meals is better for carefully selected music. The best times for music will need to be worked out by the recreation leader and others involved in any mass programming of music from a central source.

MUSIC THERAPY THROUGH SINGING

Arthur Todd (1959) has written the following cogent statement regarding singing:

> What constantly baffles me is that an activity as universally enjoyed and as simple to develop as music is so generally ignored. Community singing is

adaptable to all occasions. It cuts across the lines of age, race, economic groups and physical capacities. It is less expensive than most activities. It is good winter or summer, indoors or outdoors. It has the power to weld a group together, to turn a crowd into a community, into a "rhythmic human companionship," as Carlyle used to say.

Although the reference above is to but one kind of singing, it easily could be generalized to any setting in which two or more individuals are occupied in tedious, boring activity or in which clients are thrown together without benefit of feelings of community among them. Singing will cause the individual singers to interact with one another, cause them to be aware of the others' pitch, loudness, phrasing, expression, etc. In fact, the accomplishment of a song in a group is an absolute impossibility without intragroup concern and positive action. Group singing, however, will serve to unify a group of otherwise disparate clients, give them a joint activity and a common goal, and promote fellowship, joy, and a shared aesthetic experience. Singing together has been found to be an excellent "ice breaker" for opening group therapy sessions.

The Recreation Leader in Singing Activities

In any group activity the leader will have to employ group dynamics skills. There will be groups that will function best when the recreation leader simply becomes part of the group and singing proceeds without a leader. In these instances the leader will begin the songs and might suggest certain songs. He does not direct the singing but coordinates the group.

During the course of the singing, the goal of enjoyment is never forgotten; likewise, neither are the therapeutic goals for the group and the individuals within the group. If a decision has been made for one member of the group to be more expressive in all of his dealings with others, the leader encourages this individual to "sing out." If the opposite is the case, oversinging is discouraged, all within the context of the song.

The success of music therapy through singing depends to a large extent upon the effectiveness of the song leader but almost equally upon the composition of the group and the songs used. It is important to be aware that music is a human process, representative of the culture, economic class, and ethnic background of the client. The songs most immediately appealing to the client will be songs from his culture. This is not to say that all music cannot eventually have great effect upon him, but that for immediate responsiveness the recreation leader will have to be responsive to the background of the client in selecting music.

Types of Songs

A basic knowledge of the kinds of songs that are available for singing will facilitate selections to meet the needs of the variety of individuals with whom the recreation leader will work. The most common types are listed below:

Action Songs As the name implies, these songs call for certain types of action, ordinarily described in the lyric of the song. The recreation leader must know these actions well and be prepared to demonstrate them, in addition to leading clients in the activity. After initial shyness is overcome, these songs provide a considerable amount of fun. They also give some individuals the opportunity to perform with a minimum of embarrassment because everyone else, including the leader, is doing the same actions.

Art Songs These songs are composed for trained voices and most of the time make use of poems for lyrics. They are sung by a solo voice in most cases but are easily adaptable for group singing. The recreation leader will not have much occasion to use the art song; however, there may be a few instances when knowledge of such songs and how they are sung will permit valuable contributions to individual therapy.

Folk Songs There are legitimate and quasi folk songs. Legitimate folk songs are those that have grown out of the life and culture of a section or race of people and that have been "handed down" from generation to generation. Usually there is a guitar, dulcimer, banjo, or other "folk instrument" accompaniment style that has been handed down with the song. Some knowledge of basic accompaniment technique on the guitar, ukulele, dulcimer, etc., will permit the recreation leader to participate effectively in this form of musical expression by the client.

Quasi folk songs, on the other hand, differ from legitimate folk songs in that they are usually adapted to include any current musical fads that happen to be popular at the time of the song's release. Many of these fit easily into the "popular song" category.

Popular Songs Popular songs usually are written for immediate public appeal, often for social dancing. These songs make up the "top forty" songs of any given week and tend to be forgotten soon afterward. Such songs have great appeal for adolescents and offer an excellent means for establishing group rapport. Because the popular song is usually identified with the style of the performer who makes the song popular, it is frequently very difficult for the average "fan" (or client) to reproduce the song effectively during informal singing. It is important to exercise considerable judgment regarding the singing of popular songs, particularly when the style of presentation is the most popular aspect of the song in question. "Country and western" songs and "soul" songs are examples of types of popular songs in which the style of singing is as important as the song itself in the appeal of any performance. In the majority of cases, popular songs are seldom good for group or individual singing in music therapy. Such songs can be used in other activities, however, such as structured or unstructured youth groups' programs, dancing and listening sessions to name a few.

Procedures for Singing in Music Therapy

The procedures for using singing activities in therapy are related directly to the function and role of the recreation music leader as well as the setting under consideration. For example, in a large mental hospital with a relatively slow turnover in the patient population, the music therapy session is planned with long term goals and is viewed as one of the standing activities of the patient's day-to-day hospital life.

The singing session may be an elaboration of a group psychotherapy session which meets on alternate days with the music therapist (e.g., Monday, Wednesday, Friday with the psychotherapist, and Tuesday, Thursday with the music therapist). Just as often there are groups developed for the sole purpose of music therapy through singing. In either case, the recreation leader, regardless of his level of experience or skills, must take four factors into account: 1) therapeutic goals of the group, 2) preparation of materials and procedures, 3) settings and space, and 4) evaluation of the activity.

Therapeutic Recreation Goals These goals are usually determined by a specialist or group of specialists in a "staffing" of the clients, individually or as a group (Harper, 1959). (Examples of goals from a psychoanalytic point of view might be catharsis, insight, transference, relationships, reality testing, etc.)

The singing group may also serve the purposes of a laboratory workshop in creative risk taking. When such is the case, the music group becomes a social system in which the participants learn to strive for relevance, creativity, and a means of taking initiative through various methods of group singing.

When free, spontaneous interaction through informal singing is a goal, the participants may be led into an activity somewhat akin to psychodrama; perhaps "psycho-opera" may be an appropriate description of the resulting process. Here the clients sing out their feelings while role playing and improvising a story. This approach to therapy through singing, with some adaptations in procedure, can be equally effective in short term treatment settings.

Preparation of Materials and Procedures

If the singing activity is to be a therapeutic one, the selection of songs must be based upon more than mere whimsy. The lyrics of selected songs should offend no one, especially racial, religious, or national groups. If the song is suitable except for one or two offensive words, words should be changed rather than risking offense and regressive behavior on the part of the offended (e.g., use "darling" for "darky" where appropriate in certain Stephen Foster songs).

The age of the singers is an important factor that must be considered in song selection. The songs that tend to be best remembered are religious songs learned during childhood and love songs learned during adolescence. If, for example, the recreation music leader finds himself with a new group whose average age is about 58, and he wants to begin immediately with songs that would appeal to a majority of group members, he would select hymns representative of the religious majority in the group and the popular songs that were sung when this particular group average was about 15 years old. A simple formula for selecting immediately appealing songs is:

$$\begin{array}{c} \text{average age} - 15 \text{ (years)} = \text{year of most} \\ \text{of group} \qquad\qquad\qquad \text{familiar songs} \end{array}$$

If we use our hypothetical group to fill in the formula it becomes:

$$58 \text{ years} - 15 \text{ years} = 43 \text{ years ago}$$

If the year of calculation were 1978, the group in question would more than likely be most responsive to the songs written around 1935 (43 years ago) or the music from the era of the "big bands" (Glenn Miller, Tommy Dorsey, Artie Shaw, etc.) and the movie themes and songs that were so popular during that time (songs by Cole Porter, Richard Rogers, George Gershwin, etc.).

As might be expected, the group leader must know the songs well. He should become familiarized with music from the target period, learn the songs, and get the lyrics reproduced on song sheets. Singing activities can be done practically anywhere and with a minimum of physical requirements. Some situations are, of course, better than others.

Settings and Space

In the better organized large mental hospitals there is usually a suite of rooms set aside and designated as the "Music Therapy Clinic (or Department)." In such a place one would expect to find at least one comfortable room set aside for singing. The room should probably not look like the traditional "rehearsal room," but should be furnished so that the group members can sit or stand comfortably without crowding. Chairs should be movable, as should the piano. The latter can be accomplished easily by putting the piano on the large wheels and metal frame often called a "piano dolly" or "piano truck." The room should be well lighted and well ventilated. Most of the requirements of a good group therapy room (with the possible exception of the long table) hold for a good music therapy room. Even the familiar long (or oval) table can be used with certain singing groups (madrigal singers).

Smaller settings, such as those found in community mental health centers, will probably not have the room of the large mental hospital for music therapy activities. A comfortable place for the group to sing is still of importance. In many cases rooms can be made available through the careful scheduling of other services and the music therapy program with regard to available space.

When space is a factor, the leader may have to rely upon one of the smaller social instruments for musical accompaniments in lieu of a piano. The piano accordian, the guitar, the autoharp, the banjo, and many other instruments can be used for effective accompaniment when available space prohibits use of a piano.

Regardless of the physical facilities, the music therapy singing session can be successfully effective if the recreation leader plans carefully with other disciplines of the center and coordinates his efforts with the other mental health workers on all levels. The amount or degree of success (or lack of it) will be of importance to all associated with the clientele being served. Such success can be evaluated at the end of one period or at other designated points during the course of music therapy with clients, patients, or students.

Evaluation After a singing activity has been completed, the leader should try to analyze the session in terms of its successes and failures. If total participation had been a goal, the amount of participation must be evaluated. Was there enjoyment? Which songs went well? Which were not successful? Why? Such observations are of great value in reporting results at the staffing of the group participants and in planning subsequent activities.

SUGGESTED REPERTOIRE OF SONGS

Opening Songs

Whatever the long range purpose or therapeutic goal of any group assembled for singing, it is of utmost importance that total participation be developed as soon as possible. This is best done by opening the singing session with songs that are familiar to all of the singers. The reasons for this are fairly obvious; the singers will suffer little embarrassment from indecision about words, melody, interpretation, etc.

Starting the group can best be accomplished by simply saying the words "Ready Sing" in the rhythm of the opening words of the song. Before starting these songs only a very few opening comments are necessary (it is a singing, not a "talking," session). Make certain that all are ready. Then, hum the starting pitch and "Ready Sing" in the pattern of the first two words or syllables of the song.

An example of how to begin the song "America" would be:

Leader: Now let us sing "America" (hums the pitch of the first note),
Ready Sing (spoken in the rhythm of . . . My Country . . .)

Group: My coun—try, 'tis of thee,
Sweet land of lib—er—ty,
Of thee I sing.
Land where my fathers died.
Land of the Pil—grim's pride.

From ev—'ry moun—tain side,
Let free—dom ring!

Conducting may amount to no more than the recreation leader moving his hand(s) in the air to the basic beat of the song being sung. Formal conducting techniques are beyond the scope of this chapter. The recreation specialist, however, can be an effective leader of singing in music therapy activities by practicing and developing facility in:

1. Starting the group together (hum pitch, "Ready Sing")
2. Keeping the basic beat going by "conducting" the basic beat of the song (moving arms and hands up and down in a mood characteristic of the song being led) and maintaining eye contact with the singers
3. Bringing hands and arms down firmly at the end of the song to indicate that all singers should stop together

Additional songs that can be used in starting a group are presented in a later section of this chapter concerned with playing instruments. After rapport has been established through the singing of familiar songs, it is frequently desirable and necessary to add novelty to the music therapy session by introducing new songs to the clients.

Teaching New Songs

The most efficient way of teaching new songs (particularly to nonmusicians) is by ear or by rote. To teach a song "by ear" or "by rote" means to teach the entire song, words and music, by demonstration with no access to written or printed song materials. In other words, clients in music therapy will learn new songs from hearing the recreation leader sing these songs during the music therapy session. There are three methods of teaching a song by ear (by rote) that have been found to be most effective in music therapy:

1. The part or "chime-in" method
2. The whole method
3. The phrase method

With the *part method* the singing group is instructed to "chime-in" on a section of the song that is repeated at regular intervals. "Old Mac-Donald Had a Farm (ee-yi, ee-yi, oh!)," "Skip to My Lou," and "Swing Low, Sweet Chariot" are examples of songs with repeated sections that can be taught easily using the part method. For instance, after the leader has sung "Swing Low" several times, the following procedure could be tried:

Leader: Swing Low, Sweet Chariot
Clients: Comin' for to carry me home,
Leader: Swing Low, Sweet Chariot
Clients: Comin' for to carry me home.
Leader: I looked over Jordan, and what did I see?
Clients: Comin' for to carry me home?
Leader: A band of angels comin' after me,
Clients: Comin' for to carry me home.

After having followed this procedure, the clients could join in any parts they remembered, and finally, the group could sing the entire song without help from the leader. Such a process can take place within 10 minutes, and the therapeutic implications of any group accomplishing so much in so brief a time should be obvious.

The *whole method* approach, on the other hand, involves the leader singing the complete song through several times (perhaps over two or three sessions) before the clients attempt singing it. Proof of the effectiveness of this method is the fact that people (including the very young) learn songs, jingles, and commercials by hearing them from radio or television broadcasts. These are always heard in their complete form and are learned as such. After the leader feels that he has demonstrated the song enough, he should have the clients sing it back to him; if there are weak places, he should give assistance in those places. Any ongoing music therapy session should have new songs that are in the process of being introduced—some being sung for the group for the first time, others having been heard several times.

A third technique, the *phrase method,* starts with the leader singing the entire song; the first phrase is sung (or first two or three phrases if these are short) and the clients sing this phrase back. When the phrase can be sung with reasonable accuracy, the leader then sings the second phrase of the song and it is sung back until learned. This process is repeated until all phrases are learned, and then the phrases are put together in a final singing of the completely learned song. For instance, in "Sandy Land" the leader would sing the first two lines of the song and the clients would sing it back to him. This procedure is repeated until the entire song is learned.

Leader: Make my living in sandy land,
        Make my living in sandy land,
Clients: (Sing both lines . . .)
Leader: Make my living in sandy land,
        Ladies, fare you well.
Clients: (Sing both lines . . .)

In the case of a regularly scheduled group, meeting daily or two to four times per week, there will be songs at various levels of familiarity. Some will have been just introduced by the leader, others will be at a stage where difficult spots are being practiced, and some will be at the level where group pride will demand some refinement of the songs being sung. The group will develop considerable pride in their ability to sing a song with an above average level of fluency.

MUSIC THERAPY THROUGH MOVEMENT

There is a unity between hearing, vision, touch, taste, and smell. All of the senses are interrelated. The complete appreciation of music will include some degree of motor response. We do not merely hear the melody with our ears, we sense it through our whole body (Thurstone, 1920). The oneness of music is based on "a universal axiom that composing, performing, and listening are basically the same act of being musical" (Howes, 1965).

There are many activities, using large and small muscles, that can be performed to music. Some suggested activities are marching, skipping, hopping, galloping, clapping hands, snapping fingers, stomping feet, tapping various parts of the body (head, shoulders, knees, etc.), bouncing a ball, and jumping rope.

When it comes to the interaction of music and such activities, the leader is limited only by his own level of creativity. Each client with whom the leader works will offer a new challenge. When a member enters or leaves that group, it changes; therefore, the leader must be alert and able to adjust to the needs of the clients.

The Recreation Leader in Movement Activities

The recreation music leader can ask the clients to imitate the leader in fine and gross motor body movements of a locomotive and nonlocomotive mode. This requires the following of directions for movement with music. The clients, for example, may participate in movement activities that require peer interaction for a successful outcome, as in "London Bridge" where two children form a bridge with their arms while the rest of the group moves under it.

Another activity is to pantomime various sport or other actions in time to music. As an example, to marching songs (e.g., "Stars and Stripes Forever," "Washington Post March") the actions pantomimed include throwing a ball, batting a ball, bowling, rowing a boat, serving a tennis ball, driving a golf ball, kicking a football, etc.

The client selects, learns, and participates in patterned dances, such as folk, square, rock, modern, ballroom, and body movement sequences. The recreation music leader sequences the movement activities in terms of complexity of patterns, formations, ability to perform the body movement, etc. This continues until the client has developed a repertoire of music skills that can allow the client to participate in the movement experiences.

A Procedure to Enhance Motor Skills

The following sequence illustrates one way of using music to facilitate motor skills:

1. Leader: "Listen to the music and try to do what the song says to do."
2. Begin playing the record. As specific directions are given, such as "wiggle something," encourage clients to use various parts of their bodies. Tell them that the movement can be done in many different ways and that no one way is correct.
3. Verbally reflect the various movements that the clients make. It may be necessary to give some clients suggestions as to how to do a specific movement which is called for in the song.

An example of a song that can enhance motor skills is "If You're Happy and You Know It." Other examples are "Stop the Music," which allows the clients to demonstrate the ability to repond to pauses in the music with immobility, and "Old MacDonald Had a Farm," during which the leader can change the words to include things that produce specific speech sounds that are troublesome to the client.

Rhythm Band Activities

In organizing the rhythm band, one instrument at a time should be introduced. As the instruments are introduced gradually, the clients should experiment with the instrument so that they feel the rhythmical responses. Clients can be taught to keep time and to play with precision. Rhythms may be free, imitated, or directed. An interesting and meaningful activity is combining all of the areas of music, rhythms, singing, action song, and dancing, as is done with the song "Put Your Little Foot." This activity is an effective means of improving social relationships and physical development. The participation in a rhythm band is one of the best means of combining social adaptation with muscular control and increased attention span.

MUSIC THERAPY THROUGH PLAYING MUSICAL INSTRUMENTS

Types of Musical Instruments

All types of musical instruments can and should be made available for use in music therapy. Making these instruments available is not the "whole story," however, because the instrument, whatever its kind, must be played upon to be of use in music therapy. This means that either the recreation leader or the client will have to be able to play an instrument before it has any functional value in the therapy setting. This becomes more of a problem when considering use of the so-called formal, as opposed to "informal," instruments.

Unless the recreation leader comes to music therapy with considerable training and background in music, the greatest successes in dealing with musical instruments will come from use of the "informal" or "social and recreational" instruments. These instruments can be described as those that are relatively easy to learn to play, thereby making them particularly suitable for music therapy sessions led by one who has less than extensive musical abilities.

The accordian offers a wide range of possibilities for a leader, from the nonmusician to the accordian virtuoso. It has the added value of being completely mobile, and, when played by the recreation leader, it permits him to circulate among his clients while providing an effective accompaniment.

Rhythm and/or percussion instruments are also excellent in music therapy. They include instruments that the performer either shakes, scrapes, strikes, or causes to ring in some manner or another and are used in accompanying singing or dancing, or for just the pure enjoyment of performing rhythms. These instruments are immediately playable by almost anybody and should be introduced by the leader when he is interested in extending the client's musical behavior beyond informal singing with a minimum of effort.

Melody Instruments

The title used here would make it necessary to include any instrument upon which a melody could be played. In keeping with the notion that certain "social and recreational" instruments will be considered and other instruments not, the following instruments are suggested:

1. Recorder
2. Tonette (song flute, ocarina, other diatonic whistles)
3. Melody bells
4. Xylophone
5. Marimba
6. Mountain dulcimer
7. Psaltery

Each of these instruments can be purchased at greatly varying prices. All but the xylophone and marimba are relatively inexpensive. The generalist can use various combinations of these instruments to make up groups of any mixture desired. Of course, any of these instruments can be used in conjunction with the singing program. The performer can "play along," or accompany a singing group with very good musical and social (he is supporting the group) effects resulting. Of all of the instruments that might be used to accompany singing—individual or group—the fretted instruments are the most effective and the most popular.

Fretted Instruments

Fretted instruments are stringed instruments with raised lines, called "frets," which indicate the positions for different pitches (from high to low) on the fingerboard of the instrument. One plays these instruments by plucking or strumming the strings with the thumb and fingers or with a plastic "pick." The most commonly seen instruments of this type in the United States are as follows:

Guitar: The guitar has a flat back and indentions or "waists" that curve in on the sides. The modern guitar has six strings and is tuned in "fourths," with one exception (between and second and third or b and g strings).

Banjo: The banjo resembles the guitar in some respects in that it has a "neck," which holds a fretted fingerboard and sometimes has six strings. The five-string banjo is, however, a popular variety, and some have only four strings.

Ukulele: The ukulele is a Hawaiian instrument of the guitar family. It has four strings and is probably the simplest to play of the fretted instruments.

Other instruments that have fretted keyboards are the mandolin and the Appalachian "mountain" dulcimer.

Harmonica

Among the social and recreational instruments, there is none which can be handled more readily and more easily by nonmusicians than the harmonica. It is easy to understand the struction of the harmonica by remembering that the most important chord in the piece being played (the tonic chord) is produced by blowing. The two other important chords (the dominant and the subdominant) can be obtained by drawing the breath in. There are 10 holes, and the instrument is held with the lower notes to the left. To play a scale, begin by blowing into the fourth hole for the first tone; draw for the second tone in the scale. Hole number 5 is next in succession; blow for the third tone of the scale and draw for the fourth. The same process will produce the fifth and sixth degrees of the scale. For the seventh, eighth, ninth, and tenth notes of the scale, the blowing process is reversed to one of "draw" "blow." The illustration below indicates this process:

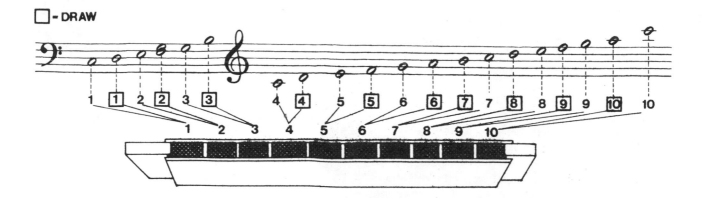

There are many styles of harmonicas on the market. The notes given in the illustration above are for the "C" instrument. Harmonicas are also built in different keys. Some instruments can play more than the simple scale. When the "sharps" and "flats" in a scale can be played upon the harmonica, the instrument may be called a "chromatic harmonica" or a "chromatica."

The chromatica consists of two harmonicas, one above the other. With the use of a lever, the player can play every note including the "chromatics" in the scale. Such an instrument permits the player to play almost any song that he is likely to hear.

Autoharp

This instrument has several advantages: it is easily portable, it can be used to accompany most any kind of singing or rhythm activities, it can be learned quickly by most people, and it is relatively inexpensive.

The autoharp (a copyrighted name by the Oscar Schmidt Company) or varieties of the instrument may have from 5 to 15 bars, permitting the playing of many "chords."

The autoharp is played by pushing down the bar for the proper chord (as indicated over the words or music of a song). The other hand strums the strings of the autoharp, usually from the long strings toward the shorter ones. The chord is changed when so indicated over the words or music of the song being played.

Playing Positions The autoharp can be played held against the body with the strings out and the small end pointed upward and slightly toward the left shoulder. The right hand strums while the left arm cradles the instrument, leaving the left hand to operate the chord bars. The instrument can also be held by a neck strap, which permits the player to suspend the instrument in a position parallel to the floor. Strum from the large strings toward the small ones.

The most common (and most comfortable) position involves resting the instrument on a table or other solid wooden surface for good resonance. The playing position remains essentially the same as above. The right hand plays on either side of the bars. The strum direction is away from the body, from the larger strings to the smaller ones.

Bar Positions The autoharp has chords in "natural key groupings." These are arranged for easy positions in whatever key is being used. Usually there are three chords associated with a particular key (the tonic, the subdominant, and the dominant). These chords usually lie easily under three adjacent fingers or are within easy reach (e.g., B-flat, C$_7$, F; C, D$_7$, G; F, G$_7$, C; etc.).

Playing the Autoharp For practice, select any round, press the proper bar, and strum once at the beginning of each stanza. Then try strumming at the important words. By using the one chord and establishing a repetitive strum rhythm that sounds acceptable to you, you are accompanying yourself (or others) on the autoharp.

Tenor Ukulele

The tenor ukulele is the easiest of the fretted instruments. The instrument is held with its longer axis parallel to the ground with the strings outward. The head of the instrument containing the tuning pegs points to the left. The strings may be tuned starting with the "top" string downward or vice versa. The pitches are G, C, E, A, when tuning from the top down and vice versa when beginning with A. The pitches can be taken from the piano.

Two-chord melodies can be immediately accompanied by placing fingers behind the appropriate frets and changing the finger patterns at the proper harmonic places. Below are the chord positions for the familiar song "Skip To My Lou."

"Skip To My Lou"

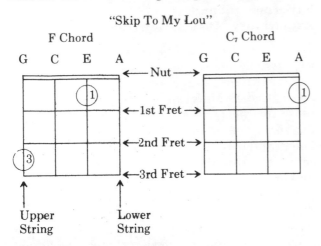

Choose your partner; ←——— skip to my Lou
F   F   F   F

Choose your partner; ←——— skip to my Lou
C₇   C₇   C₇   C₇

Choose your partner; ←——— skip to my Lou
F   F   F   F

Skip to my Lou, my Darling.
C₇   C₇   F F

Baritone Ukulele

Larger than the tenor ukulele and smaller than the guitar is the baritone ukulele. The instrument is held in the same manner as the tenor ukulele. The strings are tuned starting from the top string downward (or vice versa). When tuning downward the pitches are E, B, G, D, which also happen to be the first four strings of the guitar. The two instruments are played exactly alike except for the lower two strings, which present greater opportunities for larger chords on the guitar.

Guitar

The guitar, by virtue of its extra two lower strings, is a more versatile instrument than the baritone ukulele. The instrument is held in the same manner as the ukuleles. The strings are tuned from top to bottom on E, A, D, G (as the baritone ukulele), and the lower two strings on B and E. Below are chord patterns for "The More We Get Together."

Some songs, listed by chord, that can be sung and accompanied by any of the social or recreational instruments discussed above are listed below. You will recall that these instruments in-

"The More We Get Together"

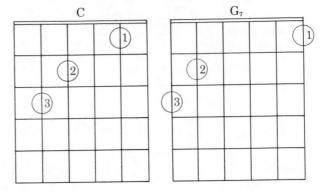

The more we get to-gether, to-gether, to-gether,
C   C   G₇   C

The more we get to-gether, the happier we'll be.
G   C   G₇C

For your friends are my friends, and my friends are your friends.
G₇   C   G₇   C

The more we get to-gether, the happier we'll be.
C   C   G₇   C

clude, among others, the guitar, the ukuleles, the autoharp, the banjo, the "mountain" dulcimer, and the harmonica. The songs that follow can be found with strum patterns and appropriate chords for accompaniment in numerous beginning methods books.

One-chord melody (G major)
    "Cripple Creek"

Two-chord melodies
    (Introducing the D₇ chord)
        "Sandy Land"
        "Hail, Hail, the Gang's All Here"
        "Paw Paw Patch"
        "Hush, Little Baby"
        "Go Tell Aunt Rhodie"
        "Old Brass Wagon"
        "Tom Dooley"
        "Bingo"

Three-chord melodies
    (Introducing the C chord)
        "Battle Hymn of the Republic"
        "Swing Low"
        "Nobody Knows"
        "This Train"
        "Goodbye, My Lover"

(Introducing the D chord)
  "Simmons"
  "Kookaburra"
  "Clementine"

(Introducing the A₇ chord)
  "Kum Ba Yah"
  "Amazing Grace"
  "Down by the Station"
  "Row, Row, Your Boat"
  "Go Tell it on the Mountain"
  "Red River Valley"
  "Goose Round"
  "All the Good Times"
  "Are You Sleeping?"
  "Little Tommy Tinker"

(Introducing the A chord)
  "All Praise to Thee"
  "Patsy Ory Ory Aye"
  "This Old Man"
  "Somebody's Knocking"

(Introducing the E₇ chord)
  "Little Brown Jug"
  "The Old Gray Mare"
  "White Coral Bells"
  "Yankee Doodle"

(Introducing the A minor chord)
  "Mister Banjo"
  "When Johnny Comes Marching Home"

(Introducing the E minor chord)
  "We Shall Not Be Moved"
  "Zum Gali Gali"
  "Standing in the Need of Prayer"

(Introducing the G₇ chord)
  "Dry Bones"

(Introducing the D minor chord)
  "Aura Lee"

(Introducing the F chord)
  "Old Smoky"
  "Greensleeves"

Other songs may be found in any community song book. Many popular music books include fingering charts for both guitar and baritone ukulele. It is suggested that these songs be practiced with all instruments available. Singing is always encouraged when social and recreational instruments are used.

MUSIC THERAPY THROUGH CREATING

Experimental and Exploratory Musical Activities

To be creative, developmentally disabled individuals may merely modify their own music behaviors without direction from the recreation music leader. More ambitious activities involve use of the clients' own materials and ideas or those the recreation music leader presents as a basis upon which to initiate and facilitate musical activities. Examples of such activities include making up new words for songs, developing new melodies, and selecting new harmonies or chord sequences. Other examples would include construction of unique instruments to create a desired sound, self-expression through modifying communication media (such as a song transformed into body movement sequences), and creation of signs and symbols for musical communication with others.

The recreation music leader's task is to facilitate the ongoing process. Alternatives and modifications should be introduced when necessary.

The Recreation Leader in Composing Activities

The recreation music leader may spend a great deal of time looking for just the right song for a client, often never being able to find that song. Therefore, it may be necessary to develop some song-writing skills. If the recreation leader develops song-writing skills, these can be used, as Ficken (1976) has noted, to prepare original songs, and also as a tool to guide a client who does the composing. When working with a client the composing experience can be shared, with the client gradually assuming more of the initiative and responsibility.

The composer's palette consists of melody, harmony, rhythm, timbre, and dynamics.

Melody can be generated in many ways including random depression of keys on the piano until a series of tones is chosen for their "likable" or "meaningful" quality.

The creating of *harmony* usually follows the melody. Harmony in the form of either chord progressions or dissonant collections of sounds (such as tone clusters, that is, when many tones are played at once) can be then developed. In regard to tone clusters, different lengths of wood can be used to depress the piano keys which thereby achieves a guaranteed reproducibility.

Rhythm not only can be explored through the original instrument, such as the piano (by the repeating of notes or the holding of notes to achieve the desired effect), but also can be added by other instruments, such as drums or sticks.

Timbre is the type of sound that is produced either by a solo instrument, such as the piano, or by groups of instruments, such as the string quartet or orchestra. The client can achieve unique sounds through the use of single instruments, combinations of instruments, the development of unique instruments, or the interaction of "regular" and unique instruments. An example of such an interaction would be the placing of a

silver dollar upon a kettle drum and then doing a soft drum roll to produce the sound of a large motor, such as a truck motor.

Dynamics, the loudness or softness of the composition, also lends to the mood of the composition by heightening the previously named effects.

An example of a simple song dedicated to the recreation music leader follows:
"Recreation Music Leader"

The Recreation Leader in Lyric Writing Activities

The freedom in lyrics allows anyone who can use words an opportunity to write lyrics. The words need not rhyme, but rhyming offers a challenge that most clients find hard to resist. Possible

RECREATION MUSIC LEADER

ᵃAs in the manner of "do, do, do, do, do" in the "People are Funny" song from the old Art Linkletter television show.
ᵇGo with "do, dee, dee, do, etc" or supply your own words.

rhyming words for "Recreation Music Leader" include: be, bee, see, fee, gee, *glee,* he, *key,* knee, me, pea (any word that ends "-py" or "-my", e.g., therapy, anatomy, atrophy), tea, we. The italicized words are often music-related words.

Music Complexity and Range

Simplicity or complexity can be accomplished by minor changes in the music structure, as is seen in the examples of the third line of the song:

Another concern is the singing range of the recreation leader's clients. For example, Larson (1977) has shown that the mean range and midpoint tone of educable mentally retarded (EMR) children are different from those of nonhandicapped children.

Mean range and midpoint of subjects

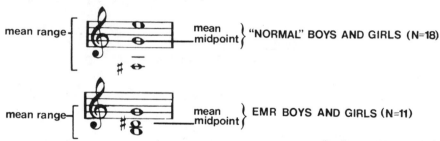

(Larson, 1977, p. 141)

The recreation music leader can use the knowledge of the range of his clients to good advantage in terms of transposing songs for singing as well as in terms of composing for them.

Below are examples of how to change the opening of the song "Recreation Music Leader," both through transposing and narrowing the range of tones (thus eliminating wide skips or jumps in tones that are often difficult for clients).

Beyond that, various dynamics and other music structures can be used to produce a quiet melody or lullaby. The third line of the song can thus be written:

The third line of the example demonstrating a driving melody (as in a passing train) is:

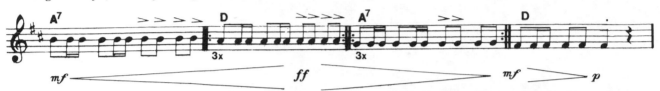

Creative ideas on the subject of composing can be discovered in many books. However, the recreation music leader may find the books by Andrews (1954), Bergethon and Boardman (1970), and Graham (1975) of particular value.

SUMMARY

The recreation leader who can qualify to work in music therapy can meet the needs of clients, families, and communities as a person who can relate music to many aspects of their problems. The recreation leader can lead developing music therapy experiences in which clients express themselves immediately and with a minimum of practice or drill. As Folsom (1968, p. 357) has stated, "... [the] teaching of worthwhile leisure time activities can be as important as vocational experiences." Although the implications of this statement may be limited, its message that the recreation leader has an important task to perform should not be overlooked. Music can be useful in the performance of that task.

REFERENCES

Andrews, A. 1954. Creative Rhythmic Movement for Children. Prentice-Hall, Englewood Cliffs, N.J.

Bergethon, B., and Boardman, E. 1970. Musical Growth in the Elementary School. 2nd Ed. Holt, Rinehart and Winston, New York.

Ficken, T. 1976. The use of songwriting in a psychiatric setting. J. Music Ther. 13:163–172.

Folsom, G. S. 1968. The developing situation. In E. T. Gaston (ed.), Music in Therapy, Macmillan Co., New York.

Gaston, E. T. 1968. Man and music. In E. T. Gaston (ed.), Music in Therapy. Macmillan Co., New York.

Graham, R. M. (ed.). 1975. Music for the Exceptional Child. Music Educators' National Conference, Reston, Va.

Harper, R. A. 1959. Psychoanalysis and Psychotherapy. Prentice-Hall, Englewood Cliffs, N.J.

Howes, R. 1965. Rhythm and man. Lecture in London Course on Music Therapy (June, 1962). Reported in Alvin, J., Music for the Handicapped Child. Oxford University Press, London.

Larson, B. A. 1977. A comparison of singing ranges of mentally retarded and normal children with published songbooks used in singing activities. J. Music Ther. 14:139–143.

Meriam, Alan P. 1964. The Anthropology of Music. Northwestern University Press, Evanston, Ill.

Thurstone, L. L. 1920. The problem of melody. Music. Q. 6:426–429.

Todd, A. 1959. Community singing. Recreat. Mag. 44:242–244.

Wood, M. M., Graham, R. M., Swan, W. W., Purvis, J., Gigliotti, C., and Samet, S. Developmental Music Therapy. National Association for Music Therapy, Inc., Lawrence, Kan.

APPENDIX
ANNOTATED BIBLIOGRAPHY AND RESOURCES

Paul Wehman, Jo Ann Marchant,
Becky Williams, Nancy Briggs, and Ron Williams

REFERENCES

The information contained in this appendix includes annotated bibliographies on references related to special playgrounds and materials, toy play, games, music therapy, and socialization. The organization of this reference list should help teachers, therapists, and other practitioners develop play, recreation, and leisure skill programs for developmentally disabled individuals.

Playgrounds for Special Populations

Austin, R. L., and Hayes, G. A. 1975. Playgrounds and Playspaces for the Handicapped. (Available from Theraplan, Inc., 1536 Pipher Lane, Manhattan, Kan. 66502. Price: $2.00.)

This basic handbook includes information on a variety of handicapping conditions, the value of active play, and design considerations important in planning play areas for the disabled. Photographs of commercial equipment are also included.

Bowers, L. (August) 1975. Play Learning Centers for Preschool Handicapped Children: Research and Demonstration Project Report. College of Education, Professional Physical Education Program, University of South Florida, Tampa.

The report explains the importance of play activities for handicapped children and discusses the results of research into playground equipment. Includes plans, discussions, and descriptions of areas.

Bowers, L. (August) 1976. Research and Demonstration Project Second Year Report. College of Education, Professional Physical Education Program, University of South Florida, Tampa.

This article includes comparisons between handicapped and nonhandicapped children's use of equipment at a United Cerebral Palsy Play Learning Center.

Dattner, R. 1974. Design for Play. MIT Press, Cambridge Mass.

This book describes the philosophy, psychology, and social functions of play. Drawings and photos of a wide variety of playgrounds are included. One chapter focuses on playgrounds for handicapped children, a special interest of the author. Many design criteria are suggested.

New York State Education Department. (undated). An Instructional Playground for the Handicapped. The University of the State of New York, Division for Handicapped Children, Special Education Instruction Materials Center, Albany, N.Y.

This report includes specifications and plans for building equipment made from old tires. A range of activities for which the equipment can be used are discussed.

Rutledge, A. J. (February) 1975. Playground Design. Parks Recreat. 10(#2):20–22, 43–44.

This article includes an informative description of Ellis' theories of play. Guidance in selecting equipment and sites is also provided.

Plans and References for Adapted and Homemade Recreation Materials

Bartholomew, R., and Meyer, B. 1976. Developing and Evaluating Learning Devices for Exceptional Children. Paper presented at the Council for Exceptional Children Annual Convention, Chicago.

This presentation described the cooperative efforts of a special educator, an industrial designer, and a toy manufacturer to develop special "learning devices" or play materials for disabled children. Design considerations were described, as well as possible gains in learning demonstrated by the children following teacher-directed activities with the new materials. None of the newly developed "learning devices" (puzzles, story boards, etc.) was carried beyond the prototype, experimental stage; that is, the manufacturer decided to not produce the materials for general distribution.

Campbell, P., Green, K., and Carlson, L. 1977. Approximating the norm through environmental and child-centered prostheses and adaptive equipment. In E. Sontag (ed.), Educational Programming for the Severely and Profoundly Handicapped, pp. 300–319. Council for Exceptional Children, Reston, Va.

This informative article is well illustrated with photographs and drawings of positioning apparatus and mobility equipment. It provides background information on developmental skills, factors to consider in choosing equipment, and other guidelines. Sources of additional information on adaptive equipment are also included.

Dorward, B. 1960. Teaching Aids and Toys for Handicapped Children. Council for Exceptional Children, Reston, Va.

This publication describes how to construct sturdy wooden toys for activities at the "early childhood" level. It includes photos of the toys and puzzles being used by the cerebral palsied children for whom the materials were developed. Construction of these toys requires some woodworking skill and equipment.

Equipment and Materials for Use in Nursery Schools for Handicapped Children. (Available from the Teaching Program for Young Children, Meyer Children's Rehabilitation Institute, 444 S. 44th Street, Omaha, NE 68131.)

A good source of information regarding manufacturers and suppliers, suggestions for adapted and homemade materials. Many photos and drawings are included, showing equipment and materials used with preschool children.

Finnie, N. R. 1975. Handling the Young Cerebral Palsied Child at Home. E. P. Dutton, New York.

This standard reference work includes suggestions for adapting and constructing play materials and equipment. It is also helpful for sensitizing the reader to the number of factors that must be considered when working with the disabled. Information on positioning children is particularly helpful.

Gerson, D. Be Big Somewhere: A Structured Play Curriculum and Specialized Toys for the Severely Handicapped. (Available from the author at Rainier School, Box G, Buckley, Va 98321.)

This curriculum manual was developed for use with a set of structured activities in a structured environment. The book describes the layout of the playroom and details of the simply modified and constructed materials and equipment. Complete training procedures and criterion tests for teaching basic play skills are included.

It Takes All Parts: An Activity Book to Develop Self-Concept in Young Children. 1977. (Available from The Capper Foundation, 3500 W. 10th St., Topeka, Kas. 66604, Attn: Benith MacPherson. Price: $3.95 plus postage.)

This comprehensive activity book was written by a team of teachers and therapists working with young physically and multihandicapped children. While the emphasis of the activities was on self-concept, a wide variety of sensory stimulation, motor development, and preacademic content was utilized. This book includes detailed daily schedules, cautions and comments, suggestions for homemade and commercial materials, etc. Many of the activities would fit into any recreation program for the disabled.

Let's Play-to-Grow. 1977. (Available from the Joseph P. Kennedy, Jr. Foundation, 1701 K St. NW, Suite 205, Washington, D.C. 20006. Price: $2.50.)

This set of booklets will probably become the standard references for many recreation programs for the disabled. One booklet suggests materials and activities for the very young or severely disabled, while the others focus on more sports-oriented activities. The series was developed originally for home use, and its style and language reflects that orientation.

Papanek, V. 1972. Design for the Real World. Pantheon Books, New York.

This fascinating book addresses issues of concern in the field of industrial design—issues that affect us all. Play equipment for handicapped children and low budget electrical appliances for underdeveloped nations are some of the many examples described by the author in his crusade to increase both designers' and consumers' awareness of the advantages of simple, economical, and functional products.

Robinault, I. P. (ed.). 1973. Functional Aids for the Multiply Handicapped. Harper and Row, Hagerstown, Md.

This excellent reference work includes all types of equipment and aids for mobility, education, and activities of daily life. Both commercial and easily adapted items are described, with photographs, references, and suggested sources.

Southwest Educational Development Laboratory. 1976. How to Fill Your Toyshelves Without Emptying Your Pocketbook. Council for Exceptional Children, Reston, Va.

This publication offers ideas for many simple-to-make toys, learning materials, and games. They are organized by areas of general curriculum content, and are more appropriate for those with minor or moderate disabilities, rather than the severely and/or motorically impaired. Many of the play materials utilize scraps and throw-aways, and may not be sufficiently durable without modification.

Technical Aids for Physically Handicapped Children. 1972. (Available from ICTA Information Centre, Bromma, Sweden.)

This book provides photographs and drawings of commercial aids, as well as adapted and homemade items. It covers mobility and positioning aids as well as play materials and equipment, and is a good source of ideas. However, it does not include specific plans or details for do-it-yourself construction.

Thorum, A. 1976. Instructional Materials for the Handicapped: Birth Through Early Childhood. Olympus Publishing Co., Salt Lake City.

This paperback book may be of particular interest to those looking for sources of early learning and preschool materials. It includes names, addresses, and brief descriptions for nearly 400 manufacturers and distributors. It also discusses various evaluation criteria and more advanced curriculum materials.

Toy Book: Self-Help Toys to Make for Handicapped Children. (Available from Alpha Chi Omega National Headquarters, 3445 N. Washington Blvd., Indianapolis, Ind. 46205.)

This booklet includes a variety of play and learning materials designed by volunteers. Some plans are very simple; others are quite complex. Both wooden and cloth toys are described. Many of the ideas may need to be modified by improving durability, size, etc., to make the materials more useful for the severely disabled.

Toy Libraries Association's various publications. (Available from the association at Seabrook House, Wyllyotts Manor, Darkes Lane, Potters Bar, Herts, England, EN 6 2HL.)

The TLA offers a series of booklets as well as a regular newsletter. This organization focuses specifically on play materials and equipment for the disabled—both children and adults. The booklets include information on selection of commercial toys, construction of homemade materials, toys for language development, magnetic toys, and so on. The entire set of booklets should be made available to all recreation programs through reference libraries, etc. For more information, write to the Toy Libraries Association, or see the article by Morton Thompson in Rehabilitation World, Spring 1977, pp. 31–32.

White, J. 1976. Stimulus box for the profoundly mentally retarded, Am. J. Occup. Ther. 30(3):167.

This article describes a "stimulus box" for a severely multihandicapped child. This item is actually a large cardboard carton embellished with a variety of stimulating materials and objects. Photos show a child placed in the tunnel-like box environment, where his very slight movements are rewarded by auditory, visual, and tactile stimuli. The article suggests the development of a more durable piece of similar equipment.

Williams, R., Briggs, N., and Williams, B. 1978. Play materials in instructional settings: Processes for increasing availability and utilization. Paper presented at a meeting of the Council for Exceptional Children, Kansas City. (Available from Exceptional Play, Inc., P.O. Box 1015, Lawrence, Kas. 66044.)

This presentation describes the design process involved in developing recreation materials for disabled children, basic criteria for evaluation and selection, the teacher's role as an informed consumer, and current research and trends related to play materials and their use in both recreational and educational settings.

Wolinsky, G., and Koehler, N. 1973. A cooperative program in materials development for very young hospitalized children. Rehab. Lit. 34(2):34–46. (Available as a reprint from the National Easter Seal Society.)

This article describes several homemade materials developed during workshops for hospital personnel in a pediatric unit. General types and characteristics of appropriate play materials are outlined, as well as specific suppliers. Although this article is now several years old, it still offers assistance to those who have an interest in severely multihandicapped young children and their play needs.

Zegers, H. Touch Toys and How to Make Them. (Available from Touch Toys, 5004 Rodman Road, Washington, D.C. 20016. Price: $2.40.)

This mimeographed booklet has detailed plans for many small manipulative toys, as well as larger environmental modifications. Originally designed for blind children—with particular emphasis on "feel," sound, smell, and sturdiness—the items may be useful for mentally handicapped persons, also. Utilization of scrap materials and recycled objects is encouraged by the author.

Selected Articles in Play and Recreation Programming with Developmentally Disabled Persons

Bernhardt, M. A., and Mackler, B. 1975. The use of play therapy with the mentally retarded. J. Spec. Educ. 9(4):409–414.

In this article play therapy is depicted as a possible method of helping the mentally retarded work out problems. A thorough review of the limited research dealing with the use of play therapy with mentally handicapped persons is included, and the authors conclude that, although it is a relatively new approach, play therapy should be attempted with this population.

Bigge, J. 1976. Leisure. In J. Bigge (ed.), Teaching Individuals with Physical and Multiple Disabilities, pp. 219–245. Charles Merrill Publishing Co., Columbus, Ohio.

Bigge suggests techniques for helping students plan, select, and enjoy participation activities, spectator activities, and appreciation activities during their free time in this chapter. Disabled children and adults need a broad repertoire of leisure skills. The kinds of projects that are suggested include: pet care, music appreciation, photography, games, horseback riding, nature study, and TV watching. References dealing with each activity are also included in the chapter.

Bishop, R., and Balters, H. 1976. The use of reinforcement in activities for the mentally retarded. Ther. Recreat. J. 10(3).

In this study six severely and profoundly retarded males were given edible reinforcement for successful performance on four recreational tasks: billiards, serving a ping-pong ball, throwing and catching a ball, and throwing a ball into a basket. A pre- and posttest design was utilized, and the results indicated that the reinforcement in and of itself was ineffective in bringing about remarkably different performance levels on the learning tasks. Thus, the need for further investigation on the value of edible reinforcement with the severely and profoundly handicapped is suggested.

Black, M., Freeman, R., and Montgomery, J. 1975. Systematic observation of play behavior in autistic children. J. Autism Child. Schizo. 5(4):363–371.

The play behavior, defined as interaction with peers and objects, of five autistic children was observed systematically in four environments, i.e., a stark environment, a theraplay unit, a playroom, and an outside play deck. The preliminary results suggested that: 1) with some children environment has little or no effect on their play behavior; 2) with multiple objects, autistic children frequently related to the objects rather than to their peers; 3) object play was most frequently at the manipulative stage and often included repetitive and negative behavior; 4) within a confined space with no objects present, autistic children frequently engaged in solitary repetitive behavior; and 5) within a confined space designed to facilitate a movement flow (theraplay), autistic children modeled and imitated and were involved in gross motor play together.

Bradtke, L., Kirkpatrick, W., and Rosenblatt, K. 1972. Intensive play: A technique for building affective behaviors in profoundly mentally retarded young children. Educ. Train. Ment. Retard. 7(1):8–13.

Intensive play is described in this article as the building of positive responses to normally pleasurable experiences. The authors suggest methods of using close body contact and physical stimulation, such as rocking, hugging, or rough housing, to break through the barriers of unawareness, fearfulness, and unresponsiveness which are general characteristics of profoundly mentally retarded children.

Burmeister, J. 1976. Leisure services and the cultural arts as therapy for mentally retarded persons. Ther. Recreat. J. 10(4):139–142.

Goals for leisure services to the mentally retarded are specified in this article, and the inclusion of the cultural arts in a diversified leisure program is justified. Music, dance, theater, and the visual arts are said to enhance normalization efforts, and it is pointed out that such activities stress cooperation rather than competition and may appeal to many individuals not interested in highly regulated activities. Suggested teaching techniques for incorporation of the cultural arts into recreation programs are included in the article.

Day, R., and Day, H. M. 1977. Leisure skills instruction for the moderately and severely retarded: A demonstration program. Educ. Train. Ment. Retard. 12(2).

In this article, a summer recreation program developed to teach leisure skills to 30 severely and moderately retarded children and adolescents is described. Three hundred leisure time activities in the areas of arts and crafts, games, hobbies, music, aquatics, nature observation and home living were delineated in the program and taught. The daily activity schedule is explained as is the programming for generalization to the homes and communities of the students. The severely retarded children in the program acquired few leisure skills in the summer session, but the moderately retarded children and adolescents mastered two-thirds of the subtasks that were attempted.

Favell, J. E., and Cannon, P. R. 1976. Evaluation of entertainment materials for severely retarded persons. Am. J. Ment. Defic. 81(4):357–361.

Time-sampling measurements were made of the free-play behavior of 11 severely retarded females in this study. They were presented with 16 different toys and with a videotape of Sesame Street on television, a rocking chair, three catalogs, and a plastic bottle filled with styrofoam. The results indicated that, although there were strong preferences among toys, there was little correlation between toy preference and price, and the professional staff were unable to make accurate predictions of toy preference. The need for further research to determine what characteristics of toys affect preferences of this population is indicated.

Flavell, J. 1973. Reduction of stereotypies by reinforcement of toy play. Ment. Retard. 11(4):24–27.

In this study prompting and positive reinforcement of toy play were employed to increase toy play responses and to decrease stereotypies (repetitive movements of any part of the body) by three severely retarded children. A multiple baseline design and reversal procedure were employed, and the results indicated that appropriate toy play with a wide array of toys was developed in these students while stereotypies decreased to zero levels.

Grove, N. 1976. Challenging opportunities for special populations in aquatic activities. Ther. Recreat. J. 10(2).

An extensive annotated bibliography of printed materials pertaining to aquatic activities is included in this article. Activities range from swimming to white water rafting and scuba diving, and the resources are designated to indicate for what special populations they are appropriate. Audio-visual aids are similarly listed as are assistive devices and adapted equipment.

Gunn, S. 1975. Play as occupation: Implications for the handicapped. Am. J. Occup. Ther. 29(4).

In this paper, play is viewed as a necessary and vital part of need-fulfilling behavior for all persons, but especially for handicapped individuals, because play elicits responses to the unknown and offers an opportunity for one to learn confidence and to be creative in facing novel or difficult situations. Theories of play are presented, with the optimum arousal theory of play presented as most significant in the rehabilitation process of the handicapped individual.

Hamre-Nietupski, S., and Williams, W. W. 1977. Implementation of selected sex education and social skills to severely handicapped students. Educ. Train. Ment. Retard. 12(4):364–372.

This article describes selected sex education and social skills programs that were used successfully with severely handicapped students in three public school classrooms. A model-test-teach design and a test-teach design were used to instruct the students in five component instructional areas: Bodily distinctions, such as body parts and sexual distinctions; self-care skills, such as premenstrual training; family members and relationships; social interactions; and social manners methods of involving parents in the programming are explained, and data are presented showing progress made in the component areas by students over a 3-year period.

Hitzhusen, G. 1975. Therapeutic recreation services for the educable mentally retarded. Ther. Recreat. J. 9(4):153–157.

A comprehensive discussion of what therapeutic recreation for the educable mentally retarded involves is provided in this article. Therapeutic recreation is viewed as a process that utilizes recreational services for purposive intervention in some physical, emotional, and/or social behavior to bring about a desired change and to promote the growth and development of the individual. Methods for correlating recreation with all aspects of the lives of EMR individuals are defined, and outstanding programs, such as the "Special Olympics" and "Families Play to Grow," are described in detail and highly recommended for use in community recreation programs.

Hoeft-Rindfleisch, T. 1977. Therapeutic recreation and the institutionalized adult male—severely and profoundly handicapped client. Ther. Recreat. J. 11(3).

In this article procedures for observing, assessing, and planning recreational activities for a retarded adult are discussed. It is suggested that general treatment objectives be developed from which long and short range goals and activities can be derived. An individual puzzle program for the client is presented in task analytic form, and data collection sheets are included.

Hopper, C., and Wambold, C. 1978. Improving the independent play of severely mentally retarded children. Educ. Train. Ment. Retard. 13(1):42–46.

This study represents an effort to improve the independent play skills of institutionalized, severely mentally retarded children in a classroom setting. Twenty reactive and nonreactive toys were introduced to four students in the classroom, and teacher modeling and prompting were used to encourage interaction with the toys. Data were collected as to whether the children engaged in appropriate or inappropriate actions on the toys during 10-second intervals. Intervention efforts to improve the quality and diversity of the object interaction skills of two of the students are described, and toy preferences of the students also are discussed.

Jarman, P., and Reid, D. 1977. The importance of recreational activities on attendance to a leisure program for multi-handicapped retarded persons. Ther. Recreat. J. 11(1).

This article reports a study to determine what effect available recreational activities had on use of the leisure room in a state institution. Forty nonambulatory clients who could wheel themselves to the game room were involved in the study. A reversal design was employed, and the results indicated that when recreational activities such as cards, records, art materials, refreshments, a modified pool table and a pinball machine were available in the leisure room, the residents consistently attended the program.

Johnson, M., and Bailey, J. 1977. The modification of leisure behavior in a half-way house for retarded women. J. Appl. Behav. Anal. 10(2).

In this study the effect of availability of materials, prizes for participation, and instruction on the leisure behavior of 14 mentally retarded women in a half-way house was investigated. The study employed a multielement baseline design combined with a multiple baseline design, and the results indicated prizes were most effective in maintaining participation in puzzles, card games, and clay and painting activities after the women had received instruction in the activities. However, prizes were not necessary to maintain participation in weaving or rug making by the women who were instructed to do these tasks.

Jorgenson, H., and Parnell, M. K. 1970. Modifying social behaviors of mentally retarded children in music activities. J. Music Ther. 7(3):83–87.

Describes the modification of inappropriate social behaviors in four moderately retarded children, all 8–9 years old with IQs from 40 to 55. The Shaker Game, the Indian Game, the Hokey-Pokey, and listening to records were used to modify hitting, yelling, pushing, and nonparticipation.

Katz, S., and Yekutiel, D. 1974. Leisure time problems of mentally retarded graduates of training programs. Ment. Retard. 12(3):54–57.

This article depicts leisure time and social problems of recent graduates of two sheltered workshops in Israel, as reported by the parents of the retardates. The most important problem was a lack of suitable companions and friends of both sexes. The next most serious problem was that there was a lack of proper facilities for leisure time activities. In general the results of the study indicate that socially the mentally retarded are isolated from the community.

Knapczyk, D., and Yoppi, J. 1975. Development of cooperative and competitive play responses in developmentally disabled children. Am. J. Ment. Defic. 80(3):245–255.

This study investigates a behavior management program for training cooperative and competitive play responses in five educable mentally retarded children. A token-praise-feedback management procedure was implemented to encourage the desired play skills in the students who had marked behavior and communication disorders, and who had previously exhibited no competitive play responses and low levels of cooperative play. Increases in cooperative play as well as small increases in competitive play were measured, following the use of a token system whereby points were given to each student for social interaction. The points were exchanged for desired prizes.

Koegel, R., Firestone, P., Kramme, K., and Dunlap, A. 1974. Increasing spontaneous play by suppressing self-stimulation in autistic children. J. Appl. Behav. Anal. 7(4):521–528.

In this study appropriate play with toys was studied in two autistic children with high occurrences of self-stimulatory behavior. An A-B-A design was employed, with A representing baseline conditions and B representing intervention in which self-stimulatory behavior resulted in the child's being told, "No!" and the part of his body with which the response was being made being briskly slapped or briefly held. The results indicated that spontaneous, appropriate play increased when self-stimulatory behavior was suppressed, but this increase in appropriate toy play was not maintained when the suppression of self-stimulation was discontinued.

Linford, A., G., and Jeanrenaud, C. Y. 1969. A systematic language structure for teaching recreative skills to the mentally retarded. Ther. Recreat. J. 3(1):8–11.

Discussion of the University of Illinois' recreation and motor performance research team's task analysis of levels of recreation responding. The analysis has been used as a guide for the teaching of play skills and is also an evaluative instrument. A typical motor profile for motor actions is illustrated.

Luckey, R. E., and Shapiro, I. G. 1974. Recreation: An essential aspect of habilitative programming. Ment. Retard. 12(5):33–35.

This article discusses the importance of recreation to the total system of habilitative services for mentally retarded individuals. Current trends in recreation programming for the handicapped are described, including the role of the parent-volunteer movement; and problems being encountered are depicted, as are continuing needs in the field of recreation for the retarded.

Matthews, P. 1977. Recreation and the normalization of the mentally retarded. Ther. Recreat. J. 11(3).

Matthews stresses that recreation can aid and facilitate the normalization of the mentally retarded by providing activities in which they can participate. He suggests that recreation can have a more significant influence on normalization if the following steps are taken: 1) the mentally retarded must have access to recreation, 2) the mentally retarded and their families must be made aware of the opportunities available to them, 3) the needed skills for participation must be taught, 4) the recreational opportunities made available must be based on the retardates' strengths, and 5) the community's perceptions and expectations of the mentally retarded must be even more affirmative than they currently are.

Maynard, M. 1976. The value of creative arts for the developmentally disabled child: Implications for recreation specialists in community day service programs. Ther. Recreat. J. 10(1):10–13.

Creative arts are said to accomplish the following goals with developmentally disabled persons: helping the student develop an understanding of the various art forms in the environment, providing an outlet for creative expression, providing an opportunity for the child to gain skills in body coordination, and providing an opportunity for problem solving and communication. This article provides a schematic model which suggests steps a recreation specialist should follow in programming for creative development in developmentally disabled children and adolescents.

Melvin, L. 1976. Aquatics games: A multidisciplinary teaching method for the handicapped. Ther. Recreat. J. 10(2).

In this article, the teaching of aquatics games is viewed in terms of a multidisciplinary approach in which transfer of learning is programmed. Such games should involve initiation of skill development in areas such as fundamental movement skills, perceptual motor development, structured preacademic skills, and academic skills. Methods of teaching handicapped persons to play games are presented, and aquatic games using the following common rule structures are described: permissive games, fantasy games with music and rhythm, games resulting in equal shares, and games involving win/lose competition.

Morris, R. 1974. Evaluation of a play environment for blind children. Ther. Recreat. J. 8(4).

This study investigates how effective a specially designed play environment would be in helping preteenage blind children develop a greater degree of orientation skill and mobility through their play activities. All equipment was fixed in place on the playground so that the students had to provide movement. Tactile maps and talking-book recordings at each map were used to provide multisensory stimulation. Varying textures and slopes were incorporated into the layout of the play area, and play items were of various sizes. Teachers and orientation specialists, along with other experts, were asked to evaluate the playground; varying opinions resulted. Concerns regarding the safety aspects of the play area and the amount of adult intervention needed comprised the largest comment areas.

Morris, R., and Dolker, M. 1974. Developing cooperative play in socially withdrawn children. Ment. Retard. 12(6):24–27.

This study compares three approaches to the development of cooperative play. The cooperative task involved two students rolling a ball to one another and the experimental conditions involved grouping two low interacting students together, one high and one low interacting student together, and the third approach involved a no-treatment condition. Social and edible reinforcement was used, and the results showed that pairing high and low interacting children together and implementing a shaping procedure produced the greatest amount of cooperative play with the ball.

Morrison, T., and Newcomer, B. 1975. Effects of directive vs. nondirective play therapy with institutionalized mentally retarded children. Am. J. Ment. Defic. 79(6).

Fourteen institutionalized retarded children were randomly assigned to 11 sessions of directive play therapy, nondirective play therapy, or no treatment in this study. Student nurses served as therapists, and the Denver Developmental Screening Test was used as a pre- and posttest. The results indicated that play therapy was effective in increasing developmental level, but directive therapy was found to be no more effective than nondirective therapy.

Newcomer, B., and Morrison, T. 1974. Play therapy with institutionalized mentally retarded children. Am. J. Ment. Defic. 78(6).

The effects of individual play therapy, group play therapy, and no intervention in the area of play skills in institutionalized retarded children are described in this article. Twelve mildly and moderately retarded children were randomly assigned so that four children received individual play therapy stimulation, four received group play therapy, and four received no type of play therapy. Gross motor, fine motor–adaptive, language, and personal-social activities were included in both the individual and group play therapy sessions. The groups receiving individual or group play therapy exhibited higher scores on the Denver Developmental Screening Test following therapy than the no-treatment group, which showed no improvement in scores. No differences were noted between group and individual therapy.

Paloutzian, R., Hasazi, J., Streifel, J., and Edgar, C. 1971. Promotion of positive social interaction in severely retarded young children. Am. J. Ment. Defic. 75(4):519–524.

This article describes the use of prompting and reinforcement to develop positive social interaction in severely retarded young institutionalized children. Ten experimental subjects were trained to imitate novel social responses of a model as a means of facilitating positive social interaction with peers. After training, these 10 children exhibited a significantly higher level of social behavior, which generalized to the ward setting. Ten control subjects showed no change in level of social behavior.

Peterson, N., and Haralick, J. G. 1977. Integration of handicapped and nonhandicapped preschoolers: An analysis of play behavior and social interaction. Educ. Train. Ment. Retard. 12(3):235–246.

This paper reports the results of an exploratory study to determine how handicapped and nonhandicapped children interact socially in an integrated preschool setting. Five nonhandicapped and eight handicapped students were observed in a structured manner over a period of time as they interacted freely, with little teacher intervention, during two daily free-play sessions. In general, the results indicate little discrimination by the nonhandicapped children against the handicapped students, and the handicapped students were found to engage in less isolate play when at least one nonhandicapped peer was present at play time.

Pomeroy, J. 1974. The handicapped are out of hiding: Implications for community recreation. Ther. Recreat. J. 8(3):120–128.

Deinstitutionalization and its impact on the field of recreation are discussed in this article. Recreation programs are said to have proven quite valuable to persons residing in group homes or other sheltered environments. Model programs in various localities are described, and it is pointed out that with minor additional installations, such as ramps, the needs of even the most severely handicapped can usually be met in existing physical facilities. Personnel and program considerations in serving handicapped persons are also discussed in the article.

Reynolds, G. 1976. Agency development of aquatic programs for special populations. Ther. Recreat. J. 10(2).

This article points out the value of aquatic activities for people with special needs and lists many diverse factors that must be considered when an agency plans aquatic programming for special persons. Such considerations involve staffing problems, public relations work which is needed, and program planning, as well as needed adaptations of physical facilities. A list of available printed resources is included in the article.

Rogow, S. 1976. Play and reality: Essentials of educational planning for blind retarded children. Educ. Train. Ment. Retard. 11(4).

The role of play in fostering concept development and perceptual development in blind retarded children is described in this article. Play, meaning exploratory, manipulative, and self-initiated activity, is considered to be the main educational vehicle of the curriculum for young blind retarded children. The importance of using tactile exploration of all play materials is discussed as is the necessity of following an established sequence of instruction to teach an activity. The value of dramatic play in developing social competence in blind retarded individuals is also explained in the article.

Romanczyk, R. 1975. Increasing isolated and social play in severely disturbed children: Intervention and postintervention effectiveness. J. Aut. Child. Schizo. 5(1).

In this paper two studies are provided which demonstrate a group treatment program to develop appropriate play in severely disturbed children. Passive shaping procedures are used to increase students' interaction with toys and peers, and teacher intervention is faded gradually as appropriate play is developed. A time sampling observational code is used to record student behavior, and continuous reliability assessment is utilized. Both studies are described clearly in a way that can be easily replicated in other classrooms.

Seaman, J. A. 1975. Effects of municipal recreation on the social self-esteem of the mentally retarded. Ther. Recreat. J. 9(2):75–78.

In this study 24 educable and trainable children were rated on a Self-Esteem Questionnaire before and after participation in a 9-week municipal recreation program. Recreation directors rated the children, and at the end of the program TMR children tended to play noncompetitive games more frequently with their peers and both groups were participating more in competitive games and sports. The EMR group was not quitting games or sports as quickly when difficulty was encountered, and this perseverance is viewed as an important factor in the development of a positive self-esteem.

Sengstock, W. L. and Jens, K. G. 1974. Recreation for the handicapped: Suggestions for program adaptations. Ther. Recreat. J. 8(4):172–177.

In this article recreators are encouraged to develop a sensitivity to the problems encountered by handicapped persons trying to master a leisure time skill. The importance of a positive self-concept is stated, and it is suggested that success be built into recreational programming. Activities should be task analyzed and taught in small steps so that a child feels successful and experiences no fear of failure. The values of feedback and positive reinforcement are explained, and illustrations are given to show how these techniques can be used in training recreational skills.

Seyfried, D. 1974. Leisure time and interest development center for handicapped children. Ther. Recreat. J. 8(1).

This article describes the Leisure Time and Interest Development Center at the University of Iowa Hospital School. The center provides structured and nonstructured activities to provide handicapped individuals with the opportunity to learn to use leisure time appropriately. A second objective of the program is to teach handicapped individuals to use leisure time in order to be able to contribute to the enjoyment of others. Guidelines for activities are included in the article, and practical experiences which should be provided in the areas of transportation, social functions, and hobbies are listed.

Strensrud, C. 1976. Recreation's role in meeting the socio-sexual needs of special populations. Ther. Recreat. J. 10(3).

This article stresses the need for special persons to have similar opportunities for developing sexuality as other persons, and describes techniques that can be employed in recreational settings to provide such opportunities. Formal education, such as training in body awareness, body functions, and parenthood, is recommended. In addition, experimental opportunities, such as integrative social activities and small parties, are suggested, as are leisure counseling and education.

Strain, P. 1975. Increasing social play of severely retarded preschoolers with socio-dramatic activities. Ment. Retard. 13(6).

This study utilizes socio-dramatic activities such as instructing children how to role play characters in familiar stories in an attempt to increase social play in eight severely retarded preschoolers. An ABAB reversal procedure was implemented, and the results indicate that the provision of socio-dramatic activities and social play levels were functionally related since increases in the amount of social play were noted only during periods when the teacher assigned roles to the children and prompted the behaviors. The techniques employed are said to be easily replicable in other classrooms.

Tilton, J., and Ottinger, D. P. 1964. Comparison of toy play behavior of autistic, retarded, and normal children. Psycholog. Rep. 15:967–975.

(See Weiner, Ottinger, and Tilton (1969) for discussion.)

Wehman, P. 1975. Establishing play behaviors in mentally retarded youth. Rehabil. Lit. 36(8):238–246.

This discussion paper emphasizes the interrelationships among curriculum, teaching procedures, and student functioning level in recreation program development. Literature up through 1974 is reviewed, and areas for future research are highlighted.

Wehman, P. 1976. A leisure skills curriculum for the developmentally disabled. Educ. Train. Ment. Retard. 11(4):309–313.

A leisure skills curriculum that depicts games, hobbies, free play, sports, and socializiation is presented. Each area within the curriculum is broadly sequenced horizontally. This curriculum outline calls for a more systematic approach to skill selection and instruction.

Wehman, P. 1976. Selection of play materials for the severely handicapped: A continuing dilemma. Educ. Train. Ment. Retard. 11(1):46–51.

This discussion article focuses on the importance of play materials in the recreation environment. Specifically, it discusses the role of configural complexity, plasticity, and novelty in toy selection. A taxonomy of toys and their related functions is also presented.

Wehman, P. 1977. Applications of behavior modification techniques to play problems of the severely and profoundly retarded. Ther. Recreat. J. 11(1): 17–23.

This discussion article describes how basic behavior modification techniques can be used to shape play skills in low functioning individuals. Physical prompting, modeling, chaining, task analysis, and reinforcer selection are discussed, and a task analysis of "Follow the Leader" is provided.

Wehman, P. 1977. Helping the Mentally Retarded Acquire Play Skills: A Behavioral Approach. Charles C Thomas, Springfield, Ill. Price: $12.50.

The initial chapter of this text focuses on the needs, problems, and theory regarding play of the mentally retarded. It includes discussions of the rationale for encouraging play, problems of play faced by the mentally retarded, play definitions, and theoretical foundations.

Subsequent chapters outline the basic principles and procedures of behavioral programming, along with providing concrete suggestions for the development of such a program. The remainder of the text is concerned with methods and techniques for developing play behaviors in the severely and profoundly retarded, ways of helping the multiply handicapped retarded learn to play, leisure time programming for the mildly handicapped, and issues in recreation program development for the mentally retarded.

The ideas and procedures detailed in this book will serve to reinforce the position that the use of behavioral programming to stimulate play skills in the mentally retarded is both necessary and desirable. Those who interact daily with the retarded and who are confronted with the task of helping the mentally retarded develop independent recreation skills will find *Helping the Mentally Retarded Acquire Play Skills* to be an eminently practical text and a solid contribution to their work and to the general well-being of those they serve.

Wehman, P. 1977. Recreation Curriculum: Hickory Hill Program. Richmond Public Schools, Richmond, Va.

The recreation curriculum was designed for teachers working with severely and profoundly handicapped students. It includes many task analyses in gross motor recreation skills, guidelines for toy selection, and information relevant to setting up a free-play program. A number of illustrative instructional programs for teaching are provided as well.

Wehman, P. 1977. Research on leisure time and the severely developmentally disabled. Rehabil. Lit. 38(4):98–105.

Two studies, one which focuses on developing isolative play and the other on cooperative play, are reported in this paper. Six institutionalized profoundly retarded individuals participated in the programs. Each study was evaluated in an across-subject multiple baseline design. Stereotypic behavior of participants was assessed in each study and reduced through increases in appropriate play.

Wehman, P. 1978. Effects of different environmental conditions on leisure time activity of the severely and profoundly handicapped. J. Spec. Educ. 12(2).

This article describes the differential effects of toy proximity, modeling, and instructions plus modeling on the free-play activity of three severely retarded adolescents. Social reinforcement was provided in all conditions. Leisure activity was substantially increased through all conditions, with instructions plus modeling being the most effective condition.

Wehman, P. 1978. Instructional strategies for improving toy play skills of severely and profoundly handicapped students. AAESPH Rev. In press.

The purpose of this paper is to identify typically encountered play problems in severely retarded children and provide specific strategies for overcoming these problems. The problems include refusal to play, play of short duration, toy throwing, inappropriate play, lack of appropriate materials, isolative play, and lack of self-initiated social interaction.

Wehman, P. 1978. Leisure skill programming for severely and profoundly handicapped persons: State of the art. Br. J. Soc. Clin. Psychol. 17(4).

This review paper analyzes and synthesizes research studies involving leisure skills with severely handicapped individuals over the past 8 years. Approximately 25 studies are analyzed in terms of population, independent and dependent variables, and results. A statement of leisure skill teacher competencies is also provided.

Wehman, P. 1978. A recreation curriculum for developmentally disabled persons. Manuscript submitted for publication.

Expanding on earlier work, the author has provided a far more detailed curriculum sequence. Over 200 leisure skills have been sequenced into toy play, passive leisure, games, hobbies, sports, and socialization. Information is also provided concerning how to implement the curriculum.

Wehman, P. 1978. Task analysis in recreation programs for mentally retarded persons. J. Leisurability, 5(1):13–20.

In this paper the role of task analysis in recreation programs is discussed in detail. An illustrative data-based social interaction program is provided, along with several gross motor recreation task analyses.

Wehman, P. 1978. Teaching recreational skills to severely and profoundly handicapped persons. In E. Edgar and R. York (eds.), Teaching Severely Handicapped Persons, Vol. IV. AAESPH, Seattle.

This chapter discusses behavioral assessment and intervention stategies relevant to setting up a free-play program. A second part of this chapter provides information concerning instructional program development in recreation. This includes objective setting, task analysis, behavior observation, and teaching procedures.

Wehman, P., and Abramson, M. 1976. Three theoretical approaches to play: Applications to exceptional children. Am. J. Occup. Ther. 32(8):551–559.

Psychoanalytic, cognitive-developmental, and arousal-seeking theories are compared and contrasted in this paper. These theories are discussed in the context of their implications for exceptional children. It was concluded that the latter two theories have the greatest potential for assessment and intervention of play with handicapped children.

Wehman, P., and Marchant, J. 1977. Developing gross motor recreational skills in children with severe behavioral handicaps. Ther. Recreat. J. 11(2):48–54.

In this article three severely retarded children were trained, through task analysis, modeling, and social reinforcement, in the use of a tricycle, sliding board, and trampoline. Data were collected through assessing the percentage of independent steps completed in each task analysis.

Wehman, P., and Marchant, J. 1978. Improving free play skills of severely retarded children. Am. J. Occup. Ther. 32(2):100–104.

This study provides data on the progressive improvement of four severely retarded children's free-play skills. Autistic, independent, and social play levels were assessed, and the program was evaluated in an ABAB reversal design. Social and edible reinforcement were employed to increase independent and social play in all children.

Wehman, P., and Marchant, J. (March) 1978. Teaching table games to severely retarded children. Paper presented at Virginia State CEC Convention, Richmond, Va.

This study describes a table game sequence for nonverbal severely retarded children. "Lotto" games were taught to four children through task analysis and forward chaining. A multiple baseline design across skills was used to evaluate program results. Parents were involved in the program to ensure generalization.

Wehman, P., Renzaglia, A., Berry, G., Schutz, R., and Karan, O. 1978. Developing a leisure skill repertoire in severely and profoundly handicapped persons. AAESPH Rev. 3(3).

In this paper two studies are provided that demonstrate the development of physical fitness and table game leisure skills. Both studies employed a task analysis data-based approach and were evaluated in multiple baseline designs. Institutionalized severely and profoundly retarded adolescents and adults participated. The exercises were sit ups, duck walking, and push ups. Table games included "Cats Eye," "Tic-Tac-Toe," and "Chinese Checkers."

Weiner, B., Ottinger, D., and Tilton, J. 1969. Comparison of the toy play behavior of autistic, retarded, and normal children: A re-analysis. Psycholog. Rep. 25:223–227.

In this study and an earlier one (Tilton and Ottinger, 1964), free-play behavior of autistic, trainable retarded, and normal children was observed and coded. The following classification was generated: repetitive manual manipulation, oral contacts, pounding, throwing, pushing/pulling, personalized toy use, manipulation of movable parts of toy, separation of parts of toy, and combinational uses of toys. As might be expected, normal children demonstrated the most advanced type of play; trainable level retarded children were more sophisticated in their play than autistic children.

Whitman, T., Mercurio, J. R., and Caponigri, V. 1970. Development of social responses in two severely retarded children. J. Appl. Behav. Anal. 3(2):133–138.

This study investigates the effect of reinforcement on the social responses of two severely retarded children. Food and praise were used to reinforce ball-rolling and block-passing actions by the students. A progressive increase in these social responses was noted during the reinforcement period, and generalization to other students in the classroom also occurred. A decrease in the social behaviors was noted when the reinforcement was discontinued, but the social interactions occurred more frequently than they had during the initial baseline period.

Wyatt, W. S., and Hunt, S. K. 1976. Using parents as evaluators of a therapeutic recreational camping program for the retarded. Ther. Recreat. J. 10(4):143–147.

In this article the value of parental participation in the evaluation of a camping experience for the mentally retarded is discussed. The parents of 139 campers were asked to evaluate the overall enjoyment of the experience by their child, the camper's general state of health when he arrived home, and the strengths and weaknesses of the program, based on comments made at home by the camper. The results obtained indicated that the parental input added a valuable dimension to the overall evaluation of program effectiveness. It is suggested that such parental interest be cultivated by professionals.

Selected Articles in Music Therapy

Alley, J. M. 1977. Education for the severely handicapped: The role of music therapy. J. Music Ther. 14(2):50–57.

The purpose of this article is to provide an overview of current issues related to the education of severely handicapped persons and to delineate music therapy attributes that increase its utility with educational administrators.

Carroccio, D. F., Latham, S., and Carroccio, B. B. 1972. Operant use of guitar-rental to decelerate head/face touching of an adult male psychiatric patient. Available from Music Therapy Retrieval Center, School of Music, Florida State University, Tallahassee, Fla. 32306.

This is possibly the only longitudinal study using operant techniques in music therapy. The study suggests interesting techniques for facilitating generalization from the experimental to the daily living situation. The schedule presented in this study has a wide use in decelerating many behaviors without resorting to punishment procedures.

Cotter, V. 1971. Effects of music on performance of manual tasks with retarded adolescent females. Am. J. Ment. Defic. 72:242–248.

Sixteen institutionalized retarded adolescent females were assigned to contingent and noncontingent music groups on the basis of work performance of manual tasks in a simulated workshop situation. The article provides an excellent example of the use of music as a reinforcer in an operant learning procedure.

Dorow, L. G. 1975. Conditioning music and approval as new reinforcers for imitative behavior with the severely retarded. J. Music Ther. 12(1):30–39.

The purpose of this experiment was to: 1) examine the effect of secondary reinforcers on the performance of imitative behaviors, 2) study the effect of the conditioning process on an approval alone contingency and an approval plus music contingency, and 3) determine the durability of newly conditioned reinforcers across a second baseline period.

Eagle, C. (ed.). 1976. Music Therapy Index. Vol. 1. National Association of Music Therapy, Inc., P. O. Box 610, Lawrence, Kan. 66044.

An international interdisciplinary index to the literature of the psychology, psychophysiology, psychophysics, and sociology of music.

Galloway, H. F. (ed.). 1975. A comprehensive bibliography of music referential to communicative development, processing, disorders and remediation. J. Music Ther. 12(4):164–196.

This bibliography is a compilation of advocatory reports, reviews, and experimental research articles referential to the use of music with communicative deficient populations, normal development, and processing and paracommunicative settings. Twelve categories, including "Brain Injured" and "Mentally Retarded," give the reader easy reference access.

Giacobbe, G. A. 1972. Rhythm builds order in brain-damaged children. Music Educ. J. 3:40–43.

This article is a theoretical discussion of the favorability of using rhythm as a medium in music to help build order in brain-damaged children.

Graham, R. M. 1972. Seven million plus need special attention. Who are they? Music Educ. J. 58(8):22–25.

This article reviews contributions music therapy can make in programs for a variety of exceptional children. The author emphasizes similarities between the program needs of these children and normal children, pointing out ways that the individual needs of all children can be met through music.

Harrison, W., Lecrone, H., Temerlin, M. K., and Trousdale, W. W. 1966. The effect of music and exercise upon the self-help skills of non-verbal retardates. Am. J. Ment. Defic. 71:279–282.

This study points out an extremely important purpose for music in relation to severely/profoundly mentally retarded individuals. Music can be used not only as a reinforcer but also to train severely retarded children in necessary self-help skills. The combination of music and exercise can be applied to toilet training, tooth brushing, all aspects of dressing oneself, learning low level type work skills (sweeping, etc.) and the development of patterns of responses to verbal commands.

Hauck, L. P., and Martin, P. L. 1970. Music as a reinforcer in patient-controlled duration of time-out. J. Music Ther. 7:43–53.

This article demonstrates the effectiveness of patient-controlled time-out in reducing the rate of unwanted behaviors. A desirable alternative to strong negative reinforcement.

Jorgenson, H. 1971. Effect of contingent preferred music in reducing two stereotyped behaviors of a profoundly retarded child. J. Music Ther. 8:139–145.

Uses of music as a reinforcer in the modification of behavior are discussed in this article. Duration of stereotyped hand movements as well as stereotyped rocking decreased when the subject was rewarded with preferred music for cessation of these behaviors.

Luckey, R. E., Carpenter, C., and Steiner, J. E. 1967. Severely retarded adults' response to rhythm and instruments. Am. J. Ment. Defic. 71:616–618.

The effectiveness of using rhythm band instruments to stimulate gross rhythmical motor activity among 12 long term institutionalized, severely retarded adults was investigated. Rhythm band activities significantly increased the subjects' rhythmical motor responsiveness to music.

Lundin, R. W. 1967. An Objective Psychology of Music. 2nd ed. The Ronald Press Co., New York.

This volume is written as a basic textbook in psychology of music. Helpful to those who want to find out more about musical behavior. Included in the volume are programmed learning, music therapy, and useful tests for the measurement of musical abilities.

Madsen, C. K., Greer, R. D., and Madsen, C. H., Jr. (eds.). 1975. Research in Music Behavior: Modifying Music Behavior in the Classroom. Teachers College Press, Columbia University, New York.

This book has three parts: Part 1 deals with issues relevant to music instruction as behavior modification and with issues relevant to research methodology. Part 2 presents procedures and techniques intended to serve as models for researchers and educators. Part 3 contains an annotated bibliography.

Nordoff, P., and Robbins, O. 1977. Creative Music Therapy. John Day, New York. (252 pages and cassette tape.)

This is the third book to be authored by Nordoff and Robbins on the subject of improvisational music therapy—a technique based on 20 years of experience with emotionally, physically, and mentally handicapped persons. Various clinical techniques and procedures are demonstrated through case studies. Guidelines are presented for judging child-therapist relationships in musical activity and musical communications.

Purvis, J., and Samet, S. 1976. Music in Developmental Therapy: A Curriculum Guide. University Park Press, Baltimore.

This book begins with concise instructions and an overview of the developmental therapy model. A series of behavioral objectives in the four curriculum areas of behavior, communication, socialization, and academics are then listed by developmental stage. Nearly 170 music therapy learning experiences which correspond to these areas follow with thorough directions for their use.

Reid, D. H., Hill, B. K., Rawers, R. J., and Montegar, C. A. 1975. The use of contingent music in teaching social skills to a non-verbal, hyperactive boy. J. Music Ther. 12:2–18.

Three experiments investigated the contingent use of music in teaching social skills to a nonverbal hyperactive boy. J. Music Ther. 12:2–18.

Three experiments investigated the contingent use of music in teaching social skills to a nonverbal hyperactive boy. The role of music in behavior is discussed in regard to the experiments.

Richman, J. S. 1976. Background music for repetitive task performance of severely retarded individuals. Am. J. Ment. Defic. 81:251–255.

Environmental manipulation in the form of specific tempo background music was used to assist in the habilitation of severely retarded persons. Thirty institutionalized retarded males were tested on a repetitive manual performance task judged to be similar to the type of tasks found in sheltered workshops. Results indicated that the regular tempo of background music facilitated the greastest improvement of performance.

Stevens, E. A. 1971. Some effects of tempo changes on stereotyped rocking movements of low level mentally retarded subjects. Am. J. Ment. Defic. 76:76–81.

Results showed that some significant changes in speeds of body rocking were produced by the environmental manipulation of music tempo.

Stevens, E., and Clark, F. 1969. Music therapy in the treatment of autistic children. J. Music Ther. 6:98–104.

This is one of the first studies on autism that applies objective methods of control, observation, and data recording. Judges used video-tape recordings to rate the subjects.

Wolpow, R. I. 1976. The independent effects of contingent social and academic approval upon the musical on-task and performance behaviors of profoundly retarded adults. J. Music Ther. 13:29–38.

This article reports the results of a study to determine the independent effects of social and academic approval rates on musical on-task (attentiveness) and performance behaviors.

MANUFACTURERS AND DISTRIBUTORS

This listing includes companies that *advertise* recreation-related materials or equipment for disabled persons. No endorsement is intended by their inclusion, and no judgment is implied by the omission of other companies. All products should be evaluated carefully by the purchaser in terms of the criteria and considerations described in Chapter 2.

Playground Equipment

Exceptional Play, Inc.
P. O. Box 1015
Lawrence, KS 66044

Exerglide Playground
  Division
Erisco Industries, Inc.
P. O. Box 1068
Erie, PA 16512

Game Time, Inc.
900 Anderson Road
Litchfield, MI 49252

Miracle Recreation
  Equipment Co.
P. O. Box 275
Grinnell, IA 50112

North American
  Recreation Convertibles
P. O. Box 758
Bridgeport, CT 06601

Theraplay Products
P.C.A. Industries, Inc.
20–24 40th Avenue
Long Island City, NY
  11101

Toys, Games, and Other Materials

Childcraft Education Corp.
20 Kilmer Road
Edison, NJ 08817

Constructive Playthings
1040 East 85th Street
Kansas City, MO 64131

Designs for Learning
P. O. Box 417
Hinsdale, IL 60521

Developmental Learning
  Materials
744 Natchez Avenue
Niles, IL 60648

Exceptional Child
  Development Center
725 Liberty Avenue
Pittsburgh, PA 15222

Exceptional Play, Inc.
P. O. Box 1015
Lawrence, KS 66044

Flaghouse, Inc.
18 West 18th Street
New York, NY 10011

Handicapped Educational
  Learning Products
P. O. Box 9763
Sacramento, CA 95823

Mosier Materials
Box 3036
San Bernardino, CA 92413

North American
  Recreation Convertibles
P. O. Box 758
Bridgeport, CT 06601

J. A. Preston Corp.
71 Fifth Avenue
New York, NY 10003

Fred Sammons, Inc.
Box 32
Brookfield, IL 60513

Skill Development
  Equipment Co.
P. O. Box 6300
Anaheim, CA 92807

Theraplay Products
P.C.A. Industries, Inc.
20–24 40th Avenue
Long Island City, NY
  11101

INFORMATION SOURCES

These professional, voluntary, and governmental organizations offer regular publications and/or other types of information related to recreation, education, therapy, etc.

1. American Association for the Education of the Severely/Profoundly Handicapped, 1600 West Armory Way, Garden View Suite, Seattle, WA 98119
2. American Association on Mental Deficiency, 5101 Wisconsin NW, Washington, DC 20016
3. American Foundation for the Blind, 15 West 16th Street, New York, NY 10011
4. American Occupational Therapy Association, 6000 Executive Boulevard, Suite 200, Rockville, MD 20852
5. American Physical Therapy Association, 1156 15th Street NW, Washington, DC 20005
6. American Speech and Hearing Association, 9030 Old Georgetown Road, Bethesda, MD 20014
7. Association for Childhood Education International, 3615 Wisconsin Avenue NW, Washington, DC 20016
8. Association for Children with Learning Disabilities, 5225 Grace Street, Pittsburgh, PA 15236
9. Bureau of Education for the Handicapped, U.S. Office of Education, 400 Maryland Avenue SW, Washington, DC 20202
10. Children's Bureau, Office of Child Development, 300 Independence Avenue SW, Washington, DC 20201
11. Closer Look, Box 1492; Washington, DC 20013
12. Council for Exceptional Children, 1920 Association Drive, Reston, VA 22091
13. Consumer Product Safety Commission, Washington, DC 20207
14. International Society for Rehabilitation of the Disabled, ICTA Information Center, Fack, S-16103, Bromma 3, Sweden
15. IRUC (Physical Education and Recreation for the Handicapped: Information and Research Utilization Center), c/o AAHPER, 1201 16th Street NW, Washington, DC 20036
16. National Association for the Education of Young Children, 1834 Connecticut Avenue NW, Washington, DC 20009
17. National Association for Retarded Citizens, P. O. Box 6109, 2709 Avenue E, East, Arlington, TX 76011

18. National Easter Seal Society for Crippled Children and Adults, 2023 West Ogden, Chicago, IL 60612
19. National Foundation March of Dimes, 1707 H Street NW, Washington, DC 20006
20. National Information Center for Educational Media, University of Southern California, University Park, Los Angeles, CA 90007
21. National Information Center for the Handicapped, 1201 16th Street NW, Room 607 E, Washington, DC 20036
22. National Recreation and Park Association, 1601 North Kent Street, Arlington, VA 22209
23. National Therapeutic Recreation Society, 1601 North Kent Street, Arlington, VA 22209
24. President's Committee on Mental Retardation, U.S. Department of Health, Education and Welfare, Washington, DC 20201
25. Public Action Coalition on Toys (PACT), P. O. Box 189, Providence, UT 84332
26. Rehabilitation Research/Information Center, Department of Vocational Rehabilitation, Commonwealth Building, 4615 West Broad Street, Richmond, VA 23230
27. Special Olympics/Let's Play-to-Grow, Joseph P. Kennedy, Jr. Foundation, 1701 K Street NW, Suite 203, Washington, DC 20006
28. Therapeutic Recreation Information Center (TRIC), University of Oregon, 1597 Agate Street, Eugene, OR 97403
29. Toy Libraries Association, Seabrook House, Wyllyotts Manor, Carkes Lane, Potters Bar, Herts, England EN6 2HL
30. United Cerebral Palsy Association Inc., 66 East 34th Street, New York, NY 10016

INDEX